STOKE NEWINGTON

THE STORY OF A
DISSENTING VILLAGE

RAB MACWILLIAM

First published 2021

The History Press
97 St George's Place, Cheltenham,
Gloucestershire, GL50 3QB
www.thehistorypress.co.uk

British Library Cataloguing in Publication Data.
A catalogue record for this book is available from the British Library.

ISBN 978 0 7509 9091 2

Typesetting and origination by The History Press
Printed and bound in Great Britain by TJ Books Limited, Padstow

STOKE NEWINGTON

THE STORY OF A

DISSENTING

VILLAGE

RAB MACWILLIAM

The History Press

STOKE
NEWINGTON

Enfield

Barnet

Harrow

Haringey

Waltham Forest

Redbridge

Havering

Brent

Camden

Islington

Hackney

Ealing

Barking and
Dagenham

Hillingdon

City of
Westminster

City of London

Tower
Hamlets

Newham

Hammersmith
and Fulham

Kensington
and Chelsea

Southwark

Greenwich

Bexley

Hounslow

Wandsworth

Lambeth

Lewisham

Richmond

Merton

Kingston

Croydon

Bromley

Sutton

CONTENTS

SLOUCHING TOWARDS STOKEY

During much of the 1970s, I lived in north London's Crouch End, then a pleasant suburb sheltering under the forbidding shadows of Highgate and Muswell Hill.

Not far from my flat, Hornsey Arts College was in the process of closing and being replaced by Middlesex Poly, and these once infamous institutions helped to generate an artistically radical, unconventional atmosphere in our little cultural backwater. Also, Crouch End's affordability, the diversity of its bars and its prevailing air of genial camaraderie created a stimulating and friendly environment. I enjoyed my few years there.

However, various events, mainly of a domestic nature, coincided in the early 1980s to suggest that I moved away from the comforting embrace of the Ally Pally. Throughout the following decade I drifted around Stroud Green, Dalston, Hackney, Shacklewell and Holloway, reacquainting myself with a dis-solute, occasionally debauched but always satisfyingly self-indulgent lifestyle. I had also been working in Fitzroy Square, Highbury Fields, Chelsea, Soho, Hounslow, Hemel Hempstead and, for a mercifully brief period, Aldershot, so I figured it was again time to settle down. In early 1991 my wife and I moved into a flat in Stoke Newington – they were affordable then – and we have lived in this splendidly eccentric little parish ever since.

As the 1980s progressed, I had become increasingly fond of Stoke Newington, in particular my strolls around the area's back streets and my regular visits to the Rose and Crown, Rochester Castle, Three Crowns and a few other pubs and restaurants, including Fox's Wine Bar. Fox's was owned by

Robbie and Carole Richards, who were widely credited with kick-starting the 'revival' of Stoke Newington Church Street. Although it had the honour of being the longest street name in London (I defy you to come up with a longer one), Stoke Newington Church Street, which was plain old Church Street until the 1930s, was then a fairly dilapidated, meandering old thoroughfare that dated back to early medieval times but which was, like a good many of its local residents, floundering in Thatcher's Britain.

In those days, it hosted several boarded up, vacant shops interrupted occasionally by a number of hopeful but wary businesses, usually small, friendly restaurants and drinking dens that never seemed to hang around for very long. Other arrivals, however, such as Bridgewood and Neitzert's violin and cello outlet and Atique Choudhury's Yum Yum Thai restaurant, continue to exist today. Some of the longer-term retailers were Whincop Timber Merchants (a fixture on the street since the mid-nineteenth century), John's Garden Centre, Rosa's Lingerie and Fox's Wine Bar, all now gone.

However, KAC electrics shop, Anglo-Asian restaurant, Gino's barber shop and the Rose and Crown, Auld Shillelagh and Red Lion bars remain, as do several other equally venerable pubs and retail establishments, but the street's overall impression was then one of relative decay tinged with genteel shabbiness. With the exceptions of the enduring Michael Naik, Philips Estates and newcomer Next Move, estate agents were then markedly less numerous, although Julian Reid, who was then employed by Church Street's Holden Matthews, currently runs his eponymous estate agency on Church Street. Indeed, it was Julian who, despite our new neighbour's pit bulls roaming across our back yard, sold us our flat.

Around the corner from Church Street, Stoke Newington High Street, which almost 2,000 years previously as Ermine Street had resounded to the menacing tramp of Roman legions marching north to quell rebellious Britons and Celtic troublemakers, and which, at the beginning of the twentieth century, had been one of north London's busiest retail centres, was also embracing a seemingly terminal decline.

At the turn of the twentieth century, an Edwardian observer had noted with reference to the High Street and the surrounding area: 'Stoke Newington is one of the brightest and pleasantest of London boroughs … its attractiveness is enhanced by its excellent shops. These, for variety and the useful services they offer, are second to none in any London suburb.' Sadly, times had moved on.

By the mid- to late-1980s, the High Street retailers included Woolworth's (near a fading Marks and Spencer wall sign, recently airbrushed out as if to erase any trace of its former presence), the well-stocked General Woodwork Supplies, Hamdy's newsagent emporium, the Gallo Nero restaurant/deli, two or three cheerfully scruffy bars, a few welcoming Turkish/Kurdish restaurants, and several smaller independently owned specialist shops – such as Parker's Pet Shop and Hammerton Hardware, both long-standing retailers but now gone – but trade appeared to have tailed off markedly over the years, although the grim police station, dating from Victorian times, usually appeared busy enough.

Other streets across Stoke Newington – such as Albion Road, Cazenove Road, Allen Road, Shacklewell Lane and Green Lanes – were also, to varying degrees, revealing signs of a trading downturn and general disrepair. This decline in Stoke Newington's fortunes even appeared to have affected many of the area's road and pavement surfaces, which were shabby and were frequently pot-holed, although this was due more to neglect by Hackney Council than to any wider sense of sociocultural regression.

This disheartening general malaise across the parish was not helped by the widespread negative perception of Stoke Newington, with even some of my more degenerate friends describing it as London's South Bronx in terms of its reputation for dangerous street encounters, random violence and other such vile imaginings. I remember at the time reading a report in the *London Evening Standard* that described Stoke Newington as being 'beyond the bounds of law and order', which may have sold a few more papers but I thought it was a bit harsh on the old place.

The relative absence of convenient public transport, accessibility and, when required, swift departure, only added to this prevailing air of negativism. There was no tube station in the immediate vicinity, the nearest being a good hike away at Manor House, and the local overground train station only travelled directly north or south, as did many of the buses. However, the ever-reliable 73 bus regularly ploughed its way from Victoria up through Oxford Street, King's Cross and Islington to reach this abode of the damned.

Even black cabs, particularly in the West End, normally refused the fare for what was a relatively short journey: 'Sorry, mate. I'm heading home now.' We had to jump into the back, shut the door and then state our destination. Legally, cabbies then had no option but to comply, but their grumbling was accompanied by their deliberate acceleration over large speed bumps, simply to make the journey as uncomfortable as possible for the passengers. I guess the reason for their reluctance was not timidity (a cab driver?) but because they knew they wouldn't pick up a return fare in Stoke Newington.

I recall saying to my wife that a sure sign that our little area was on an upward trajectory would be the sight of a black cab driving up Church Street with its yellow 'For Hire' light on display. In 1994 I saw my first such cab, ironically as I was making my way back from the Homeless Festival in the local park. Something had to give, and within only a few weeks the 'crusties' and a good many squatters seemed to have all but disappeared. Even local self-styled 'anarchists' Class War appeared to have faded away. The old order was rapidly changing.

It was becoming evident that the outside world's perception of a decrepit and dangerous Stoke Newington was gradually being superseded by the pros-pects of a revival in the area, prompted and promoted by a number of factors: by the efforts of local pressure groups, such as the Hackney Society and the Stoke Newington Business Association, and their acquisition of funding and grants for the area, as well as securing selective Conservation Area status; by the growing awareness and celebration of such splendid old buildings as St Mary's Old Church, Sisters' Place and the Georgian houses on Church Street and elsewhere, the Unitarian Chapel and London's oldest terrace (mid-seventeenth century) on Newington Green, as well as the area's many other buildings that invoked a wealthier and more optimistic past, such as Sanford Terrace and Clissold House; and by a recognition of the variety and accessibility of the area's open public spaces, in particular Clissold Park, Stoke Newington Common, Abney Park Cemetery, Newington Green and, slightly further east, Springfield Park with its unparalleled view across Walthamstow Marshes, one of the last remaining semi-natural wetlands in Greater London.

Further signs of the area's re-emerging vitality and adventurous spirit were demonstrated by the popularity of the annual Church Street Festival, which began in the mid-1990s, as well as the Hackney Show on Hackney Downs. Although less dramatic, but equally important in re-fostering a sense of 'belonging', was the emergence in Church Street and other places in the area of newly created memorial plaques, bicycle rails, small volunteer-led public gardens, Christmas street lights and other ideas and activities that individually were minor contributions to the area but which collectively implied a progressive feeling of community awareness and a growing pride in the old parish.

Other significant uplifting factors were the explosive growth of a varied and vibrant local music scene – particularly rock, folk, reggae, soul and blues, with occasional bursts of classical Baroque (Battuta) and opera (Opera Cabaret). Jazz was provided at the renowned Vortex Jazz Bar, opened on Church Street in 1984. Other early bars and venues included The Pegasus on Green Lanes (rhythm and blues from Juice on the Loose was a regular Friday date), the Rochester Castle's punk and blues live acts in the late 1970s and The Four Aces in Dalston Lane, which arrived in 1967 and which quickly became London's leading reggae, ska and soul club. As time progressed, several others clubs and venues incorporated live music, almost all from the growing number of new bands and performers in Stoke Newington.

This was complemented by a reawakening interest in, and celebration of, the written word. Daniel Defoe, Edgar Allan Poe, Joseph Conrad and Alexander Barron had all lived here, and authors are highly regarded in this parish. Special mentions must go to the deserved success of the Stoke Newington Book Shop, which opened in 1988, the unveiling by Mehmet Ergun of the makeshift Arcola Theatre in a side street off Stoke Newington Road, and the Stoke Newington Literary Festival, which would have had its eleventh anniversary in 2020 but for Covid-19 (*see* Postscript).

Also gratifying was the eager willingness and co-operation of local bars and venues, including both the Old and New St Mary's churches and the civic Assembly Rooms on Church Street, to stage gigs featuring local performers as well as diverse literary and musical events, and the gradual appearance of intriguing, useful little shops and quirky small businesses, alongside the refurbishment of some of the older, somewhat seedier bars (although these last 'improvements' were far from universally welcomed).

There were also positive indications, particularly at the northern end of the High Street, of the growing integration of faith and ethnic groups in the area, exemplified by the co-operative co-existence of the Muslim and Ultra-Orthodox Jewish populations and community centres in and around Cazenove Road. I recall during the 2011 'Hackney Riots' that a large crowd from Mare Street headed up to Stoke Newington in an attempt to spread the disruption. The potential invaders were swiftly repelled by a line of Turkish and Kurdish restaurant employees forming a defensive line across the High Street while clutching their meat cleavers. A second line of resistance, although not required (the Kurds had seen to that), was formed by a hastily assembled group of Muslim and Hassidic youths who had gathered together further up the road and who appeared determined, physically if necessary, to defend their mutual territory.

Yet another major reason for the area's upturn in recent years was that many of the local inhabitants and recent arrivals also seemed different to the norm. As well as the ever-expanding ethnic and cultural incomers and the ease of their acceptance into the existing neighbourhood, there were eccentrics, anarchists, hustlers, buskers, amiable and voluble drunks, and contrarians of all persuasions, often to be found in public houses. Stoke Newington's close proximity to central London, and the area's disputatious nature and history, attracted writers, journalists, musicians, visual artists, radical politicians and vociferous opinion-formers, many of whom mixed and intermingled with similarly minded, companionable local people whose fondness for Stoke Newington life often also revealed a cheerfully cynical attitude to the local Council at that time.

There were, of course, beggars and the homeless sitting on the streets, but these unfortunate people were, as a rule, not treated with dismissal or disdain but with the friendly humanity they deserved, and they normally responded in a like manner. A number of groups and organisations were formed to help those who had fallen on hard times. As an example, North London Action for the Homeless began in the early 1990s in a synagogue (built on the site of a former Baptist chapel) in Amhurst Park and then moved to St Paul's Church on Stoke Newington Road. Reliant on external funding, grants and volunteers, NLAH provided, and continues to offer, regular meals, clothing, medical assistance, housing advice and much else. There are today several similar organisations in the area.

Less definably, but as important as all the heartening signs of Stoke Newington's return to grace, was the growing awareness among local people of the area's historical legacy, which had always exerted a powerful presence, albeit in temporary abeyance. All of these initiatives, encounters, discussions, creative activities, eccentric behaviours and voluntary community groupings resulted in a conducive atmosphere for, once again, dissent to flourish in this parish. Aside from a few notable exceptions, this was a forward-looking, optimistic dissent and one that has contributed to today's revitalised, if rather different, Stoke Newington.

However, it occurs to me that you may think I'm painting an excessively rosy picture of how this parish handled the changes of recent years and, to a degree, you may be right. In an inner-city area where employment is for many people a welcome but unreliable and sporadic activity, where social deprivation, injustice and governmental indifference often exist next door to affluence and self-indulgent luxury, and where shabby, often poverty-stricken council estates are to be found round the corner from streets containing million-pound houses, there will inevitably be occasions when social hostility and related confrontation can occur. It is in no one's interests to pretend otherwise, and it can happen anywhere.

As an example, I recall a good few years back when I was invited (for some reason) one Saturday afternoon to an event described as a 'village fete' being held in the grounds between Old St Mary's Church and Clissold House. With the yummy mummies and helicopter dads indulging themselves in full-size chess games, enjoying the home-baked cakes, the kids dressing up as fairy tale figures, story-telling, small stalls selling home-knitted clothing, quizzes, backgammon competitions and all the rest of it, I felt I could have been in deepest rural Berkshire. I soon left, and was walking home along Church Street when I was stopped by police and directed home down a side road. There had been a violent clash between groups of youths that had involved the use of knives, resulting in several stabbings and serious injuries, and the corner of the High Street had been closed to the public.

On the way home, I asked myself which of these two events represented the 'real' Stoke Newington. The truth is that, during those years, they both did. The 'fete' seemed to be an attempt, instituted by a number of probably well-intentioned people, to reintroduce bourgeois 'normality' into the area, while the stabbings episode, although obviously prompted by other factors, felt like an unconscious but understandable reaction to the arrival in the parish of a new, more privileged population. When people from very different cultural and socioeconomic backgrounds live in a small built-up area, the potential for trouble is often present. However, vicious street violence involving weapons is now a rarity in this area, although not unknown, and Stoke Newington feels a safer place. These scenes represented a polarity in Stoke Newington that today appears to have resolved itself into a tolerance, if on occasion a grudging one, of the behaviour and opinions of other, more advantaged residents.

Despite that afternoon, despite the external and prevailing negative perception of the area – or perhaps because of them – and despite the crime, the punch-ups, the muggings, the screaming street arguments, the menacing stares from small gangs of youths, the early threat of the pit bull population and all the rest of it, the longer I lived in this area, the more I enjoyed being here. Eventually, after a few years as a resident, and with my background as a writer, editor and publisher, it occurred to me that this area of around 50,000 people was a small town, and that most small towns had their own newspapers. Unless one included the *Hackney Gazette* and the occasional advertising-led promotional sheets, Stoke Newington did not then possess such an organ of opinion, commentary and reflection.

This being the case, I helped to establish in the late 1990s *N16 Magazine: The Voice of Stoke Newington*: a free, quarterly, editorially led magazine. For the following twelve years of its existence I was its publisher, and I also initiated and was director of the N16 Fringe — an annual weekend of mainly free music in venues and bars across Stoke Newington — during most of the magazine's life. As you may imagine, I learned a good deal about this locality from both these ventures and, in the pages of this book — *Stoke Newington: The Story of a Dissenting Village* — I draw heavily from the experiences, interactions and friendships I formed while running the mag, as well as from a significant number of other sources, historical and contemporary.

In the thirty years since my permanent arrival in Stoke Newington, most of this area has re-evolved into an undeniably more middle-class and less fractious part of London, yet its radical atmosphere of dissent and its argumentative but companionable spirit lives on. Stoke Newington has been and remains a most unusual and fascinating place.

For all these reasons, and a good many others, I took great satisfaction from writing this book. I hope you take as much pleasure from reading it.

(I delivered the final draft of this book to the publisher just before the full impact of the Covid-19 pandemic became apparent. I subsequently corrected on the page proofs any factual errors caused by the pandemic. On page 201 I include a brief explanatory Postscript on how the book's publication was affected by Covid-19.)

WHERE IS STOKE NEWINGTON?

If I were to describe present-day Stoke Newington as being less of a London area than 'a state of mind', I'm pretty sure that you would regard such a proposition as, at best, self-deluding and as, at worst, pretentious nonsense. To an extent, I'd agree with these criticisms, but there is more than an element of truth in this assertion, so I'll restrict myself to saying that Stoke Newington does seem to be a good deal more than the sum of its parts.

By this I mean, first, that Stoke Newington is perceived by many of its longer-term residents as, for all its faults, possessing its own special identity and that it generates a strong attachment to the area as well as a sentiment of loyalty in many residents, and does so with an iconoclastic style that few other places in London can sustain. Second, and as I discovered at *N16 Magazine* when we received emails and letters from Stokey born-and-bred readers across the world, 'out of place' does not mean 'out of mind', judging by the nostalgia, homesickness and residual fondness for the place that was clearly manifested in their memories and stories.

It's all a bit strange, but this parish can and does generate a sense of belonging that is not normally evident elsewhere. This being so, its informal boundaries are fluid, and there are many people – including residents of Upper Clapton, Stamford Hill, Dalston and other neighbouring areas – who do not live within the formal boundaries of Stoke Newington but who describe this parish as being their home.

◆ ◆ ◆

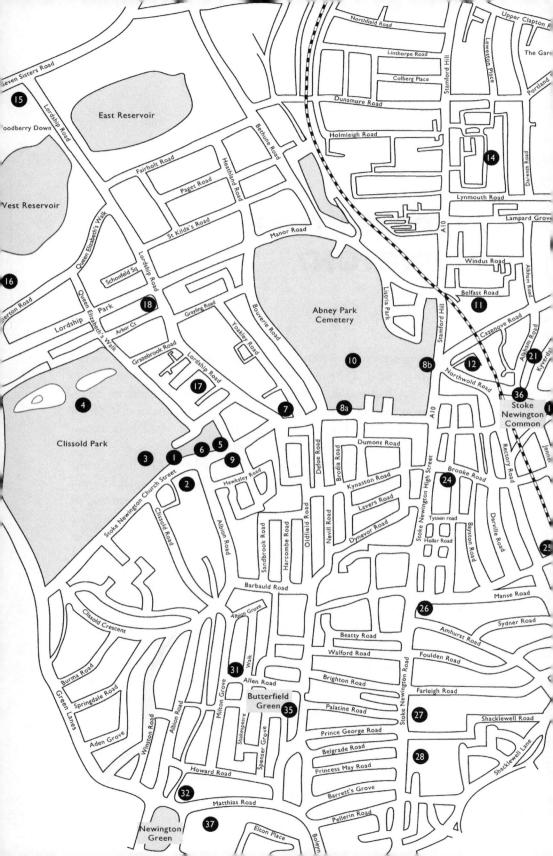

1: ST MARY'S OLD CHURCH

2: ST MARY'S CHURCH

3: CLISSOLD HOUSE

4: LAKES: RUNTZMERE AND BECKMERE

5: STOKE NEWINGTON LIBRARY

6: STOKE NEWINGTON ASSEMBLY ROOMS / TOWN HALL

7: RED LION / ROUND HOUSE

8a: CHURCH STREET ENTRACE, ABNEY PARK

8b: MAIN HIGH STREET ENTRANCE, ABNEY PARK

9: SISTERS HOUSE

10: ABNEY PARK CHAPEL

11: STOKE NEWINGTON RAILWAY STATION

12: GIBSON GARDENS

13: MARC BOLAN BIRTHPLACE

14: STAMFORD HILL ESTATE

15: WOODBERRY DOWN ESTATE

16: CLIMBING CENTRE

17: LORDSHIP ESTATE

18: ST MARY'S LODGE

19: CLAPTON COMMON

20: CLAPTON LIBRARY

21: 16 ALKHAM ROAD

22: SITE OF FORMER BROOKE HOUSE

23: CLAPTON TRAM DEPOT

24: OLD FIRE STATION

25: RECTORY ROAD RAILWAY STATION

26: ST PAUL'S CHURCH

27: SOMERFORD ESTATE

28: SIMPSON'S FACTORY

29: THE BECKERS ESTATE

30: MOSSBOURNE ACADEMY

31: ALLEN ROAD / 'ALBERT TOWN'

32: UNITARIAN CHURCH, NEWINGTON GREEN

33: NIGHTINGALE ESTATE

34: CLAPTON RAILWAY STATION

35: BUTTERFIELD GREEN

36: STOKE NEWINGTON COMMON

37: MARY WOLLSTONECRAFT SCHOOL

As Stoke Newington began to outgrow its medieval parish status, so also did its boundaries expand and become more clearly defined, as I will explain as this book progresses. However, the area most commonly agreed as representing the formal limits of today's parish was delineated in 1900 by Stoke Newington's creation as a Metropolitan Borough, and it was refined after its induction in 1965 into the London Borough of Hackney.

Prior to 1900, the parish of Stoke Newington had long virtually encircled, roughly to its south-west, the self-administering area of South Hornsey. The now-redundant signpost indicating 'Town Hall Approach', on Milton Grove as one travels along Albion Road, refers to South Hornsey's administrative centre. The physical inclusion of another parish within Stoke Newington had long been an anomaly but, immediately prior to the Metropolitan Borough legislation, this intrusion proved advantageous.

Some doubts had previously been expressed concerning Stoke Newington's suitability as a candidate for a Metropolitan Borough as it contained, by some degree, the smallest population among the contenders. However, if it added South Hornsey to its constituency, Stoke Newington could then more easily pull its weight alongside the big boys. That's what happened, and South Hornsey found itself dissolved and under the administrative control of Stoke Newington.

The main boundary change thereafter was its formal extension beyond the eastern boundary of Ermine Street (the ancient, straight Roman road known variously as Kingsland Road, Stoke Newington Road and Stoke Newington High Street) to include Stoke Newington Common (an area of open land previously known as Newington Common and Cockhangar Common) and a small section of what had beforehand been West Hackney. Along with the Common came sections of Cazenove and Northwold Roads and several other north–south roads leading to Evering Road, before again turning west and re-joining the previous boundary on Rectory Road.

This may seem to you as an irrelevant geographical diversion to Stoke Newington's history, but it is important for the purposes of this book to have as accurate a knowledge as possible of what constitutes the Stoke Newington borders, given the number of historically important areas elsewhere in Hackney. As it is, on occasion I veer away from the area – for instance, to Hackney Downs, Clapton Common, Lower Clapton Road and Dalston Lane – to refer to other parts of Hackney Borough that are not strictly within Stoke Newington but which, particularly in terms of dissent and related activities, have impacted significantly on the behaviour and opinions of residents within its boundaries.

Therefore, although I concentrate below on Stoke Newington's postcode of N16, I also make brief visits to N1, N4, N15, E5 and even tiptoe into E8. However, as I proceed I will provide you with prior warning that I am about to venture abroad.

STOKE NEWINGTON BOUNDARIES IN 2020

The following pleasant little excursion will lead you around the area included, more or less, in the N16 postcode. This code is usually regarded as containing the present-day Stoke Newington, and the parish is normally on the right-hand side of my directions as you travel round. I will mention any changes to this as we proceed. It's nothing like as complicated as it may appear.

Beginning at Stoke Newington railway station on Stamford Hill Road, travel south to Cazenove Road. Turn left here and make your way past Alkham, Kyverdale and Osbaldeston Roads. Then turn right and proceed south along Fountayne Road until you reach the road's end at the eastern edge of the Common. Wiggle across to Norcott Road and head south for a block until you encounter Brooke Road, where you turn left and then take the right-hand turn at the junction on Evering Road. Travel west along to Rectory Road railway station at the end of Evering Road, and then make a left at the traffic lights onto Rectory Road. Follow Rectory Road to your left, ignoring the one-way right turn back to the High Street.

Ignore the left-hand turn to Hackney Downs. At the junction with Amhurst Road, continue straight across the traffic lights to Shacklewell Road, passing Shacklewell Green and keeping to the right at the roundabout. (If you look to the left here, you will see St Mark's Church, which is impossible to miss as it is the largest parish church in London, is bigger than Southwark Cathedral and is known as 'The Cathedral of the East End'.) Keep going past the mosque to your right, and you then arrive at Kingsland Road (or Ermine Street, south of Stoke Newington Road). Go straight across at the traffic lights onto Crossway, turn right at the next lights at Boleyn Road and continue until you reach the bend of Matthias Road, which you follow past the Factory and school to your left, until you find yourself at Newington Green. (Curiously, if you turn left on Kingsland Road, stay on the right-hand pavement, go past the Rio Cinema, turn into Gillett Square, emerge from the other end of the Square, turn right and go over the traffic lights, you are back on Boleyn Road. On this short stretch of Kingsland Road, which is really Dalston, N16 is to your right and includes the Rio and Gillett Square, while E8 faces you on your left, across the street.)

Go around Newington Green (three sides of which are in N1), turn left at Green Lanes, and you are back in N16. Stoke Newington occupies the north side of the Green including the Unitarian chapel. Keep travelling northward along Green Lanes, passing Clissold Park, Brownswood Road, The Castle Climbing Centre and the Reservoirs, until you arrive at Seven Sisters Road (which is in N4).

Turn right along the Seven Sisters carriageway, passing on your right Woodberry Down estate and the right-hand turn at the first set of lights for Lordship Road. Turn right into Amhurst Park as the main carriageway veers left, travel along Amhurst Park, with Stamford Hill railway station to your left, till you arrive at the busy Stamford Hill junction, where you make a sharp right turn at the lights. You are now back on Ermine Street (the straightness of the road is a clue), so keep moving south in a straight line until you are back at Stoke Newington railway station, where you began this enjoyably convoluted trip. You may now go to the nearest bar (the Wheatsheaf on Windus Road is about as close as you can get, while the Bird Cage and Mascara Bar are just up the road) and have a few drinks, as you deserve these.

In this book, I occasionally include Upper Clapton and Stamford Hill as part of Stoke Newington, as it is an interesting area. To follow this route, continue straight ahead from the Stamford Hill traffic lights, pass by Clapton Common, and follow Upper Clapton Road southward until it reaches the Lea Bridge Road roundabout. Here, you turn right (or west) onto Kenninghall Road, and then either veer left for Hackney Downs or continue straight ahead, a short journey that takes you back to Evering Road and the delights of Stoke Newington.

Finally, and as a stylistic point, you may occasionally find confusing in this book my use of the word 'parish', which I employ in two similar but slightly different ways. In some cases, the word refers to the formal, older vestry boundaries of Stoke Newington. In others, it is a word I have always used – in a more general, affectionate sense – to encompass Stoke Newington and its immediate surrounds. The context should clarify the difference. (If this is the only thing that confuses you, I'd be delighted.)

INTRODUCTION

We always did feel the same,
We just saw it from a different point of view.

'Tangled Up in Blue', Bob Dylan

In 1953, the architectural historian Nikolaus Pevsner neatly captured the essential spirit of Stoke Newington when he wrote, in *The Buildings of London*, 'Stoke Newington is not entirely London yet'.

Notwithstanding its urban location and physical integration into the sprawling mass of the city, this perversely unique area has never allowed its independence to be absorbed fully into London's collective unity. Although Pevsner employs the academically cautious word 'yet', such an absorption today and in the foreseeable future appears unlikely.

Unlike other suburban areas, Stoke Newington has today avoided the loss of its historical identity, and it has managed to retain its distinctive character, despite the many countervailing pressures and despite its geographical location close to the heart of one of the world's largest cities.

In order to discover why this is the case, I examine in this book the historical and contemporary reasons underlying this spirit of independence, and I attempt to reveal why, throughout its history, Stoke Newington has been and remains such an unusual and special place.

◆ ◆ ◆

on, once a tiny medieval hamlet just north of the city, is today
iticultural area located in inner-city London. In 1965 it was
ilated, along with the metropolitan boroughs of Hackney and
Shor.... nto the London Borough of Hackney. As such, it now forms
the north-eastern part of Hackney, which borders the Boroughs Islington,
Haringey, Waltham Forest, Newham and Tower Hamlets.

Within Hackney, the metropolitan borough of Stoke Newington is today
sandwiched between Haringey to the north and Islington to the west. This
locational description of contemporary Stoke Newington makes it appear
simply as another small district of north-east London and as a fairly banal
component of this great sprawling capital. The reality, however, is very different.

This parish is widely known and appreciated for its cultural and historical
importance and its impact on British social and political life, and this has
been, and remains, of much greater significance than its relative size may
suggest. Stoke Newington's proximity to London and to the old borough
of Hackney, particularly in recent years, helps one to understand the reasons
for this.

For much of the later part of the twentieth century, Hackney was considered to be one of the most socially and economically deprived regions in
the UK but, over the last twenty years or so, the borough has gentrified at an
almost alarming rate and, although there remain areas of relative poverty, it
has overcome its previously dismissive ranking. Indeed, much of Hackney, for
example Shoreditch and more recently Stoke Newington, is today regarded,
particularly by younger people, as one of London's most desirable, innovative
and exciting areas.

Since the start of the new millennium, Stoke Newington has shrugged off
its late-twentieth-century reputation as a run-down and depressed inner-
city London area and has become an aspirational, 'hipster' venue, with its
bars, restaurants and chic designer shops attracting a new breed of visitors
and inhabitants. Known by many as 'Stokey', this little 'village' (as some still
see it) has maintained its identity through some hard times, and is currently
something of a cultural magnet for these mainly bourgeois newcomers. In
this respect, Stoke Newington is doing no more than replicating the respect
and reputation that it once enjoyed and which marked it out as a remarkable
place for over 500 years, from its emergence as a retreat for wealthy London
merchants and dissenters in the sixteenth century until its twentieth-century
inclusion in the 'Great Wen'.

As with many inner-city areas, Stoke Newington is no stranger to social deprivation, crime and all the other downsides to contemporary urban existence, but its history as an area of resistance to external interference, its culture of dissent and its enduring tradition of offering a welcome to people from differing cultures, ethnic groups and social backgrounds has ensured that this particular 'village' can well handle and adapt to most of today's urban blights.

By the sixteenth century, Stoke Newington was close enough to the expanding City of London for it to be able to offer a retreat to moneyed merchants whose daily activities committed them to the noisy, cramped and often disease-ridden vagaries of city life, as well as to its mainly upper-class and aristocratic inhabitants who also involved themselves in the capital's social and commercial affairs.

For these people and others like them, during its early years Stoke Newington was developing into a rural dormitory suburb of the city. Meanwhile, in common with other villages of the time, the less privileged inhabitants – the burgeoning presence of tradesmen, agricultural workers, servants, 'masterless men' and the otherwise economically and socially disadvantaged – existed side-by-side with the wealthy new arrivals, with both groups generally co-existing to their mutual advantage.

In this book I trace the evolution of Stoke Newington and its southern neighbour, Newington Green, from these late-medieval origins as a popular retreat for wealthy merchants, rich urban dilettantes and aristocrats into an extended village which, in the seventeenth and eighteenth centuries, was to transform itself into a byword for religious dissent. Thereafter, and to the present day, the Stoke Newington area has preserved this 'dissenting' tradition, but has enhanced and continually modified its contrarian nature away from purely religious matters to adopt political and cultural positions that have been and remain at variance with 'the establishment' and its widely accepted principles and attitudes.

While elsewhere 'dissent' was widely regarded as divisive and even dangerous, in Stoke Newington it was, and is, positively relished. Although in this book I consider and discuss several other intriguing aspects of the area – including matters literary and cultural, the ever-changing nature of land use and development, the local economy, architecture and unusual buildings, relationships with nearby Clapton and Stamford Hill, popular activities and entertainment, personality profiles and so on – 'dissent' is the principal perspective from which I will be narrating the story of this nonconforming and constantly changing urban village.

◆ ◆ ◆

'Dissent' – from the Latin *dissentire* – is defined in the *Shorter Oxford English Dictionary* as 'not to assent; to disagree with or object to an action … to think differently'.

It is one of those all-inclusive words, the dominant meaning of which, depending on the period under investigation, ranges, at one extreme, from a mild objection to what is considered a disagreeable suggestion to, at the other extreme, the adoption of physically violent activity in the defence of one's principles against the attempted imposition of a contrary, often widely held, set of opposing beliefs. Today, the term 'dissent' tends to the former usage, but 400 years ago the word's meaning was emphatically concentrated on the latter.

In seventeenth-century England, in the aftermath of the Reformation and during the continuing decline of feudalism, the term 'nonconformist' was applied to the growing number of 'independent' thinkers who questioned not only much of the Anglican Church's teachings but, on occasion, its very existence. In those times, given the inflexible and mutually dependent relationship between religion and state, profound social upheaval was the inevitable result of this clash between dissent and orthodoxy.

These religious nonconformists were virtually all Protestants as, after King Henry's break with the Roman Papacy in the 1530s, Catholics were considered as extreme 'recusants' (from the Latin *recusare*: to refuse), and were regarded as legitimate targets for the state's and God's wrath. Given their relative scarcity in England, however, 'papists' were in no position to dissent publicly from anything, as they were obliged to worship in the utmost secrecy. Indeed, Stoke Newington apparently contained no Roman Catholic inhabitants, or the Catholics kept quiet about it, throughout the entire seventeenth century. Similar strictures applied to the few Sephardic Jews (from Spain and Portugal) in the country.

So long as they kept themselves to themselves, these two groups were on safer ground than were the dissenters, as, although Catholics and Jews were treated by the state as dangerously suspect foreigners, their adherents in England were considered as 'aliens' to be kept at arm's length rather than, as were the Protestant nonconformists, condemned as blasphemous traitors.

As attitudes and circumstances changed with the first glimmerings of liberalism and modernity, and as the relationship between the state and its people gradually developed into a degree of religious toleration, so also did the meaning of 'dissent' begin to assume a new emphasis and an application to a wider constituency. The word became applied to contrarians in the political and cultural life of the nation, and, particularly in relatively recent times, 'dissent' has again widened its focus. When considering, for example, the various waves of immigration, particularly during the twentieth century, I have stretched still further my definition of 'dissent' and have subsumed it under the catch-all term 'different'.

◆ ◆ ◆

Today, Stoke Newington's ethnic, social and cultural diversity can be observed on a daily basis simply by strolling around its streets. There are a good many other similar areas in London and elsewhere in the UK. However, few other places in London and beyond can today claim a virtually continuous dissenting heritage dating back to before the mid-seventeenth-century English Civil War (or, if you prefer, War of the Three Kingdoms).

Stoke Newington provided a secure post-Civil War home from the mid-seventeenth to early-nineteenth centuries for such radicals, writers and nonconformist preachers as Isaac Watts, Daniel Defoe, Mary Wollstonecraft, Anna Laetitia Barbauld, Cromwellian senior army officers Charles Fleetwood and Alexander Popham, Unitarians Dr Richard Price and Charles Morton, Methodists John and Charles Wesley, Quaker anti-slavery abolitionists Samuel Hoare and James Stephen, prison reformer John Howard, Baptists, Congregationalists, Methodists, Puritans, Presbyterians, Republicans, anti-monarchist Parliamentarians, foreign exiles and a good many others whose religious and political views differed significantly from the norm.

Jewish people, who had been expelled from England by Edward I in 1290, had been invited back under Oliver Cromwell's Protectorate in the 1650s, because he wished to make use of their expertise in matters financial and their profitable trading acuity. (It has also been suggested that, as Cromwell was a believer in the impending Apocalyptic Last Judgement, he wanted to be present when the Jewish people were forced to atone in front of God for their 'sins'. Given the Protector's relative level-headedness, however, this seems a rather fanciful notion.)

Jewish businessmen were certainly financially adept but, as dislike of Jewish people was rife in medieval times and finance was one of the very few professions at that time open to them in England, they had to excel in financial affairs or they would face the alternative of poverty. One of the reasons for Edward's earlier expulsion of the Jews had been that his courtiers and fellow aristocrats owed large sums of money to Jewish lenders. Expelling these people was one way of cancelling these debts, although this could be seen as a panicked response to sound business practice, which included the probability of conversion into long-term repayment of debt. The principal cause was clearly virulent anti-Semitism, as these 'Christians' believed in the 'Christ-killer' status of Jews and all too easily afforded credibility to 'blood-libel' slurs.

However, a number of Sephardic Jews remained in England, often in small villages such as Stoke Newington. The 30,000 or so Ultra-Orthodox Jews who today live in Stamford Hill are Ashkenazi (mainly from Ukraine and Germany), and their recent history before reaching England was a harrowing and difficult story, as I will relate in Chapter Seven.

◆ ◆ ◆

Newington Green's Unitarian church was opened on the southern boundary of the parish in 1708. Initially, it was built as a Presbyterian place of worship but gradually it had become a home to Unitarians and, as such, today it remains committed to these anti-Trinitarian beliefs.

In the same area there also flourished the dissenting academies, which taught a variety of subjects and did not require, as did the two English universities of Oxford and Cambridge, a knowledge of Latin and Greek nor, more importantly, a commitment to the Anglican Church. These academies hosted, and in some cases educated, sympathetic intellectual luminaries of the calibre of John Locke, Daniel Defoe, John Stuart Mill, David Hume, Benjamin Franklin, Thomas Jefferson, Tom Paine and others of a similar ilk.

Although from the early eighteenth century Anglican religious intolerance was becoming more relaxed, and religious dissent was correspondingly diminishing in its impact as a contentious issue between Anglicans and non-conformists, the position of the established Church remained a powerful one. Political, cultural and economic dissatisfactions, however, continued to be expressed and Stoke Newington willingly maintained its role as a protector of individual beliefs. The quasi-heretic meaning of 'dissent', although in some circles retaining a strong foothold, was evolving into its wider, more complex definition.

The dissenting tradition continued in 1840 with the opening of Stoke Newington's Abney Park Cemetery, one of London's 'magnificent seven' cemeteries that were established to cope with the rapid population growth of the time and the inability of London's small churchyards to contain this expansion. Abney Park was the only non-denominational, unconsecrated cemetery of the new seven burial grounds and, with its 32 available acres, it was considered sufficiently large for its task.

After the closure of Clerkenwell's nonconformist graveyard Bunhill Fields, known as 'God's Acre' and which had long been the only burial space in London for all nonconformists, who were not permitted to be buried in the City of London, Abney Park became the final resting place of later dissenters, opponents of the prevailing status quo and objectors to the mores of the time.

Also, during the nineteenth century – largely as a consequence of local and national government initiatives and legislation, the speedy growth northward of the conurbation of London and the arrival of the railway and other internal trans-port links – the population of Stoke Newington expanded in dramatic fashion, as did its land use, communication channels and social complexity. By the early twentieth century, the quiet, essentially middle-class village, which had existed only a century or so beforehand, was fast becoming – in an architectural and spatial sense, at least – an integral component of urban inner north-east London. But 'dissent', as ever, remained a signature factor in Stoke Newington life.

In this book and, as I have mentioned, during recent years, I apply the term 'dissent' not only to the pre-existing population but also – in the simple and non-contrarian sense of 'different' – to the relatively new inhabitants of Stoke Newington, particularly to those Asian, Jewish, Kurdish, Turkish, Afro-Caribbean, African, European and other immigrants who, during the twentieth century, made their homes here. These people were welcomed into the area by the pre-existing populations who helped them to settle into their new home, while applying little pressure on these overseas arrivals to abandon their own cultures.

This has been a process of vibrant 'multiculturalism' rather than an attempt to assimilate them into the host nation's values and beliefs. For instance, the regular demonstrations on the High Street by many Kurds concerning the continuing imprisonment of ex-PKK leader Abdullah Öcalan, and the heated protests by predominantly people of Afro-Caribbean backgrounds at the highly suspicious death of Colin Roach while in Stoke Newington police station, were generally regarded in this area with acceptance and understanding.

I also apply this more elastic but equally important definition of 'dissent' to other twentieth-century people and groups, particularly over the last fifty or so years, whose activities may or may not have been illegal but who saw in Stoke Newington a place in which they could 'disappear' and, to this degree, lead 'normal' lives. These people shared with the religious dissenters of the sixteenth and seventeenth centuries a perception of this part of London as the only area within the capital that, for over 500 years, has remained unchanged in its tolerance of the strongly held and different beliefs of its residents.

The infusion and growth of 'different' cultures in Stoke Newington has injected into the area a refreshing willingness to consider and challenge many of the elsewhere prevailing conventional viewpoints. Encouraged and enthused by Stoke Newington's historical dissenting tradition, and by today's local and frequently expressed sentiment that Stoke Newington may be 'in' but is not 'of' London, this 'village' continues to provide fertile ground for the continuance of such a healthy, if contentious, tradition.

This being so, and given the freedom I have permitted myself with my liberal interpretation of the word 'dissent', I intend in the final chapters to concentrate almost as much on these recent events in Stoke Newington's disputatious history as I do on the dissenting activities of the preceding centuries.

I include here, for example, squatter movements, radical writers and artists and other similar contemporary protest groups. As for artistic dissenters, this area contains an abundance of creative contrarians, as I will mention. Also, particularly in the 1970s and '80s, houses, terraces, council flats and old villas across Stoke Newington were squatted, mainly by younger homeless people who had nowhere else to live in London. Squatting was then not unusual in other parts of the city but, given the area's dissenting heritage, Stoke Newington was the squatters' preferred option.

There were also 'revolutionary' groups, such as the Angry Brigade, or the 'Stoke Newington Eight', who were arrested here, as well as IRA cells whose presence and bomb factories were discovered in the area. And who was the fugitive member of the Baader-Meinhof group who was working for the Council in Clissold Park? Again, although they could certainly not be described as 'revolutionary' or 'dissenters', one cannot ignore the fact that Stoke Newington was the 'manor' of the Kray Twins, as was testified by the existence of the Regency Club in Amhurst Road and the murder of Jack 'the Hat' in Evering Road.

Although one may find the Krays' and their henchmen's activities morally repugnant, it would be difficult to omit them entirely from a discussion of Stoke Newington. Throughout this book I will refer to these people, as well as to the new artistic, literary and musical 'dissenters', and the events and festivals, to have emerged from this area in recent years and which have flourished here or have embraced a wider public stage.

◆ ◆ ◆

As this book is something of a personal introduction to Stoke Newington, and as it is intended as an overview of many centuries of the area's existence, it is necessarily a selective and relatively brief account of what I consider to have been the formative events, people and periods in the parish's history.

The book's relative brevity, and its emphasis on 'dissent', preclude from my consideration a number of factors that other residents of the area may consider important, but in the following pages I attempt to discuss those features of Stoke Newington's history that suggest a 'sense of place' rather than offer a comprehensive and definitive reference to the area. Those readers who wish to discover more on particular aspects will find in the Further Reading section the most fruitful avenues for further enlightenment on specific details.

The issues that Stoke Newington has faced in recent years – racism, crime, street and gang violence, national and class hostilities, ethnic grievances and urban integration among others – will, to a greater or lesser extent, continue, as they are common to all contemporary inner-city areas. These issues may not be fully understood by earlier 'dissenters' but they would probably appreciate that these frequently ignite argument and disagreement in the Stoke Newington area, and they would no doubt offer a sympathetic hearing to all involved in such disputations.

Although there has been a good deal more than 'dissent' to the story of Stoke Newington, nonconformity has underpinned its history from medieval times to the present day, as I reveal in the pages that follow.

CHAPTER ONE

STOKE NEWINGTON: THE EARLY YEARS

In the Ice Ages, the glacier sheets passed south, crushing everything in their paths. They stopped just north of Stamford Hill and large parts of the Palaeolithic floor are undamaged ... Man appears to have retreated in front of the advancing cold. There is no evidence that Palaeolithic people ever returned.

The Growth of Stoke Newington, Jack Whitehead

During the 1860s and 1870s, much of Stoke Newington's fertile soil – a combination of gravel and brickearth sitting on London clay that had long supported its buildings, farmlands and pathways – was being dug up to an unprecedented extent and depth.

These frenetic excavations were caused by the high number of burials at the new Abney Park Cemetery, the arrival of the Stoke Newington overground railway station, which required the construction of railway cuttings and level surfaces for its trains and coaches, and the surge in local house-building, which insisted on solid foundations and basements. Much of this activity was being carried out on and around Stoke Newington Common (then a part of West Hackney parish), which was in 1872 bifurcated by the new Great Eastern Railway Line from Enfield to Shoreditch. Shovels were also busy at work elsewhere across this fast-expanding parish, including the land around today's Alkham, Osbaldeston and Fountayne Roads as well as elsewhere in the area.

During the course of this backbreaking effort, it became apparent that a number of the artefacts discovered by the labourers were unusual objects and that they required the experienced attention of archaeologists, who had been arriving here. At a depth of almost 2m below the surface, and mainly in locations on and around the Common, the archaeologists unearthed sharp flint instruments, adzes, axe-heads, broken animal bones and antlers, all of which indicated that human hunter–gatherers had once lived in this area. But when were these implements in use and who were these early residents of Stoke Newington?

When the experts examined these discoveries, their analyses dated these tools and animal remains to the Palaeolithic (Stone Age) Period of 200,000 years ago, although some sources suggest an even earlier date. It seems that a group of primitive early humans – the forerunners of *homo sapiens* – had a settlement on what is today the area around the Common, which was then part of a flat plain, surrounded by swampy land, and which was significantly larger than today. These early proto-humans existed partly on the flesh of the animals that they drove into the nearby marshy lands or a river – which was possibly the ancestor of the Hackney Brook – to trap and kill these no doubt ferocious wild beasts.

THE HACKNEY BROOK

The Hackney Brook was an ancient stream with its source near Holloway. It had developed into a substantial river by the time it arrived at Stoke Newington where, as late as the 1830s, it was up to 10m wide when in flood, and even in dry weather it flowed at a rate of 400 cu ft of water every minute.

It ran eastward around the north of what are now Clissold Park and Abney Park Cemetery, crossed Stamford Hill beside the cemetery's main gates – with stepping stones and then a bridge provided for those wishing to cross the road at that point – and circled round the north of Stoke Newington Common. It then struck south across today's Brooke and Evering Roads, the west side of Hackney Downs, Hackney's Mare Street (where another ford crossed the street, under today's railway bridge) and Hackney Wick, before entering the River Lea at Old Ford where, when again in flood, it could reach 30m in width.

By the 1850s, the Brook was travelling through newly built-up areas and had become an unpleasant, disease-carrying open sewer. In 1860 it was culverted under the direction of Sir Joseph Bazalgette and was linked into London's subterranean sewer system, where today this old river remains. Several street names, such as Glazebrook Road in Stoke Newington and Well Street in Hackney, are evocative reminders of the open passage of the Hackney Brook.

In one of its occasional fits of lunacy, Hackney Council in 2016 briefly considered reopening the river between Mare Street and Hackney Wick for purposes of swimming, canoeing and kayaking, but common sense prevailed in this case and the old waterway continued its underground course untroubled by human interference.

On a visit some years ago to the Museum of London, the first exhibit I encountered was a life-sized diorama of these Palaeolithic people on Stoke Newington Common. This was located close to the main entrance and was presumably one of the museum's leading exhibits. I subsequently learnt that the archaeological evidence, and the great age of the various implements, have led to the Common's historical status as one of the most important Palaeolithic sites in Europe. As a result, I began to treat what was the then-scruffy, overgrown Stoke Newington Common, which sits only a block away from where I live, with the respect that one reserves for a treasured family heirloom.

◆ ◆ ◆

However, and putting to one side its ancient Stone Age origins, the area that is today agreed as the original site of a continuously occupied Stoke Newington was first formally assessed and recorded in the late eleventh century.

In 1086, twenty years after he and his Norman troops (the name 'Norman' betraying their Norse Viking origins) had invaded England, King William I, or William the Conqueror, received from his aides the 'Great Survey' that he had commissioned. This work is the oldest public record in England, and it contained detailed information on more than 13,000 places in his new domain. It concerned itself with most of England and Wales: its land distribution and ownership, townships, manorial estates and copyholdings (short-term feudal leaseholdings granted by the lord of the manor), the nature and beneficiaries of local and individual taxation systems, and other information of a similar nature.

This monumental work of research, designed to discover the fiscal and landholding basis and relationships underpinning these Saxon territories that William had so recently appropriated, came to be labelled the 'Domesday Book'. Unsurprisingly, the name stems from the Middle English 'doomsday' as, similar to the doctrinal finality of The Last Judgement, its findings and conclusions were considered immutable, at least by the country's Norman overlords.

The Domesday Book revealed *inter alia* the presence of the tiny hamlet of 'Neutone' ('new town in the wood') almost hidden from sight in a clearing in the Forest of Middlesex, close to the Roman-built, first-century Ermine Street and located around 3 miles north of the Bishopsgate entrance to the City of London. After the Conquest, the ancient forest was proclaimed a Royal Forest that also included common land. It stretched for 20 miles across the north of the city and was described as 'dense with foliage concealing wild animals – stags, does, boars and wild bulls'. The Domesday Book noted that Neutone consisted of four 'villeins' (bonded feudal serfs), thirty-seven 'cottars' (peasants who lived in a cottage owned by a farm) and was occupied by around 100 people, with much of the settlement being surrounded by extensive, thick woodland.

Although informed historical conjecture suggests that Neutone had been continuously occupied since the early Saxon period established a couple of hundred years previously ('Middlesex' meaning 'mid-Saxon'), William's survey was the first written description of the hamlet and inhabitants of what was to become, almost a millennium later, today's thriving inner-London 'village' of Stoke Newington.

♦ ♦ ♦

After William's brief, abrupt intrusion into its anonymity, Neutone reverted to type, and for another couple of hundred years or so it again virtually disappeared from public gaze, seemingly content to remain in its relative obscurity among the open fields and the gradually disappearing woodland. The hamlet was to resurface in the later medieval period under a new name – Stoke

Newington ('stoke' meaning 'timber' or 'tree stump') – with only a small increase in its extent and its population but, alongside the village's peasantry, serfs and general labourers, there was a growing number of wealthier, more culturally diverse and more politically influential residents than had existed under Norman rule.

During its seemingly sleepy social interregnum, however, the village had not been entirely inactive. In the year 939, before William arrived on the scene, the Saxon King Athelstan, grandson of Alfred the Great, had granted in perpetuity to the Prebendary ('Dean' and 'Chapter', or ecclesiastical over-lords) of St Paul's Cathedral an area of twenty-four 'hides' (the Old English word 'hide' amounting to approximately 100 acres), which was 'next the Wall of London'.

This expansive gesture to his spiritual peers comprised much of the Manor of Stepney, then one of the largest and most powerful manors in England, and which included the parishes of St Augustine's in Hackney and St Leonard's in Shoreditch. A small part of this regal gift also granted to St Paul's the village of Neutone, situated a mile or so to the north of these parishes.

By the early twelfth century, Neutone had acquired a rudimentary mano-rial structure and a small chapel or church that, over time, came to be known as St Mary's Church. The precise date of the church's establishment must remain speculative, as its early records were destroyed along with the orig-inal St Paul's Cathedral in the 1666 Great Fire of London. The parish, with an overall area of 325 acres, was formally instituted in 1314 when its first rector, one Thomas de London, was appointed. St Mary's Church was by then the local manorial place of worship, although its oldest recorded burial monument, which is now long gone, was erected in memory of one Matilda Elkington in 1473.

In medieval times the early parish boundaries were, to the west, the old pathway of Green Lanes and, to the east, London Way or Ermine Street, the latter leading to Cambridge, Lincoln and, eventually, York. These two ancient roads were linked together by the winding, gravel thoroughfare of Church Street. To the north and south the boundaries were largely open fields and woods, and these merged with the neighbouring parishes in a fluid and fre-quently undefined manner.

The land and fields to the north of Church Street were largely 'demesne', an old French word meaning 'belonging to the lord of the manor', and these fields were well maintained and carefully planned. To the south of Church

Street the land distribution was less organised, as there were several estates, such as Pulteney and Stonefields – and, in the early eighteenth century, the Palatine – and these were smaller landholdings under the control of less experienced managers than was the demesne. Also, directly south of the church lay the 'glebe' land, which was tended by the church rector and was part of his 'benefice', or salary.

During the early years of the Tudor era – which lasted from Henry VII's victory over Richard III at Bosworth Field 1485 until the death of Elizabeth I in 1603 – the village of Stoke Newington, and its southern neighbour Newington Green, whose existence was first publicly recorded in 1480, slowly emerged from relative slumber. The surrounding woodland was gradually diminishing in size due to deforestation, thereby permitting the expansion of cultivatable land for crops and grazing fields for animals, and also the profitable sale of the timber. With the village's proximity and ease of travel to the City of London, its open landscapes and clean air, the availability of more than sufficient land for building decent homes, and its tranquil solitude, Stoke Newington – then containing fewer than 100 households, which were concentrated at the eastern end of the street and dotted along the London Road – began to prosper.

By the mid-sixteenth century, it had evolved into a favoured destination for a day out and as a refuge from the city for merchants, traders and aristocrats, some of whom began to construct in the parish large brick-built houses and mansions with spreading gardens and pastures, and to take up residence here. Generally, these wealthy arrivals were welcomed by the inhabitants of Stoke Newington, whose incomes were supplemented by catering to the newcomers' needs and requirements.

Other than the arrival of these newcomers, there seems to have been very little to report about the parish of Stoke Newington during the first half of the sixteenth century. In this respect, it was probably a bit like today's radio programme *The Archers*: it was located in the countryside, people gossiped to each other about parochial matters, everyone knew each other, they all gradually grew older and, generally, not a great deal happened. Or perhaps I'm being unkind to the then-inhabitants of Stoke Newington (or to *The Archers*).

Nevertheless, this small community continued with its policy of deforestation and the manufacture of bricks (which, given the abundant brickearth in much of the local soil, was a common, profitable business across the area). The inhabitants also plied their various trades, enjoyed their archery, rabbit coursing and hunting of various small animals, and drank their ales in the local alehouses, such as Le Bell on the Hoop (established in 1405), the Hinde, the Falcon and the Cock and Harp, which became, after 1603, The Three Crowns.

The reason for the Cock and Harp's change of name was that, owing to the intricate complexity of monarchic succession, after the death of the childless Queen Elizabeth in 1603, James VI of Scotland was her closest living relative and thus also became James I of England, thereby replacing the Tudors with the Stuart dynasty. The new King, along with the Lord Mayor and Sheriffs of the city who had ventured out to Stamford Hill to welcome him, had popped into the Cock and Harp on the London Road for a few beers after James's lengthy, triumphant journey down from Edinburgh to his London coronation, and the bar's landlord was not slow to notice a marketing opportunity.

These pubs were on or around Church Street, and there were another five licensed premises in the parish, most probably on the London Road, to service the needs of the passengers on the horse-drawn coaches and the long-distance travellers. As the taverns began to proliferate under the new Stuart regime, so too did the objections to the parish vestry increase from the emerging Puritan dissenters in Stoke Newington, who were mainly teetotal abstainers and who disapproved of alcohol.

(From the feudal period until the late nineteenth century in England, the term 'vestry' referred to a regular meeting of selected parishioners who were charged with the discussion and dispatch of parochial business and related matters. The vestry can be seen as the equivalent of today's local government authority, with their name deriving from where they normally assembled: the vestry, the part of a church in which were kept the parish records and ecclesiastic vestments. However, they frequently also held meetings in other venues, a favourite being public houses.)

As well as enjoying local taverns, many locals worked on the fields, market gardens and orchards, the last two being skills they had learnt from Protestant refugees who had arrived from Europe, as the City of London was fast expanding and running out of space to accommodate its people, never mind having room to grow anything. Indeed, it is estimated that, between the years 1550 and 1600, the city's population rose from 70,000 to 200,000 residents. These people relied on fresh food imported from outside the city walls, and Stoke Newington supplied the capital with fruit – apples, pears, plums and cherries – and such vegetables as artichokes and asparagus for the wealthier city dwellers. Stoke Newington was also happy to satisfy the thirst and hunger of the drovers of cattle and sheep, some from as far away as Scotland, who regularly passed down Ermine Street or Lordship Lane through the village on their way to a London slaughterhouse.

Church Street remained at the centre of village life in the Tudor period. Aside from Ermine Street and Green Lanes, means of communications and roads in the 1500s were minimal, although ever-changing footpaths were fairly common. The route between Church Street and Newington Green was known as Church Path and was described as 'a medieval bridleway', although sections of the path exist today. Also, a 'little lane' – Cut Throat Lane – carved its ominous way from what is now Lordship Road, through today's Oldfield Road, Wordsworth Road and Newington Green, and concluded its meanderings on or close to Cock Lane, as present-day Shacklewell Lane to Crossway was then called. Further up the High Street, the narrow footpaths of Sanford Lane (still so named today) and Bull Alley (today's Cleveden Passage) permitted access to Stoke Newington Common.

By the early sixteenth century, larger homes were appearing in the area. The **Manor House** was an impressive old Tudor structure built in 1500, and was located next to St Mary's Church, on the ground where today stands the 1930s Stoke Newington Town Hall (small sections of the original Manor wall are still visible, behind thick glass frames, in the Town Hall). In 1571, William Patten (*see* below) relinquished the lease of the Manor House to John Dudley, a relative of the Earls of Leicester. Despite scant documentary evidence for this encounter, it's said that Dudley invited Queen Elizabeth I to the demesne and took her for a stroll along his lands behind St Mary's Church. The elm-lined path along which they ventured is today a road, on the eastern edge of Clissold Park, which is named Queen Elizabeth Walk in commemoration of this regal amble.

After Dudley's death in 1580, his wife later married Thomas Sutton, whose name exists to this day in Sutton House, in which he lived for several years (*see* below*)*, and he stayed at Stoke Newington Manor House for only four years. Founder of Charterhouse School, his reputation in the world of business, and his general moral practices, can be surmised from a popular play of the period, as Sutton was the model for the greedy, lustful Volpone (Italian for 'sly fox') in Ben Jonson's 1605 satirical drama of the same name.

The Manor building extended to today's Edward's Lane, and further along Church Street were the agricultural equipment sheds and outbuildings that were located, unsurprisingly, in today's Barn Street. Opposite St Mary's Church stood the clerical home, the **Rectory**, the site of which was occupied in the mid–nineteenth century by the new St Mary's. Over the following two centuries, there would be built other imposing mansions on Church Street, but at this point the street was essentially comprised of wooden cottages and open fields.

One of the East End's oldest and historically most important buildings was constructed with local brick walls at the beginning of the sixteenth century by the Dean of St Paul's, and contained an impressive courtyard, gatehouse and chapel. Although not within Stoke Newington parish, it was just over the eastern border in the parish of West Hackney, only a ten–minute walk away from Ermine Street. Originally called King's Place, it later became known as **Brooke House,** and it sat near the junction of today's Brooke Road and Upper Clapton Road, just before the Lea Bridge roundabout and approximately on the site of today's BSix Sixth Form College.

It has been suggested that the land originally belonged to the Knights Templars and that, after their dissolution in the early fourteenth century, it was passed to the Knights of St John of Jerusalem. The earliest building to have been erected on the land was during the reign of Henry IV in 1409, when it became known as the King's House. A century later, the estate was granted to the Percy family, the Earls of Northumberland; in 1531 the mansion was reacquired by Henry VIII as a royal palace, was expanded by Thomas Cromwell and, after Henry's death in 1547, it was rented to such personages as Sir Ralph Sadlier, who had previously built and lived in nearby Sutton House.

SUTTON HOUSE

A Tudor manor house, and the oldest surviving domestic building in Hackney, Sutton House was built in 1535.

Located in Homerton, just a couple of miles south of its contemporary Brooke House, it was built for Sir Ralph Sadlier, secretary to Thomas Cromwell and Secretary of State to King Henry VIII. Originally known as Bryck House, its current name was a mistaken reference to Thomas Sutton, who lived next door before moving to Stoke Newington Manor House. Its design was H-shaped and three-storeyed but changed over the years – including a division into two houses in the eighteenth century and the addition of Wenlock Barn in the early twentieth century – and it was acquired by the National Trust, still its owners, in 1938.

The building thereafter passed through various hands and, when the ASTMS trade union left in 1982, Sutton House deteriorated and became home to squatters. When the Trust suggested its conversion into flats in the mid-1980s, the 'Save Sutton House' campaign persuaded them instead to embark on a full-scale restoration project, with the House opening to the public in 1994. Today, it also boasts an award-winning garden on the adjacent land, once owned by a car-breaking company.

Sutton House now functions as a museum, art gallery and cafe, with a section set aside for weddings, discussions, historical group meetings and for community and educational use. This Grade II* listed building is a carefully maintained homage to the area's long history.

Other late-sixteenth-century occupiers of Brooke House included the Earl of Oxford, Edward de Vere, who was reputed to have been the author of several of Shakespeare's plays. De Vere also occupied the mansion in Church Street that was demolished to make way for the 'Sisters House'. In the late sixteenth century, Brooke House was acquired by the Greville family, who held the Brooke baronetcy and who gave the house its enduring name.

Brooke Road, which today travels over Evering Road, south of Stoke Newington Common, to meet the High Street, began at the northern corner of the Brooke estate and was known as 'The World's End'. Four hundred years ago it was a cart-path to the mansion's farm buildings, and it veered its rural way north-west across fields, hedges and a bridge over Hackney Brook on its way to the Common.

By the mid-eighteenth century the house had become a private lunatic asylum. Seriously damaged by Second World War air raids, Brooke House was acquired in 1944 by Hackney Council, who completely demolished the building in the mid-1950s. When the building's age was confirmed after an archaeological investigation, Brooke House was a heap of rubble, and with its destruction disappeared much of the physical evidence of the area's history.

Other large mansions in the area included **Shacklewell House**, of a similar vintage to Brooke House, which faced onto Shacklewell Green and was owned by the Heron and then the Tyssen family, who also owned much of the land and brickfields to the north of this area and who were the lords of the manor. The name 'Shacklewell' derives from the nearby presence of a well, the water from which apparently possessed healthy, life-enhancing properties.

Shacklewell House, which was situated around today's Seal Street area, was demolished in the mid-eighteenth century. There were other late-medieval mansions in the Stoke Newington area, particularly around the larger village of Hackney, but these have been unable to resist the advance of time and the nineteenth-century spread of urbanisation from London.

The following centuries – the seventeenth and eighteenth – witnessed the building of potentially more durable large homes and estates in Stoke Newington, and I will discuss these in Chapter Two. These were often built by, and intimately connected to, the growing number of wealthy dissenters arriving in the area, and to the radical religious, literary and educational anti-establishment positions that they represented. However, before the conclusion of the sixteenth century other events of both local and wider importance had been initiated in this village before dissenters had started to make their lasting impressions on Stoke Newington.

AN OLD CHURCH RENEWED

It's safe to assume that most residents of today's Stoke Newington will know the name 'William Patten', as it's difficult to miss the imposing Victorian primary school and community centre that bears his name and whose mosaic-designed front wall faces onto the south-eastern end of Church Street. It's probably also a safe bet that few of these people are aware (and why should they be?) that he was responsible, nearly 500 years ago, for ensuring the continuing existence of one of the parish's finest remaining medieval buildings, Old St Mary's Church.

'A LEARNED GENTLEMAN AND A GRAVE CITIZEN'

Described thus by a contemporary, William Patten (1510–98) was appointed in 1552 by St Paul's Prebendary as the first non-clerical lord of the manor of Stoke Newington. Prior to this, he was Collector of Customs in his native London, a JP for Middlesex, a government official in several senior capacities, a member of the Society of Antiquaries, a scholar, an author and a renowned Humanist (a student, in the tradition of the Dutchman Erasmus, of ancient Greek and Roman literature and culture). Patten was also reputed to have translated the Bible into six languages.

In all these learned respects, Patten – also described as a 'celebrated historian' – was something of a prototype for the intellectual middle- and upper-classes who were then in the process of discovering the pleasant, healthy attractions of Stoke Newington life. Although never a 'dissenter', it is quite likely that, if William Patten had lived in the village alongside these nonconformists in the following century, he would have contributed much of value to their discussions and sympathised with their reasoned and reasonable stance as religious outsiders.

The manor house and, in particular, the church had suffered from many years of neglect when Patten took over. He spent much of his time refurbishing the manor house to the standards required to sustain his exalted position. In 1563 he turned his attention to the dilapidated St Mary's Church. He oversaw the church's restructuring, repairing the crumbling walls and adding stained-glass windows, a new aisle, external towers, a vestry, a chapel and a small schoolroom. By so doing, he reversed the decline of the building, and he significantly increased the church's size and the space available for worshippers. He converted the building into what was, in his vision and design, the first post-Reformation Anglican church in England. Above the south entrance he added a flat stone that carried the words '1563, Ab Alto' ('From Above'), which remains there today.

Although major alterations were carried out during the centuries that followed, it was to be 150 years after Patten's work before the church again required further refurbishment. These later renovations were required to ensure the enduring stability of the old building, but without Patten's earlier unstinting efforts it is conceivable that Old St Mary's Church may not have survived until the present day.

THE POWER OF GRAVITY: THE NEW RIVER

Some forty years later – around the onset of England's Stuart Age – work commenced on another project that, although in scale dwarfed by Patten's rebuilding of Old St Mary's, was until recent years an equally familiar and popular landmark in Stoke Newington. It was also much needed.

Today, only a few yards from Old St Mary's is the Church Street entrance to Clissold Park, the development and history of which I will be discussing in Chapter Three. As you walk towards the neo-classical facade of Clissold House, you may wonder about the bridge and short stretch of stagnant water to your left, which appears to be a river but which ends just after the bridge. After a loop away from the House and two short bridges later, it again comes to a halt. This elongated pond is, in fact, all that remains in Stoke Newington of an engineering triumph of the early seventeenth century: the New River.

In the early 1600s, London was a dirty, plague-ridden city and one that required constant, clean drinking water. The Thames was filthy, as were the several other rivers and rivulets that fed into it, so it was decided to construct a new river – or, rather, an aqueduct – that would provide fresh water for the city. Sir Hugh Myddleton introduced a scheme whereby such a river could have its source in the Hertfordshire countryside and, as pumps of this nature were not then available, it would reach London by a carefully calculated calibration of the generally downward-sloping contours of the landscape: in other words, it would be directed along its path solely by the force of gravity.

This scheme was approved, and in 1608 work began on what was called the 'New River'. With around 600 labourers every day digging out and forming the aqueduct to the precise instructions of Myddleton, and beginning its journey near Ware – where it was sourced from local springs, wells and a diverted section of the River Lea – the New River was completed by 1613, a remarkable achievement in those virtually machine-free days. As its source was 20 miles to the north of the city, and its height not much more than 100ft above the level of the Thames, the length of the river extended to 40 miles as it negotiated its winding way through today's Clissold Park towards its destination at Sadler's Wells. The river descended only 25ft over its 40-mile journey, or around 7in per mile. (A 'new cut' in 1814 reduced the river's length to 27 miles.)

The New River entered Clissold Park from Green Lanes, looped around the bottom half of the Park, past Clissold House, turned west along the internal southern edge of the Park parallel to Paradise Row on west Church Street, and then crossed Church Street by running under Paradise Bridge and then Park Bridge before it resumed its journey through Highbury, where it was eventually culverted.

In 1830 the New River Company bought 42 acres of land in Woodberry Down in Stoke Newington, on the site of former brickfields. By 1833 they had built two reservoirs – Eastern and Western – which had a total water capacity of 90 million gallons, as well as a pumping station. After a serious cholera outbreak in 1846, filter beds were built in 1852 next to the reservoirs to purify the water, as by now it was becoming polluted by the time it reached Stoke Newington.

The New River was a popular swimming attraction in the area before the increasing dumping of rubbish in the water led to its culverting, aside from the small area that remains in Clissold Park. It was also, for its time, a masterpiece in engineering design, and its legacy continues to the present day (*see* box).

WOODBERRY DOWN RESERVOIRS

When the reservoirs were constructed, they lay in an area of open land, pasture and woodland. By the late 1860s, there were several large mansions in the area, some of which backed onto the New River and overlooked the reservoirs, and the land was gradually being developed for housing. Today they are virtually surrounded by houses and buildings, including the Woodberry Down Estate (the story of which is in Chapter Six).

By 1946 the pumping station and filter beds had ceased to exist, and the New River terminated at the reservoirs. The Metropolitan Water Board bought from the Church Commissioners the freeholds of both reservoirs in 1958, and in 1971 the Board issued plans to demolish the pumping station and sell the land for development. A vigorous public campaign – 'Save Our Reservoirs' – was initiated to combat these plans, and the land was saved and the building listed in 1974. In 1996 the pumping station – in appearance, a neo-Gothic version of a medieval Scottish castle – was opened as a climbing centre that is today regarded as one of the country's finest, although the old filter beds underpin Myddleton Grange housing estate on the western side of Green Lanes.

Thames Water, then privatised, tried again in 1992 to sell off the land and reservoirs, but local campaigners once more succeeded in preventing this. Also, the water in the reservoirs had been treated regularly with chlorine and sodium phosphate, and this was brought to a halt. The wildlife began to return to the reservoirs.

Today, the West reservoir is a popular water sports and environmental educational centre, while the East reservoir, under the management of London Wildlife Trust, is now a nature reserve that was opened to the public in

2016 under the name Woodberry Wetlands. The New River Path was also constructed and made accessible to the public, and the Path runs along the northern rim of the reservoirs from Bethune Road to Green Lanes.

What was once an essential public service is today an open public space, and one which makes a significant contribution to the popular appeal of the Stoke Newington area.

ORIGINS OF DISSENT IN STOKE NEWINGTON

Meanwhile, as these works were progressing, Stoke Newington was becoming an ideal refuge, in particular for well-off nonconformists who were finding that the City authorities and its orthodox Anglican clergy were becoming irritating obstacles to their desire to express their views concerning independence of thought and expression, the relationship between man and God, and to worship in the manner that they wished.

Several of these wealthy newcomers had arrived in Stoke Newington from Europe. In the sixteenth century, Stoke Newington was home to Flemish, Italian, Cypriot, Dutch and other European merchants and traders, and these people had first-hand experience of the profound impact of the Lutheran and Calvinist new Protestant theology and the often savage social reactions, particularly from the Roman Catholic Church, to the rejection of church ceremonies and beliefs. The word 'Protestant' was originally coined by the Catholic Church as a dismissive term, as these proponents of this new faith were always protesting about something or other.

Protestants believed fundamentally in the 'Word of God' as revealed through reading the scriptures rather than, as with Catholics, through the adoption of and adherence to traditions that often had little or no biblical reference or foundation (said the Protestants). They objected to the assumptions and fundamental irrelevance of the earlier scholastic teachings promoted by Thomas Aquinas, the invention of purgatory, the power and ubiquity of bishops, the denial of the possibility of adult baptism, the increasing practice by many Catholic priests of simony (the selling of ecclesiastical indulgences) and similar practices.

They also denounced the Anglican Latin liturgy – preferring sermons and communal hymn-singing to be preached and sung in English – and rejected ritual music and ceremonial trappings, unnecessary ornamentation, and all aspects of Anglican doctrines and practices that interfered with an individual's direct relationship with his or her God.

Calvinists, or Reformed Protestants, also welcomed the widening acceptance of predestination and of justification by faith alone. St Paul had proposed, in his Epistle to the Romans, a form of predestination and, with the later agreement of St Augustine, this was the cornerstone of Calvinist belief, although it became an increasingly controversial and divisive issue within the Protestant movement.

Some of the other new English-born residents of Stoke Newington had travelled around Europe and had also been introduced to these continental, post-Reformation developments and new ideas in religion and philosophy, and had become similarly disenchanted with the teachings of the Anglican Church.

In the opinion of the Church of England, which had virtually been an arm of the English state since Henry VIII's split with Rome and the subsequent dissolution of the English monasteries, many of the religious beliefs that were being discussed in places such as Stoke Newington were considered blasphemous and dangerous, as they presented a serious challenge to the Church and to the social/monarchical structure of the time. Some of these new 'sectarians', as they were becoming known, were millenarians, deists, unitarians or even atheists, and others had expressed republican sentiments.

By the early years of the seventeenth century, these heretical and monarchy-threatening notions were considered anathema by the prevailing new Anglican Church teachings – a curious combination of Catholic ceremonial ritual worship and quasi-Calvinist theology – and the Anglicans began to label proponents of nonconformist opinions, which differed from the 'orthodoxy' of Anglicanism, as 'dissenters'. In the following chapter, I mention several of the most influential (and notorious) of these groups – from Ranters to Levellers and from Fifth Monarchists to Quakers – in order to illustrate the wide variety of dissenting beliefs in England during the religious maelstrom of the mid-seventeenth century.

Meanwhile, Stoke Newington was beginning to embrace and enhance its status as a rural retreat and a meeting place for leading religious dissenters. Many of these people were to play significant roles in one of the most disastrously divisive and socially implosive periods in British history: the English Civil War and its long and troubled aftermath.

CHAPTER TWO

CIVIL WAR: THE EMERGENCE AND SPREAD OF DISSENT

No bishop, no king, no nobility.

James I and VI

But we need not doubt the sincerity of the great number of preachers who proclaimed that Parliament's cause was God's, and that — whatever Charles I's subjective intentions — his government was objectively forwarding the cause of the Roman Antichrist. The royalists were the antichristian party.

The World Turned Upside Down, Christopher Hill

When King Charles I was executed in London on 30 January 1649, his beheading was considered by many at the time as one of the most profoundly shocking events in England's history. In fact, and with the benefit of hindsight, this unprecedented regicide was merely the curtain falling on the first act of the tortuous drama that constituted the English seventeenth century. As the century progressed, further acts would unfold and several other actors would assume centre stage before the final curtain dropped on the last scene of this era's turbulent and bitterly socially divisive events.

However, after all the trouble and strife, after all the violence and bru-
tality had receded, and after all the smoke had drifted away from this most
traumatic of periods, the seventeenth century gradually became regarded as
the years that oversaw not only the end of feudalism and the assumed divine
right of monarchs, but also established the preconditions for constitutional
parliamentary democracy, religious tolerance, freedom of expression and a
good deal more that today many take for granted.

As Christopher Hill observed, the period 1603–1714 was 'the century of
revolution', and it was one that – despite the ferocious internecine hatreds
of the period, and in no small measure due to the persistence of the often-
despised 'dissenters' – gave birth to the modern British state.

In this book I do not intend to add to the enormous body of literature
that has been published on the two Civil Wars, and I will refer to the War
mainly when it impinges – as it frequently does during the Cromwellian
Protectorate, and in the reigns of Charles II, William and Mary and the early
Hanoverians – on the Stoke Newington area.

♦ ♦ ♦

In the early 1600s, Stoke Newington remained a small rural settlement surrounded by open fields and dwindling woodland, but it was becoming a
wealthy little place. Other nearby hamlets, particularly Upper Clapton and
Newington Green, were also enjoying a rising prosperity, and part of the
reason for this continued to lie in the area's profitable role as a fresh food
exporter to the City of London. Its fields and market gardens had benefited
from European incomers, particularly the Dutch, who had brought with
them new fertilisation and planting skills that far outperformed the parish's
previous farming techniques.

However, the principal reason for the parish's financial good health lay in
the continuing arrival of moneyed dissenters, who were building ever-larger
homes with extensive gardens in Stoke Newington, where there was still plenty
of land available for these purposes. Throughout the conflicts of the century,
Stoke Newington remained anti-Royalist and staunchly pro-Parliamentary,
as one would expect given the nature of its growing new constituency and
its location. Most of southern England – in particular London – as well as
East Anglia and the country's north-eastern coastline was of a similar radical

persuasion (indeed, Hull had been the first English town to close its gates to Charles I and his Royalist army) while, generally speaking, the north and west of England tended to a pro-Royalist stance, although a number of dissenting sectarian groups had their origins in the northern towns.

A PROLIFERATION OF SECTS

The Protestant sectarian groups, which were particularly active during the 1640s, included Anabaptists, Behmenists, Enthusiasts, Familists, Fifth Monarchists, Grindletonians, Muggletonians, Philadelphians, Puritans, Sabbatarians, Seekers, Socinians, Ranters and probably a few more, most of whom had faded away or had merged with others between the late 1640s and the early years of the Restoration.

I find it almost inconceivable that I mention the Ranters and the Puritans as sharing a religious grouping, or even the same planet, as the former saw themselves as each possessing the spirit of God and therefore being incapable of sin. Under leader Abiezer Coppe, they did not generally believe in the afterlife, and spent much of their time drinking alcohol and fornicating. The Puritans were, well, Puritans. However, I suppose that unity against a perceived common foe can lead to strange bedfellows.

(As an aside, a cartoonist friend and I once conceived of a cartoon series featuring the adventures of a group of Ranters who had entered a 350-year time warp on a north Middlesex pasture land and who had awoken in Clissold Park in today's Stoke Newington. The Ranters would have had much in common with several residents of today's parish.)

The political ideas emanating from other dissenting Protestant groups, particularly the Levellers and Diggers, are today seen as having been, in many respects, well ahead of their time. The Levellers instigated the 1647 Putney Debates and were advocates of representative democracy. Although active in the New Model Army, the Levellers did not favour direct action for political ends, unlike the Diggers. The Diggers (or 'True Levellers') were led by Gerrard Winstanley, who famously wrote that land should be 'a common treasury for all' and he preached, and briefly practised, communal living. On a monument erected in Moscow by Lenin in 1917 that names seventeen of the world's greatest revolutionaries, Winstanley's name appears on this pantheon. A prophet without honour in his own country ...

Other groups – such as Baptists, Congregationalists, Presbyterians and Unitarians (although, as anti-trinitarians, Unitarians were normally Socinians) – survived, and were later followed by Methodists. Today, these are worldwide religious organisations, and have long been represented in Stoke Newington and its surrounds. However, the most influential grouping in Stoke Newington, from the seventeenth till the twentieth centuries, was 'The Society of Friends': the Quakers. Later in this chapter I will be discussing the important and enduring role of the Quakers in Stoke Newington.

By the second half of the seventeenth century, Stoke Newington was a slowly expanding area with Church Street remaining at its core. The Manor House, however, was showing its age. I mentioned earlier that John Dudley, erstwhile lord of the manor of Stoke Newington, died in 1580. After his death his daughter, Anne, married Sir Francis Popham, and the lease of the manor was assigned to them. Francis, a committed Parliamentarian, died in 1644, and his son Alexander, who under Cromwell became a colonel in the New Model Army, bought out the manorial lease and remained there during the Protectorate as lord of the manor. He bought back the lease and manor from Charles II after the Restoration but, as the early-Tudor building was becoming increasingly dilapidated, he sublet it and moved away from the area, although he retained his status as the manor's lord.

Other substantial homes had appeared on the street, but, at the century's end, the two largest mansions on Church Street were in place. These neighbouring buildings faced imperiously onto the street, and their lawns, gardens and orchards extended several acres north to Hackney Brook and encroaching on the slopes of Woodberry Down. Their occupants were some of England's leading aristocratic nonconformists and dissenters. These estates, for such they were, became known as Fleetwood House and Abney House.

FLEETWOOD HOUSE

On Church Street, the land that is today occupied by the fire station, as well as Fleetwood and Summerhouse Roads, was once the extensive front garden of Fleetwood House.

In 1628, Sir Edward Hartopp, MP for Leicester, bought a sizeable chunk of land on the northern side of the street, and he and his son (also Edward) supervised the construction of a spacious, three-storey red-brick mansion. Edward the younger, a nonconformist who had been instrumental in raising and overseeing a regiment for Cromwell, died in 1658, when the mansion and land became the property of his widow, Dame Mary Hartopp, son John and daughter Mary, all confirmed dissenters. Dame Mary married Charles Fleetwood in 1664. He moved into the mansion and it then became known as Fleetwood House.

Fleetwood was one of the most eminent Puritan nonconformists (*see* box) in England. At the age of 26, in 1644 he was appointed a colonel in Cromwell's army, and he was promoted six years later to lieutenant general. The following year his wife died, leaving him with two young children, and in 1652 he married Bridget, Cromwell's eldest daughter, whose first husband, the famed General Henry Ireton, had been Cromwell's friend, but the previous year Ireton had died shortly after the Siege of Limerick.

THE ENGLISH PURITANS

In the sixteenth and seventeenth centuries, English Puritans were, like other sectarian dissidents, people who wished to purify the Church of England of all its continuing Roman Catholic sacraments and practices. By the late 1630s, many Puritans had emigrated to North America, particularly to New England. Those who remained had much in common with Scottish Presbyterians, who wished to see England and its Church adopt the strict Reformed Protestantism of John Calvin, which had been brought to Scotland by John Knox.

During the Civil War and its aftermath, English Presbyterians were one of the largest parliamentary dissenting groups, alongside Independents. The latter simply desired the toleration and non-persecution of all Protestant groups, and they had formed the dominant part of the Rump Parliament that had decided on the execution of Charles I. However, some earlier histories of the English Civil War refer to the period as the Puritan Civil War. It was a confusing period.

After the Restoration, the passing of the 1662 Uniformity Act led to the self-imposed 'Great Ejection', which saw almost 2,500 preachers leave the Anglican Church and establish their own places of worship, until these were also later banned. These preachers were mainly Puritan, but also Congregationalists, who shared many Puritan beliefs. Perhaps their attitudes can best be encapsulated in the timeworn phrase: 'Work hard and glorify God.'

More Puritans went to North America and, when greater tolerance was eventually afforded to Protestant nonconformists, like several other pre-Civil War dissenting sects, Puritans gradually merged into the mainstream of English religious and political life. However, several of their Calvinist beliefs are still today upheld by such groups as the Free Church of Scotland and others.

In 1652 Fleetwood was promoted to Commander-in-Chief and then Lord Deputy in Ireland, until he was called back to England to join the Protector's inner sanctum. At this point, he was almost certainly offered, by Cromwell – to take effect after Cromwell's death – the dual roles of full control of the army and head of the Commonwealth. In other words, he was to succeed him. After Cromwell died in 1658, no documents could be found to support his wishes to this effect, so Fleetwood then had to accept the ineffective Richard, son of Cromwell, as his superior, although his subordination was a short one.

After the Restoration, Fleetwood retired to Norfolk, where his second wife, Bridget, died in 1662, now leaving him responsible for a total of seven children. He was fortunate, or perhaps prescient, in that he took little part in the second Civil War, did not attend the trial of King Charles I and did not sign the death warrant, so he was not a 'regicide'. Nevertheless, he kept out of harm's way and laid low for a while. When he married Dame Mary Hartopp, he moved with his seven children into the idyllic surroundings of the Hartopp mansion and grounds in the centre of Stoke Newington. Assessed at '25 hearths' (the number of fireplaces in a house, which was used to calculate 'hearth-tax'), what was now known as Fleetwood House was the largest house in the area.

Robert Crumb, the US cartoonist and satirist of the 1960s 'hippy' movement, once observed that 'the family that lays together, stays together', but Crumb's maxim had been enacted and validated some 300 years previously in Stoke Newington. Fleetwood House contained sixty rooms, which was more than sufficient space for large and growing families. This was just as well, as John and Mary Hartopp then married two of Fleetwood's children. As a result, Fleetwood House was thereafter, in effect, split into two homes: one for the Hartopps and the other for the Fleetwoods.

Fleetwood was now consolidating Stoke Newington's reputation as England's centre of dissent in the late seventeenth century. He held regular meetings at the House and elsewhere in the village with several influential dissidents. One was Dr John Owen, the Independent minister who preached before Parliament the day after the execution of Charles I, was appointed Vice-Chancellor of Oxford University in 1652 by Cromwell, conducted Henry Ireton's funeral and ran his own Independent church in London, of which Fleetwood was an early member.

Another was the Presbyterian Dr Thomas Manton, one of Cromwell's main chaplains and rector at St Mary's in Stoke Newington between 1645 and 1657. Manton then moved to St Paul Church in Covent Garden, from which he was 'ejected' in 1662. He was followed as Stoke Newington rector by Dr Daniel Bull, another fiery nonconformist who was ejected from his position after the Restoration and who became a Presbyterian minister at a house in Church Street. Later, Manton was imprisoned for his dissenting views and for breach of the Clarendon Code (*see* box), and he was buried at St Mary's in 1677.

These nonconformists and others from the area frequently ran into trouble with the established church and government. For instance, young John Hartopp openly advocated that the then Duke of York, who was Charles II's brother and the soon-to-be King James VII, should be banned from the throne, an act for which he was censured and heavily fined. Then, along with Fleetwood and John Gould (a local merchant who worked in London), he was indicted under the Seditious Conventicles Act. And so it continued until the 1689 Toleration Act, passed under the brief reign of James VII, permitted such meetings and loosened, to a degree, the constraints that bound dissenters.

Fleetwood died in 1692 and was buried in the dissident resting place of Bunhill Fields. However, this old Puritan could rest in peace, as he had helped, in no small measure, to establish a new generation of nonconformism in Stoke Newington.

CLARENDON CODE

One of the factors – and there were many of these – that eased the path to Charles II's Restoration in 1660 was The Declaration of Breda, which he issued in April 1660 from the town of Breda in the Netherlands. Among other guarantees contained in the Declaration were:

i: a general pardon would be issued, except for all regicides who had been actively involved in the execution of Charles I, for crimes committed during the interregnum (the Protectorate) for all who recognised Charles as the lawful king, and

ii: religious toleration where it did not disturb the peace of the kingdom.

The new 'Cavalier Parliament', mainly composed of Anglican royalists, decided that the holding of public office by non-Anglicans was a threat to the 'peace of the kingdom'. During the years 1660–65 they passed four Acts against Catholics and Protestant dissenters, which became known as the Clarendon Code:

- Corporation Act of 1661. All municipal officers had to take regular Anglican communion, thereby excluding all nonconformists from public office.

- Act of Uniformity of 1662. The Book of Common Prayer was made compulsory for all preachers, with the result that many nonconformist preachers left office in 'the Great Ejection'.

- Suppression of Seditious Conventicle Act of 1664. This forbade all meetings of five or more people for worship, unless licensed. This prevented dissenting groups from advertising and holding meetings.

- Five Mile Act of 1665. This forbade nonconformist ministers from entering their town and place of worship, if it was within five miles of their residence.

These Acts were passed by Parliament but with the knowledge and connivance of Charles II. So much, then, for the promises that were made in The Declaration of Breda.

ABNEY HOUSE

Thomas Gunston, son of a successful London draper and nonconformist, was born in Stoke Newington in 1667 and lived in comfort on the south side of Church Street not far from the 'Red Lion'. From his house he could see the expansive meadowland between Lordship Lane (today's Lordship Road, then an old drovers' path leading to Woodberry Down) and Stamford Hill so, with his inherited financial resources, in 1694 he acquired much of this land and began to build a grand mansion immediately to the west of Fleetwood House. The new building, with 40 acres of land, was completed in 1695, five years before the death of Gunston at the age of 34.

Gunston had bought from Alexander Popham the leasehold of the old Manor House. Popham had already started work on the demolition of the house that, in 1709, would be replaced by the elegant buildings of Church Row. Gunston's purchase terminated the Popham family's interest in Stoke Newington.

Lady Abney, Gunston's sister, then inherited the land, the manorial lease and the handsome, red-bricked, seven-bay, two-storey mansion, with its tall chimneys, tree-lined paths, gardens and bowling green, all set well back from Church Street. The mansion was named Abney House, and her husband Sir Thomas Abney – director of the Bank of England, Lord Mayor of London and a Puritan dissident (although his roles required occasional conformity to the Church of England) – became lord of Stoke Newington manor.

While Gunston was constructing Abney House, he had struck up a close friendship with fellow nonconformist Isaac Watts – known variously as a poet, theologian, 'father of the English hymn' and a 'Dissenting Divine' – but, after Gunston's premature death, Watts moved on to preach elsewhere in London, as well as at the new Stoke Newington Independent chapel in Edwards Lane in 1722. After the death of Sir Thomas in 1722, the manor passed to his sister Mary who, in 1734, invited Watts back to Stoke Newington for a brief visit. In the event, Watts remained at Abney House until 1748 – his 'brief visit' lasting for sixteen years – when he died and was buried in Bunhill Fields.

On Mary's death in 1750, the estate and the manor lease passed to her youngest daughter Elizabeth, who remained unmarried until her death in 1782, when her will left all proceeds of the estate to nonconformist charities. In 1783 the building, land and manor were acquired by Jonathan Eade. On Eade's death in 1811, he was interred in St Mary's and he was the last lord of the manor to occupy Abney House. His sons, William and Joseph, then acquired from the Church authorities a long lease and became joint lords of the manor.

Around the same time, 1814, an Act of Parliament was passed that permitted the feudal relic of copyhold to be converted into freehold. William and Joseph Eade then set about dividing up the estate and selling it in parcels. The year 1814 saw the beginning of a housing boom in the village, with builders attracted by the extension of the period of leasehold to ninety-nine years, and this is approximately the point at which I begin Chapter Three of this book.

Next door in Fleetwood House, the Hartopp family had all died or left the village by the mid-1760s. The building then passed through various hands, the last occupants being the Ripley family in 1797. They moved on in 1824, and they leased the building to Susanna Corder and her Quaker Girls' School, which remained at the house for the following fourteen years. However, the 1814 Act, and its expansionary impact on Stoke Newington, led inevitably to Fleetwood House's demolition in 1872. Abney House had survived until 1843 as a Wesleyan theological college, but it had suffered a similar fate.

All that remains today of the Abney House estate is the iron gateway and railings that, since 1840, has been the Church Street entrance to Abney Park Cemetery, which occupies much of the land on which once stood the splendid buildings of Fleetwood and Abney Houses.

◆ ◆ ◆

In the immediate post-Restoration period, Stoke Newington was home to a number of other Civil War veterans, most of whom had had been less eminent in the War than had been Fleetwood.

For example, Thomas Venner was a local Fifth Monarchist, at the time a sect that possessed a substantial number of adherents. The Fifth Monarchists believed in the Book of Daniel's prophecy that, following the four 'monarchies' of Babylon, Persia, Macedonia and Rome, the fifth monarchy would be the return of Christ, who would then rule for eternity over all human beings. Their fervency was hastened by the imminence of the year 1666, as '666' was, in the Book of Revelation, 'the Number of the Beast'.

In 1661, Venner led a group of fifty determined, similarly minded Fifth Monarchists on a 'small-scale' attempt to capture the City of London. It was, to say the least, a courageous attempt. Although eventually and inevitably surrounded, Venner and his men survived a siege for four days before they were finally caught and Venner was executed.

Henry Danvers was a colonel in the Parliamentary army and, when being escorted to the Tower in 1661 on a sedition charge, he escaped his captors. He was also in trouble on other occasions, culminating in supposed involvement with the 1685 Monmouth Rebellion, a trial from which he again escaped, this time permanently to the Netherlands. Danvers died there in his bed in his late sixties.

Colonel Daniel Axtel, another local and avowed anti-Royalist, was in command of the men guarding King Charles I during his trial and subsequent execution. In 1660 he was arrested, tried as a regicide and executed. In 1678 the Stoke Newington house belonging to Axtel's son was searched, as he was suspected of seditious activities. Axtel Minor disappeared to the Carolinas shortly thereafter, never to return.

As Stoke Newington and its surrounding area had quickly been recognised by both nonconformists and the new regime as a dissenting hot spot, this small village no doubt attracted dissenters and informers in equal measure. However, although the wealthy residents and aristocrats of the parish have left records of their activities, the activities of the poorer and less noteworthy are not so easily obtained, which is why this book appears preoccupied with the nobility and their ilk.

It's possible that there may have been several other doomed anti-Royalist subversive activities by these 'lower orders' but it's more likely that the ordinary people – the tradesmen, farm and market garden workers, brickfield labourers and the others who kept this place together – were less concerned with dissenting intrigues than they were with making a decent living. The latter was not a problem as, by the late seventeenth century, Stoke Newington was slowly expanding, both along Church Street and down the High Street, and it was becoming a wealthy rural village, much like its southern neighbour Newington Green.

◆ ◆ ◆

DISSENT IN NEWINGTON GREEN

Described in the late seventeenth century as 'the well-to-do edge of radical Protestantism', Newington Green sits today on the southern border of Stoke Newington and Islington's Mildmay ward, the north side being within today's Stoke Newington.

Within Mildmay, such street names as Boleyn Road and King Henry's Walk suggest a connection with King Henry VIII, and the corpulent monarch did indeed own a hunting lodge in the area. The ward is named after Sir Walter Mildmay, one-time Chancellor of the Exchequer under Elizabeth I and founder of Emmanuel College, Cambridge. His grandson Sir Henry Mildmay was a Parliamentarian MP who attended the trial of Charles I. Arrested after the Restoration for 'regicide', he was granted leniency as he had refused to sign the King's death warrant, but nonetheless he was stripped of his knighthood and estate, and sentenced to life imprisonment.

During the late seventeenth century, Newington Green was a small agricultural village surrounded by meadowland. Earlier in the century, the Green had been described as 'a most rude wilderness with large old trees' but in 1742 it was railed in and improved. In the early nineteenth century, the Green was recalled by John Stewart Mill, who lived there as a young boy between 1810 and 1813 with his father James, as 'an almost rustic neighbourhood'.

It had also acquired a reputation for religious dissent, with its preachers and dissident intellectuals sheltering under the aristocratic protection of the Stoke Newington Fleetwood, Abney and Hartopp families. It was home to a number of distinguished 'dissenting academies' that had been formed across England, and particularly London, in the aftermath of the 1662 Uniformity Act. The first tutors in the academies were often nonconformist ministers who had been 'ejected' as a result of the Act, although many preferred the more conducive atmospheres of Glasgow, Edinburgh and Utrecht.

As the only two English universities – Oxford and Cambridge – then required adherence to the doctrines of the Church of England, several of these academies were attended by dissident pupils, who also preferred to learn their subjects in English and not, as in the English universities, in Latin. The most popular early academy in Newington Green was Charles Morton's Academy, which taught such subjects as geography, history, classics, maths, natural science, politics and modern languages. His pupils included Daniel Defoe (of whom, more shortly) and Samuel Wesley (the elder). Morton was a Puritan who ended his career at Harvard. A later tutor was Rev. James Burgh, author of *The Dignity of Human Nature* and *Thoughts on Education.*

On the northern Stoke Newington side of the Green stands the Unitarian church that, as is stated above the entrance, was built in 1708. Originally constructed by the Rational Dissenters – and used on occasion as a Presbyterian and even an Anglican place of worship – it was designed to look like a dwelling place so as not to alert the religious authorities. The 'Newington Green meeting-house' became firmly Unitarian in the 1750s, and today still holds regular services as the Unitarian 'New Unity' church, the oldest nonconformist place of worship in London that is still in use.

The church's most famous minister was Richard Price, a Welsh-born philosopher, mathematician, author and nonconformist who arrived in 1758 and lived at 'no. 54, The Green', which is in a small terrace on the Green and which, as it dates back to 1658, remains the oldest existing terrace in London. Price was a dissenting polymath, a universalist and a renowned preacher, and he was at various times visited by, among others, William Pitt the Elder, David Hume, Adam Smith, John Howard and Tom Paine. He also provided sanctuary from Anglican wrath for Joseph Priestley, hiring him as his librarian in 1772.

Also a close friend of Benjamin Franklin, who had invited Price to join his London-based Club of Honest Whigs, and an acquaintance of Thomas Jefferson and John Adams, the second president of the USA, Price championed the cause of the American Revolution. His 1776 work supporting the Revolution – *Observations on the Nature of Civil Liberty* – became a national best-seller and, already a Fellow of the Royal Society, he was awarded the Freedom of the City of London.

Price's sermons and pamphlets of 1789, often written with Priestley, were often in support of the French Revolution, and he praised the revolutionaries' 'universal benevolence', which had 'progressed enlightened ideas'. For his attitude to the Revolution, he was criticised by several leading politicians and intellectuals, most notably, in 1790, by Edmund Burke in Burke's *Reflections on the Revolution in France*. Burke's comprehensive response has seen him claimed as the 'father of British conservatism', as the book established the basic principles of contemporary conservatism, and it has remained continuously in print. That same year, Price's Newington Green supporter and friend, Mary Wollstonecraft (*see* box), published a book that championed, and expanded on, Price's views.

Wollstonecraft was not the only local defender of Price's stance on the French Revolution. Just down the road, at the Angel Tavern in Islington, Mary's friend Tom Paine was also replying to Burke, and his resulting book *Rights of Man*, published in 1791, became an instant success, outselling John Bunyan's *Pilgrim's Progress* and being translated into Gaelic, an honour that not even Bunyan could claim.

Richard Price, outstanding preacher and philosopher, died in April 1791. He was ten years later succeeded as minister by Rochemont Barbauld, husband to Anna Laetitia Barbauld (*see* box on p.66). The Toleration Act, passed in 1689, had applied only to Protestant dissidents who believed in the Holy Trinity.

However, the 1813 Doctrine of the Trinity Act finally granted Unitarians the legal right to worship, and to this day the church is open to all believers. Price's memory lived on, as, at the turn of the twenty-first century, the Unitarian minister Cal Courtney revived the annual Richard Price memorial lecture.

The church today remains a beacon of enlightened thought and a home for free thinkers of many kinds. As an example, prior to the Anti-Iraq Invasion March in London in 2003 it was a meeting place for Jews, Muslims, atheists, self-proclaimed pagans and many others who shared a principled stand against the disastrous action. Another instance was in 2008 – the church's 300th anniversary – when, under Cal's successor, Andy Pakula, the church refused to officiate at marriage ceremonies until same-sex unions were legally permitted. The tabloid press scornfully referred to it as 'the Gay Rights church'. However, Cal and Andy were simply following in the humanitarian footsteps of Richard Price, and in the spirit of Unitarianism generally.

MARY WOLLSTONECRAFT: AN EARLY FEMINIST

'Who made man the exclusive judge, if woman partake with him of the gift of reason?'

Published in 1792, *A Vindication of the Rights of Woman* may not have been the first book in the English language to demand equality for women but it was certainly the most influential, and its author, Mary Wollstonecraft, is today frequently claimed as the founder of modern feminism.

Born in an Essex farmhouse in 1759, through circumstance she assumed responsibility for the well-being of her drunken father and the education of her siblings. Her determination and sense of independence led to her opening in 1784, at the age of 25, a school for girls in north London's Newington Green.

Although originally an Anglican, she began attending the Unitarian church and listening to Richard Price's sermons, at which believers of all persuasions were welcomed. (I recall attending a talk at the Unitarian church a few years ago, only to be informed by a rather fussy gentleman that I had to move from my pew and sit elsewhere: apparently, the seat – the second from the front on the left – was for feminists only, as it was once where sat Mary Wollstonecraft.) Wollstonecraft particularly admired the Rational Dissenters, who had been instrumental in building the church, as they were honest, hard-working and they respected women.

However, Price became her closest intellectual companion and someone with whom she could share and discuss her increasingly radical views.

Wollstonecraft's book, *Vindication of the Rights of Man*, was published in 1790 and can be seen as a defence of Price's writings and speeches on the French Revolution and as a response to Edmund Burke's critique. Her next book, *Vindication of the Rights of Woman*, published two years later, invoked support and condemnation in equal measure. In the book, she stated: 'I do not wish women to have power over men, but over themselves,' proposed that women should have equal representation with men in Parliament, and argued that boys and girls should be educated together at the state's expense. The book was welcomed by many radical thinkers in Britain and America, but it was savagely attacked by Burkeian supporters such as Horace Walpole, who later described Wollstonecraft as a 'hyena in petticoats'.

That year, Wollstonecraft moved to Paris, where she was acclaimed for her principled stand in the battle for women's rights. She moved in with an American sympathiser, Gilbert Imlay, with whom she had a daughter. However, his infidelity added to her growing depression and, after her return to London in 1795, she attempted suicide by jumping into the Thames, but was rescued. Eventually she met and, despite her publicly stated opposition to the institution, married the anarchist and atheist William Godwin, and the couple moved to Somers Town, near King's Cross. She died in 1797, ten days after giving birth to her second daughter, who was to become Mary Shelley, author of *Frankenstein*.

On the rear wall of today's Newington Green Primary School facing onto the Green, a blue plaque states: 'Mary Wollstonecraft. Writer, teacher and feminist. Opened a school for girls near this site in 1784'. A statue of Wollstonecraft, created by sculptor Maggi Hambling, was unveiled in 2020 on the Green, an appropriate, if artistically controversial, memorial to a woman who emerged from Stoke Newington's relative obscurity to achieve worldwide renown, and is regarded today by many feminists as the original voice of liberated gender equality.

CHURCH STREET IN THE EIGHTEENTH CENTURY

Meanwhile, to the north of Newington Green, at the start of the eighteenth century Stoke Newington's Church Street and its surrounding area was assuming an air of civilised, bourgeois gentility. The new terraced houses that were beginning to appear, initially at the old street's western end, were perhaps a mild reproach to the two aristocratic but somewhat ostentatious mansions, and a reminder that the size of a building is not a direct reflection on the cultural refinement of its occupants.

The eastern end of the street had, in the 1670s, witnessed the destruction of a number of timber houses and their replacement by brick dwellings, prompted partly by the easy availability of bricks but probably more so by the devastation caused to the wooden buildings in the City by the recent Great Fire of London. The City authorities had declared, in order to minimise a future fire risk, that all new and replacement houses had to be rebuilt of non-flammable brick and tile, with wooden roof joints hidden behind brick, and window frames set back by the thickness of a brick. The parish vestry decreed that this should also be the case in Stoke Newington.

On the land previously occupied by the Manor House and which, on its western side, neighboured St Mary's Church, a team of builders erected a terrace containing nine houses. Although the last house carries a date of 1709, the terrace – known as Church Row – had probably been completed by 1700. A carpenter, Job Edwards, also built five smaller brick houses to the east of Church Row and which culminated in a lane, called, in his memory, Edwards Lane, on which stood the gateway to the old Manor House.

The Church Row houses were handsome, double-storeyed and possessed decorative gate pillars. Occupants of this terrace included Benjamin D'Israeli, grandfather of the (near) eponymous author and twice Conservative Prime Minister in the later years of the nineteenth century, and the grandfather was visited there by the book publisher John Murray and other leading literary figures.

The same house was later owned in the 1840s by Frederick Mullet Evans, proprietor of *Punch,* and his regular guests included Dickens, Wilkie Collins and Thackeray. Judging by contemporary photographs, Evans was keen on hosting large, lavish parties at his home. Around the same time, two other houses in the terrace were occupied by the Moline family, who were active in local Quaker affairs. In the early- to mid-eighteenth century, John Howard (*see* box), the inspiration for the Howard League for Penal Reform, also lodged in Church Row. Several other notable literary worthies lived in Church Row but the terrace, a splendid addition to the local architectural landscape, was demolished in the early 1930s to make way for the new Stoke Newington Town Hall.

JOHN HOWARD

Philanthropist and social reformer John Howard was born into a prosperous dissenting family in Hackney in 1726, and he was educated at John Eames's Dissenting Academy in Moorfields.

On the death of his father in 1742 and his assumption of a substantial inheritance, Howard undertook a European tour and, on his return, he lodged with Sarah Loidore in Stoke Newington's Church Row. Loidore nursed him back to health after he became seriously ill and, despite the fact that she was 30 years older than Howard, the couple married. An unassuming man and Calvinist dissenter, he was viewed as 'eccentric', which may today have been labelled as Asperger's syndrome.

After Sarah's death three years later, Howard set off for Lisbon, was captured by a French privateer and imprisoned, before returning to England in a prisoner exchange deal. His commitment to prison reform is likely to have stemmed from this experience. He moved to his family estate in Bedfordshire, and in 1773 he was appointed High Sheriff of the county. He toured prisons across the country, talking to jailers and prisoners, and was shocked by what he witnessed, including the inmates having to pay fees to the unpaid jailers and the deeply unhygienic state of the prisoners' conditions. His evidence and personal experiences assisted not only the introduction of 'single-celling' but also the passage in 1774 of two Acts of Parliament that abolished jailers' fees and improved prisoners' health. In 1777 he published *The State of the Prisons in England and Wales*, in which he argued for penal reform and the abolition of capital punishment.

Between 1775 and 1790, he travelled almost 80,000km across Europe, visiting numerous prisons, and he died from typhus in Crimea. In the late 1860s, the Howard Association was formed to continue his legacy, and in 1921 it became the Howard League for Penal Reform, still the largest and most influential such organisation. John Howard societies also flourish across North America.

He was the first civilian to have had his statue erected in St Paul's Cathedral. The inscription reads: 'This extraordinary man had the fortune to be honoured whilst living, in the manner which his virtues deserved … for his eminent services rendered to his country and to mankind.'

Across the street from Church Row had stood an old house that, by 1717, had been demolished and had been converted by local bricklayers into a terrace containing four small brick houses. A plaque on the wall states, 'On this site stood a medieval mansion, built c 14th century.' After four sisters moved into this terrace in 1813 it became known as Sisters Place, of which two remain as houses. After a good deal of attention and refurbishment by its owners in the later years of the twentieth century, the terrace is a rare extant example of Queen Anne architecture with external fine brickwork and interior period style. This is the oldest inhabited building in Stoke Newington.

Further to the west along south Church Street, where today it joins Albion Road, the Rose and Crown sits on the east corner of the junction, which was once the eighteenth-century Halstead House, demolished in the 1930s. The Rose and Crown was one of the oldest taverns in Church Street, dating back to 1612, when it occupied today's eastern corner. It was rebuilt in the late nineteenth century, and, after the demolition of Halstead House, the pub crossed the road to its present location, and it retains many of its 1930s features in its listed interior.

On the Green Lanes side of the parish 'glebe' land, there was constructed a row of houses that in 1738 was named Paradise Row. By 1723 several of these houses were in place and, by 1764, there were fifteen, mostly three-storeyed, five-bayed houses in the Row, each with extended back gardens. The centrepiece was named Paradise House, and was a single, unattached building with a pedimented porch, Corinthian pillars and projecting wings.

Paradise Row faced out across Church Street to Newington Common (today's Clissold Park) and the New River which, at the east end of the Row, left the Park, ducked under Church Street via Paradise Bridge and headed south. In the eighteenth and nineteenth centuries, Paradise Row must have been a peaceful spot, with a view over the Park and meadows as far as the slopes of Woodberry Down. The Row appealed to City merchants, bankers and traders, and many of the inhabitants were Quakers who, at the time, were Stoke Newington's most active and important citizens. Joseph Lister – 'the father of modern surgery' – lived here as a boy, and Harriet Beecher Stowe, author of *Uncle Tom's Cabin*, visited friends in Paradise Row. The Row was something of a Quaker intellectual hothouse.

Strolling back along the street in an easterly direction past what is now Old St Mary's, under the shadow of the new St Mary's Church, and past the Town Hall, public library and Edwards Lane, is the former Fox's Wine

Bar, the site of what was once the Manor House School, which was built in 1806 and demolished in 1880.

Built by the Rev. John Bransby, the school's subsequently most famous pupil was the novelist and Gothic horror story writer Edgar Allan Poe, whose adoptive family moved to the area in 1817. The 6-year-old Poe attended the school for three years, and in his short story *William Wilson* he described Stoke Newington as 'a misty-looking village of England', the school as 'a huge old house', and he mentioned the resounding sound of St Mary's church bells. The family again moved on, and Poe died in New York, aged 39.

Just past today's Barn Street was the Abney Congregational Church, built in 1706. This was the second such chapel, as the original was torn down in the late seventeenth century to make way for the Abney House grounds, and it was directly opposite the site of the former Falcon pub, today's Gujurati House, which was first licensed in 1722. The Congregationalists, who had their first meeting in Stoke Newington in 1662, moved again in 1836 to a new building opposite today's fire station. It was an impressively large building with twinned pillars and an imposing portico at the entrance but it was badly damaged by bombing during the Second World War. A much smaller chapel was built inside the existing shell, but the congregation declined and, in 2000, it was replaced by a block of flats.

Further down Church Street – on the south side, and situated between what was the Vortex Jazz Bar and the side of a building that offered, in fading letters, a 'ghost sign' extolling the merits of a local stationer's fountain pens, while, next to it, is an original Banksy graffito depicting the royal family – there is an open space that reveals an eighteenth-century house set back from the street. Interestingly, Hackney Council was apparently unaware of the international fame of the street artist Banksy, whose commission was designed to grace the cover of a forthcoming album by 1990s rock band Blur, and they sent an employee to the site to obliterate the work.

The workman was halfway through obscuring the Banksy with black paint when a woman rushed out from an adjacent shop and, citing the artist's fame, implored the man to stop. When he checked with his employer, an embarrassed Council agreed with the protester, with the result that it today remains a rare, semi-censored Banksy artwork, but with half of it obscured by black paint.

The old eighteenth-century house, at 135 Church Street, is Bliney House, a five-bay Georgian home and a fine example of the architecture of the period, built in 1769 by Henry Sanford, who was also responsible for constructing Sanford Terrace on Stoke Newington Common. Behind this building today is a row of later, small houses and a nursery school. The Quaker and slavery abolitionist William Allen lived here with his second wife between 1816 and 1827, while next door, at 137, lived another local Quaker, Frederick Jansen.

Between Bliney House and Marton Road (the next street along on the south side) there is another small row of old houses (numbers 117 to 105), which are today mainly small shops. One of these houses was a nineteenth-century beer shop, which was previously the Horse and Groom tavern and has been since the late 1980s the site of the Auld Shillelagh bar. Beside the Shillelagh is an old, narrow alley – Hussey's Lane – which leads onto Cut Throat Lane (now Kynaston Road) and, to the east, Pawnbroker's Lane, which joins the High Street via today's Kynaston Avenue. Another of these old houses (no. 111) is home to a long-established flower shop, now also a busy cafe.

Next door to this shop, no. 113 has a small, seemingly undistinguished blue door (and one that is easy to miss unless one notices the blue plaque above it), which was for many years one of the entrances to the home of the Stoke Newington author, poet, editor and dissenter Anna Laetitia Barbauld, one of the leading literary figures of her age (*see* box below).

'VIRAGO' BARBAULD

Regarded in the late eighteenth century as one of England's finest poets, authors and political dissenters, praised by Wordsworth and Coleridge, and compared to Samuel Johnson and Joseph Addison, Anna Laetitia Barbauld was a prolific early feminist writer and essayist.

Daughter and grand-daughter of Presbyterian preachers, Barbauld was born in 1743, and her early published works included the highly successful *Poems* (1773), *Lessons for Children* (1776) and *Hymns in Prose for Children* (1781), and in her poetry she criticised the slave trade. In 1774 she married the Unitarian minister Rochemont Barbauld, grandson of a French Huguenot, who in 1802 became minister at the Newington Green Unitarian church. In 1790 she wrote a pamphlet attacking the government's decision not to repeal anti-dissenter legislation, which prompted Horace Walpole to call her 'Virago Barbauld', while Wordsworth praised here as 'the first of our literary women'.

The couple moved in 1802 to Stoke Newington's Church Street, and six years later Rochemont, suffering from a fit of mental illness, committed suicide by drowning himself in the New River. In 1812 Barbauld published *Eighteen Hundred and Eleven*, a scathing critique of Britain's imperialist adventures that concentrated on British involvement in the Napoleonic Wars. The savage criticism the book provoked was of such an intensity as to shock her and induce her retirement from public life. She continued to live in the same house in Church Street, where she was active in local community women's groups until her death in 1825. She was buried in St Mary's churchyard.

Her posthumous reputation suffered during the Romantic movement, including dismissals of her work from several of her previous notable admirers, and she became a mainly neglected figure until the rise of feminist criticism in the early 1970s, which again perceived Anna Laetitia Barbauld as one of the leading literary and political figures of her age.

Crossing to the north side of Church Street, Lordship Road (once Lordship Lane) is one of the oldest roads in the parish, and it carved a straight path through the empty demesne fields and meadows, over Hackney Brook and up to Woodberry Down. Today, it crosses Manor Road, negotiates its way between the two reservoirs and Woodberry Down estate, and connects with Seven Sisters Road.

The road leaves Church Street beside the Red Lion pub (first mentioned in 1697), which sits in a small triangle beside Red Lion Lane (where sits the last survivor of a group of four eighteenth-century houses) and Lordship Road. To its rear was the former parish watch and fire engine house and the cage for punishing miscreants, at a time when the vestry controlled policing of the parish until the formation of the Metropolitan Police in 1829. It then briefly became the local police station. It was known, for obvious visual reasons, as The Round House.

Continuing on the north side towards the High Street, the next roads are Yoakley Road, which was known as Park Street until 1938 and was originally a footpath leading north to Manor Road, and Bouverie Road (built in the mid-nineteenth century), separated by the Clarence tavern.

Further along is Abney Park Cemetery (*see* Chapter Three), a couple of smaller streets, including Fleetwood Street, built on the grounds of the old estate, and Summerhouse Road in which, during the late eighteenth century, was 'the Summerhouse' villa, the home of James Stephen (*see* box), a leading anti-slavery campaigner. Then, at the eastern corner of Church Street, sits the Three Crowns tavern and the High Street.

JAMES STEPHEN, THE ABOLITIONIST

James Stephen's father moved the family from Poole to Stoke Newington in 1774, and Summerhouse, a large villa house on today's Summerhouse Road, became the young James's home. Having studied at the London Bar, in 1783 he moved to St Kitts in the West Indies, where he was appointed Solicitor-General. On a visit to Barbados he witnessed the trial for murder and execution of four black slaves, which was a gross miscarriage of justice. Stephen was appalled by this and, on his return England in 1794, he became a committed abolitionist.

He joined the anti-slave trade 'Clapham Set', met William Wilberforce and his sister Sarah, and he married Sarah in 1800, moving to the family home in Stoke Newington. Wilberforce was a frequent visitor to the house, as were Anna Laetitia Barbauld and local Quaker abolitionists William Allen, Joseph Woods and Samuel Hoare Jr, the last two being founder members of the Committee for the Abolition of the Slave Trade.

Stephen became Wilberforce's chief legal adviser in the campaign against the slave trade, and he drafted Wilberforce's 1807 proposed Slave Trade Act, but it proved unsuccessful. Stephen then became an MP, a member of the London Abolition Committee, wrote the two-volume work *The Slavery of the British West Indies*, and was a prominent advocate for abolition. He was an eloquent and powerful public speaker, and his work paved the way for the parliamentary passing of the second Abolition Bill in 1833, the year following Stephen's death.

He and Sarah were buried in St Mary's Church graveyard. His tomb, along with that of Barbauld, was recently declared by English Heritage a site of Special Historical Interest.

Opposite Yoakley and Bouverie Roads on the south side of today's street is Defoe Road, which was laid out in the 1860s and contains the St Mary's Assembly Rooms. In the early years of the eighteenth century and well before Defoe Road existed, facing onto Church Street stood the home of one of Stoke Newington's most famous literary dissenter: Daniel Defoe (*see* below).

The street then passes the old Congregational Church and two other streets – Kersley and Lancell – which in the eighteenth century were part of a prosperous market garden. Further down are two three-storey, early eighteenth-century homes, and then we are again back on the London Road.

DEFOE THE DISSENTER

Daniel Foe was born in London in 1660, the son of a wealthy, Presbyterian dissenting London butcher. He was educated at Charles Morton's Newington Green Dissenting Academy where, as a Presbyterian, he attended the Unitarian church. In 1684, he married the daughter of a rich London merchant, a union that lasted forty-seven years and produced eight children.

He joined the disastrous 1685 Monmouth rebellion against James II but received a pardon, and he became a close ally of William of Orange after 1689. Meanwhile, he grew prosperous through his various trading and business dealings – which included wire, wine, brick and tile, and raising civets for perfume – although he was rarely out of debt and was in 1692 declared bankrupt and arrested. After his release he toured around parts of Europe, and by 1695 he had become 'Defoe', believing that 'Foe' was insufficiently notable for a man of his social stature.

In his writing he revealed a prolific talent in verse and political pamphleteering. He achieved success with *The True Born Englishman* (1701), and he had written *The Shortest-Way with the Dissenters* (1703) as a humorous satire on the Tories, Church and 'occasional nonconformists' such as his soon-to-be Stoke Newington neighbour Sir Thomas Abney. However, it was taken seriously by the government and Queen Anne, who pursued a hard line with nonconformists, and the Tories were enraged. They fined and imprisoned him for seditious libel, and sent him to the pillory at Charing Cross, where it is said he won over the initially hostile crowd who had come to hurl rotten fruit, and ended up by cheering him as he recited 'A Hymn to the Pillory'.

In 1701, he established *The Review*, a magazine/newspaper, which was published thrice-weekly until 1713, and he was then employed by the English government as an agent in Scotland, from where he reported back to London on the unfolding events before the impending 1707 Union. He appeared unsympathetic to the Scottish public's antagonism to the Union – 'a Scots rabble is the worst of its kind' – but his observations were useful to the Unionist cause particularly when, still working undercover, his Presbyterian beliefs found Defoe working as an adviser to the General Assembly of the Church of Scotland. However, on his return to England he was taken to court by the opposition Whigs and, once again, imprisoned by the Tory government. When the Tories fell from power, Defoe – a master at the art of switching allegiance for purposes of self-preservation – began working for the Whigs.

He moved to the rural peace and quiet of Stoke Newington in 1709, at first renting rooms where he wrote *A History of the Union of Great Britain* (1709). In 1714, he organised the construction in Church Street of a large, three-storey house, with a stable block and a sizeable garden, which was bounded by Hussey's and Pawnbroker's Lanes and which was his home for the rest of his life. It stood at the corner of what became, in the 1860s, Defoe Road.

Defoe acquired the land from the Pulteney estate, which was owned by John Drury, and he listened attentively as Drury told him about his son Robert who had been shipwrecked in Madagascar and who had spent fourteen years on the island before being rescued. Also, Defoe had almost certainly read about the Scottish Royal Navy officer Alexander Selkirk and his five years, from 1704 to 1709, as a castaway on Juan Fernandez Island in the South Pacific. These tales, and perhaps other similar accounts, were the inspiration for *Robinson Crusoe*, published in 1719, hailed as 'the first English novel' and a book that is second only to the Bible in its number of language translations. The title/name came either from a lad named Caruso, a school-mate at Morton's, or from when Defoe was hiding in a graveyard after the failure of Monmouth's insurgency and noticed the name 'Robinson Crusoe' carved on a gravestone.

The success of *Robinson Crusoe*, and the publication and similar reception of the picaresque novel *Moll Flanders* in 1722, allowed Defoe the luxury of comfortable withdrawal from his previous erratic existence, although he remained an outspoken dissenter. He continued to write, publishing *Journal of the Plague Year* (1722), *A Tour through the Whole Island of Great Britain* (1724), and books and pamphlets on a wide variety of subjects from politics to travel. He was again arrested and released, and continued in this erratic manner until he died in 1731. The official cause of death was 'lethargy', probably a stroke, and he was buried in Bunhill Fields.

Over the course of his seventy-one-year lifespan, Defoe was a lifelong Presbyterian dissenter, political operator, journalist, internationally regarded novelist and author, and much else besides. He left behind a name and reputation that will remain an integral part of Stoke Newington's history and folklore.

UP AND DOWN THE ERMINE ROAD

Before the housing boom of the late nineteenth century, buildings in Stoke Newington High Street were mainly concentrated around, or close to, its junction with Church Street. To the north lay the main road to Stamford Hill, while across from Church Street was the, as yet, relatively building-free area around Cockhanger Green (Stoke Newington Common) in West Hackney parish.

On the western side of the High Street, just round the corner from The Three Crowns tavern and north of Church Street, there are three three-storey, imposing buildings, dating from the 1720s, with two houses sitting slightly back from the street and the middle one with a small forecourt close to the street, at what is now 187–191 Stoke Newington High Street.

SLAVE TRADING AND SLAVERY

Although Stoke Newington was then home to several influential anti-slavery campaigners and abolitionists, one man who had been involved in funding the building of numbers 187–191 Stoke Newington High Street had a rather different view on slavery. Edward Lascelles, who rose to become head of customs in Barbados, and members of his family were heavily involved in the trafficking of large numbers of African slaves across the Atlantic to Barbados. When Lascelles died in 1727 he was, largely because of the profits from his involvement in slave-trading activities, one of the richest men in England.

In 1833, slavery was declared illegal and was formally abolished by the British parliament. However, in the early 1820s the abolitionist William Wilberforce had on occasion visited the elegant estate of his friend Henry Lascelles, whose wealth had been founded on Edward's slave-trading over 100 years previously and who was then MP for Yorkshire, and the Lascelles family continued to own more than 1,200 slaves in Barbados. Wilberforce wrote, 'I sincerely believe many of the owners of West-Indies estates to be men of more than common kindness, utterly unacquainted with the true nature and practical character of the system with which they have the misfortune to be connected.'

In his book *Bury the Chains: The British Struggle to Abolish Slavery*, Adam Hochschild suggests that the underlying rationale for such statements may have been class-based:

> For one thing, class ties meant that upper-crust abolitionists had always had an easier time attacking the slave trade than attacking slavery itself. Those who carried on the trade were rough, uncouth men from a different social world, sea captains and sailors. Absentee owners of slave plantations, on the other hand, included friends, fellow M.P.s, members of the same London clubs.

There is little doubt that Wilberforce and his fellow abolitionists were sincere and committed activists in the anti-slavery cause, but perhaps some things were at that time best brushed to one side in their unremitting quest for the common good?

No. 187 Stoke Newington High Street had, by the mid-eighteenth century, become home to a wealthy Quaker, John Wilmer, who had an obsessive fear of being accidentally buried alive. As a result, on his death in 1764 Wilmer was buried in a vault in his garden with a bell tied around his wrist, in order to summon aid when he awoke from his supposed 'death'. No one ever heard the ringing of the bell. His name, however, lives on to the present day, as his garden is now a public car park that is entered from Church Street via Wilmer Close. The house then became an invalid asylum (the name was carved into the wooden frame of the door surrounding the entrance) formed by another Quaker, Mary Lister, in 1825 for 'respectable women', and then remained in institutional use, from 1909 until 1945, as the Stoke Newington Hospital for Women.

Its neighbour at no. 189 was, from 1864, the Stoke Newington Dispensary founded earlier that century by a group of well-off local men with the intention of providing health care for local poor people. One of the original founders was the banker and financier Nathan Mayer Rothschild, one of a small number of rich Jewish families who lived in Stamford Hill and Upper Clapton but who in the 1850s moved to the outlying suburbs of London. The dispensary remained in use in this house until the founding of the National Health Service in the late 1940s.

The third house in this group, no. 191, was, variously, the Infant Orphan Asylum, a private house in 1850, and, in 1884, the London Female Penitentiary, which trained prostitutes in domestic work while imparting to these 'fallen women' the benefits of Christianity. In 1896, the Penitentiary, fearing the title may be misleading, changed its name to the Female Guardian Society, and it continued with its work here until 1939.

Across the road from the Church Street junction, on the corner of High Street and Sanford Lane, is the Coach and Horses pub, which, although like most of Stoke Newington today is a nineteenth-century building, was first recorded as an inn in 1723. Also licensed in 1723, there stood another pub, now long gone, which was first recorded as The Bull and which was located a few yards north of the Coach and Horses on Bull Alley, today's Clevedon Passage.

On the corner of Garnham Street is the Jolly Butchers pub, first recorded in 1761 as the Spread Eagle and which has been much renovated and enjoyed over the years. On the outside of the pub, on the wall on Garnham Street, there is a fading mosaic/mural that depicts Georgiana Cavendish, Duchess of Devonshire, making her way through a butcher's market while campaigning for the Whigs in the 1784 general election. The Tory press circulated the story that she was trading kisses with the traders for their votes in the election. Such an exchange would certainly have brought a grin to their faces: hence the pub's name 'Jolly Butchers'.

Still further north, on a path leading to today's Common, were almshouses dating from 1740, opposite which was built in 1861 a Methodist chapel that, a century later, became a synagogue. Proceeding up the High Street to Stamford Hill on the eastern side, just beyond the Hackney Brook crossing were several shops offering the services of, variously, a carpenter, blacksmith and a wheelwright. The Weaver's Arms stood at the corner of today's Cazenove Road, the bar's name reflecting its popularity with Huguenot weavers, who no doubt much enjoyed their day out in what was then the countryside.

These skilled Huguenot artisans, normally residents of Shoreditch and Spitalfields, were expelled from France by Louis XIV in 1685 when he issued the Revocation of the Edict of Nantes, a savage attack on the country's Reformed Protestant Church and these Calvinist weavers sought and were granted refuge in Britain. For their and other visitors' entertainment, the Weaver's Arms provided a bowling green that ran from the rear of the tavern towards the Common.

While to the western side of the High Street, and north of Hackney Brook, there was largely farmland, building development had taken place close to the Common, which by the mid-eighteenth century had evolved into its roughly triangular, present-day shape. Local brewer Henry Sanford had by 1788 constructed twenty-nine homes – Sanford Terrace and Sanford Place – that faced the Common on its western fringe. Sanford Terrace, with its attractive Georgian facade, continues today to survey the Common, or at least the one-way road system and the railway cutting that both carve their way through this old expanse of open public land, although the other buildings were demolished in the mid-twentieth century to make room for council housing.

In 1970 Stanford Terrace became a *cause célèbre*, as Hackney Council was intent on complete demolition of the Terrace to expand the encroaching council flats, but it was thwarted by the tireless efforts of local conservationist pressure groups, and the old buildings today retain their proud presence, gazing over what remains of the original Stoke Newington Common.

Back on Ermine Street, and still heading north, the old parish of Stoke Newington reaches its northern boundary around today's Manor Road, and becomes what was then the wealthy, generally upper-middle-class village of Stamford Hill. As the road ascended, on the eastern side were occasional villas and large houses that were owned by merchants, bankers and the like, and which had unimpeded views over the surrounding landscape. To the west, there remained largely open fields.

'O, RARE TURPIN HERO ...'

By the early eighteenth century, Stamford Hill Road was increasingly being used by horse-powered goods wagons, carts with heavy loads of vegetables and similar traffic, and the surface was susceptible to erosion and was in a dilapidated condition. Even when dry it was tricky to negotiate, but in wet conditions the hill could be slippery and dangerous.

Residents voiced their objections and, in 1713, an Act of Parliament ena-bled the formation of a Turnpike Trust on Ermine Street that stretched from Enfield to Shoreditch. The turnpike operators organised two toll gates – one at the top of Stamford Hill and the other at Kingsland – and they were responsible for obtaining money from all who used the road, repairs and maintenance, lighting, and the appointment and supervision of watchmen.

The services of watchmen were soon required but there was little they could do to prevent the frequent, unplanned arrival of what was then the scourge of many English roads: the highwaymen of the 1730s. Although he plied his trade across north London and the immediate countryside, the legendary Dick Turpin lived for a while on Hackney Marshes, and Stamford Hill Road was apparently no stranger to his incursions. I say 'apparently', as Turpin's career and adventures have been much exaggerated and even mythologised. His horse, Black Bess, was the invention of a later storyteller, there is no evidence for his ascribed welcome to passing traffic as being 'Stand and Deliver', and so on. However, it would have been surprising if he had not scented the passing wealth on Ermine Road, so he was almost certainly a visitor, if an infrequent one.

The other notorious highwayman of the time was Tom King and, although the encounter has been claimed by other locations, it was on this road that Turpin accosted King and, pointing his pistol, demanded money from him. King began to laugh, Turpin then recognised him and apologised, and they joined forces as the Butch Cassidy and Sundance Kid of the area.

Turpin was arrested shortly after he accidentally shot King dead, and briefly escaped. He was executed in York – another of his favourite hang-outs – in 1738.

'POOR PALATINES'

There are a couple of other bars that exist on the High Street to the south of Church Street that, although perhaps much renovated over the years, can lay claim to historical existences as coaching inns that long pre-date their current appearance. Heading south from Church Street, one of these bars is the Rochester Castle, which opened under this name in 1801 and was con-structed by a builder from the eponymous Rochester in Kent on the site of the early eighteenth-century Green Dragon tavern. Still heading south, just to the north of where South Hornsey began is the imposing White Hart that, as the White Hind, was catering to travellers' thirsts back in the 1650s. Several others have come and gone over the centuries.

Travelling to the southern end of Stoke Newington – as far as Shacklewell and Crossway – Ermine Street was, judging from contemporary maps, in the late eighteenth century dotted with occasional buildings, and laid out behind them were mainly open fields. However, on the west of the street was the Palatine estate, which occupied the southern part of the parish and was situated to the north and east of Newington Green.

In 1709 London was hosting thousands of Germans, many of whom were fleeing war, famine and persecution in their homeland of the Palatinate region of south-west Germany. Although most of these immigrants were poor and unskilled, public opinion was divided between those who wanted them sent back, partly due to fear of losing their jobs, and others who took pity on their plight and referred to them as 'Poor Palatines'. Daniel Defoe was among the latter, arguing that British tradesmen and labourers had nothing to fear as the Germans would enhance 'publick Wealth'.

The Queen Anne government had offered them help, as they were Protestants escaping Catholic oppression. Most of these Germans were doing just that, but some were victims of Protestant states while a few others were Roman Catholics and, in any event, America was seen by the refugees as a safer home. Later that year, the government banned more immigration from Germany. Nevertheless, Stoke Newington parish offered assistance to four Palatine families, and the vestry oversaw the building of homes for these people on the Gravel Pit land, or Parish Fields, to the south-east of the parish. At the time, all rental income from the estate went to the maintenance of St Mary's Church, but this money was later distributed to other churches in the area.

By 1750 there existed on the Palatine estate – roughly bounded by today's Boleyn, Cowper, Brighton and Stoke Newington Roads, with Barrett's Grove cutting a path through the middle – 7 acres containing six houses and a larger building, Palatine House, set back from the main road, as well as two taverns. By 1780 there were ten houses on the estate, and the leader of the Methodists, John Wesley, frequently used Palatine House as a retreat from the rigours of preaching. As the estate grew, in 1820 the young Quaker Anna Sewell, author of *Black Beauty*, lived with her mother in the converted coach house next to Palatine House. Today, only the names Palatine Road and Palatine Grove remain as a reminder of the estate.

♦ ♦ ♦

In the following chapters I will be discussing the profound impact of the nineteenth century on Stoke Newington, and assessing all the reasons for its growth from a quiet, rural middle-class village of 2,000 people in 1800 to its expansion in 1900 into a teeming inner-London suburb containing 50,000 residents. I will also be looking at some of the features that have contributed to this: the 1814 new legislation on building and the consequent explosion in home building, the dissenter burial ground of Abney Park Cemetery, the development and popularity of Clissold Park, the arrival of the railway, the increasing proximity to London, the arrival of early immigrants, and more.

However, having made frequent mention of Quakers in this book, I should first discuss their significance for Stoke Newington, particularly in the earlier years of the parish.

SOCIETY OF FRIENDS

Peter Daniels is a poet, Quaker, ex-librarian at the Friends' Meeting House in London's Euston Road, and a neighbour of mine in Stoke Newington. In an article in *N16 Magazine*, he described 'Quakers' thus:

> Quakers have a radically simple religious outlook, based on meeting in silence to discover a deeper sense of God, without elaborate ritual or priestly hierarchy. Women and men participate fully: all people are equal before God, and each person is unique and precious. This belief has led to Quakers (or 'Friends') being much involved in work for peace and social justice.

This brief description reflects the attitudes and beliefs of many contemporary thinkers, but the Quaker history is a fascinating one. For our purposes, it is sufficient to say that Quakers have been meeting in Stoke Newington for over 300 years.

One of the most important and enduring of the dissenting 'sects' that proliferated in the religious turmoil of mid-seventeenth-century England was the Religious Society of Friends. They were dismissively referred to by a local judge as 'Quakers' because of their shaking and trembling during worship, so the name was adopted by members of the movement as both apt and, as an early indication of their determination, an inverse rejoinder to figures of authority and, as such, a badge of pride.

The Quaker movement formed around George Fox in the late 1640s, and within a decade they had attracted thousands of adherents, including many members of other radical sects such as the Seekers, with the message that the 'inner light' is already within us. Quakers were austere and level-headed, and did not recognise social distinctions, the latter illustrated by the universal 'thou' as a form of address to people at all social levels and also by the number of women leaders in the movement. I use the term 'leaders' advisedly as, unlike many other dissident groups, Quakers did not and do not recognise hierarchical authorities such as elders or priests. Such was their strength of numbers, it was suggested that rather than Quakers abolishing priests, they instead abolished the laity.

After the Restoration, and particularly in the early years after the passing of the Acts of Uniformity and Seditious Conventicles, the Quakers were imprisoned by the hundred and persecuted by the authorities. Indeed, such was the degree of attempted repression of the Friends that the new legislation was popularly known as the Quaker Acts. However, these actions by the 'Cavalier Parliament' served only to strengthen the resolve and obduracy of the Quaker movement.

George Fox often stayed at Mary Stott's house in Dalston, then a small village, in order to keep away from London, and in 1668 he helped set up a Quaker girls' school run by Mary in nearby Shacklewell, also then a tiny hamlet. In 1698, the first of what was to become regular Quaker meetings in Stoke Newington was held in two rooms in Church Street on the site of today's Clarence pub. A few years later, Daniel Defoe built his home opposite these Quaker meeting rooms, and Defoe was sympathetic to those attendants and to Quakers generally, writing pamphlets praising them and their activities.

The meetings stopped in 1741, as many Quakers were moving to Stamford Hill and attending the closer Tottenham meetings. Also, several of Stoke Newington's wealthier Quakers – such as the Hoare banking family (Jonathan built Clissold House when living in Paradise Row), Joseph Beck (one of the two men who saved Clissold Park) and William Allen (abolitionist and chemist who lived in Church Street) – worked in the City of London and attended the original Friends' meetings in Gracechurch Street.

However, in 1821 the Gracechurch Street building burnt to the ground, and the Quakers built their new premises in Stoke Newington in today's

Yoakley Road, then called Park Street. The building contained a large meeting room with a gallery, and at the rear was established a Quaker burial ground. It stood next to a row of ten spacious Quaker almshouses, funded by an earlier Quaker, Michael Yoakley. The rooms and almshouses remained in Yoakley Road for the following 130 years, as Stoke Newington's Quakers were active in both local endeavours and such wider issues as prison reform and the anti-slavery movement, and were visited by, and had discussions with, similarly minded reformers and abolitionists, including Elizabeth Fry and William Wilberforce.

A local initiative was Susanna Corder's Quaker Girls' School, established in Fleetwood House between 1824 and 1838. While waiting for the new Stoke Newington meeting rooms to be completed, Susanna commissioned what must be the first-ever school bus to transport her pupils to meetings in Gracechurch Street. Although Susanna described her school as being for 'the children of Friends', it was less respectfully referred to by locals as the 'Newington Nunnery'.

Also, in 1860 Stoke Newington Friends hosted Nahneebahweequay, an Ojibway from Canada, who travelled the Atlantic to petition Queen Victoria about the abuse of native land rights. And, in keeping with Quaker insistence on sex equality, in 1874 local resident Louisa Hooper Stewart established the Women Friends' Total Abstinence Union. The avoidance of alcohol was a major issue at the time among social reformers.

Indeed, by the end of the nineteenth century Stoke Newington contained a higher concentration of Quakers than anywhere else in London. However, despite Quakers winning the Nobel Prize in 1947 for their relief work in post-war Germany, and their later conflict-resolution activities in Yugoslavia, Northern Ireland and the Middle East, attendances at meetings declined in the later twentieth century as the Quaker population of the parish moved to the suburbs.

The Yoakley Road almshouses were demolished in 1959 and the meeting house was sold to the Seventh Day Adventists in 1966. The burial ground is still owned by the Quakers and the remaining land is now Lister Court, a block of council flats. The Adventists permitted Quaker meetings to continue for a while, but the local Friends then moved to the Scout Hall in Bouverie Road (once a Baptist Church), the Sea Cadets building on Church Street and the old Clissold Natural Health Centre before, in 2000, finding a longer-term meeting space at the refurbished St Mary's Community Centre on

Defoe Road. I suspect that the irony of holding nonconformist meetings in an Anglican-linked building was not lost on the Quakers, and nor was the coincidence that they were only across the road from the Clarence, the building where they began their local meetings over 300 years previously. After several years in Defoe Road, they again moved.

The Quaker movement, however, is a durable one and there has been an increasing interest in the beliefs and activities of the Friends in recent years. The weekly meetings are today held at Clissold House.

CHAPTER THREE

BEFORE THE RAILWAY: THE NINETEENTH CENTURY

If it were not for the fact that the New River Company chose for its reservoirs the site between the Green Lanes and the Bethune Road and placed its filter beds on the western side of Green Lanes; that the grounds of the Abneys' house were converted into a cemetery; and that the grounds of Mr Crawshay's Mansion were so wisely acquired for a public park, the whole of the area known as Stoke Newington, no doubt, by this time, would have been completely built over. As it is, there is probably no area so close to the City of London that is so favoured with open spaces.

Street Names of Stoke Newington, W.F. Baxter

When you turn off today's Green Lanes and begin travelling up the western end of Stoke Newington Church Street, you can be forgiven for thinking that you've entered a time warp and are heading towards what seems to be an idealised old English village.

Soaring above the trees is a church steeple, while to your left stretches a wide, tree-lined park that, as you approach this rural hamlet, is safeguarded by a substantial eighteenth-century mansion. Although to your right are a couple of blocks of twentieth-century flats beside a few significantly older houses, as you near the early medieval church, sitting opposite an elegantly curved nineteenth-century terrace next to the high-steepled neo-Gothic Church, and continue on to a small roundabout beside a modernist 1930s town hall, the feeling persists that you have strayed into a village off the beaten track.

As you proceed along the narrow, winding main street, past its late-Victorian library, small shops and Georgian houses, this illusion begins to fade, but this short journey remains the most compelling and appropriate introduction to Stoke Newington. And this western approach would feel like just another built-up, inner-London suburb were it not for the welcoming expanse of Clissold Park.

PARK LIFE

When Clissold Park opened in 1889 it was described as 'one of the most beautifully laid-out and planted parks in London' but it had been a struggle to achieve this open public space.

Earlier that century, and after twenty-five years of parliamentary domination by Tory governments, in 1830 the Whigs returned to power. One of their stated objectives, which included parliamentary reform and the abolition of slavery, was the establishment of a committee to investigate the opening of substantial 'public parks', amenities that were becoming a priority for urban communities across the country, and no less so in Stoke Newington.

The first such public parks in London – Victoria Park (1845) and Finsbury Park (1868) – were close by, but the boundaries of this small parish then contained little in the way of suitable public land and insufficient open space to compete with its neighbours. However, the principle had been established, and Stoke Newington's achievement would soon overshadow those of its two rivals.

Clissold House was commissioned in 1790 by Jonathan Hoare, a member of the Hoare banking family and one of several influential Quakers in Stoke Newington, including his brother Samuel, a prison reformer and one of the founders of the Society for Effecting the Abolition of the Slave Trade, the brothers being residents of Paradise Row. The house was built by Jonathan's nephew Joseph Woods, a Quaker architect and botanist. Then known as 'Paradise House', the mansion was completed in 1799. The estate encompassed Newington Common and a section of the New River, which looped round the front of the house, ran parallel to Church Street, and then flowed under the street by today's Clissold Crescent on its way to its destination at Sadler's Wells.

In 1800 Hoare encountered financial difficulties, and he sold the house and estate to Thomas Gudgeon, who in turn sold it in 1811 to William

Crawshay. One of Crawshay's daughters, Eliza, fell in love with the Reverend Augustus Clissold, an Anglican curate at neighbouring St Mary's Church. Despite her father's forcefully expressed objections to the young curate's Anglican beliefs and his banning of the young man from the house, the couple met in secret until 1835 when William Crawshay died. Eliza and Augustus (by then, both well past the first bloom of youth) were married, and the couple changed the name to 'Clissold Place'. On Clissold's death in 1882 the house reverted to the Crawshay family, who sold it four years later to the Ecclesiastical Commission.

The Commission, well aware of the financial value of the land in a fast-growing Stoke Newington, then intended to sell off the land for housing and building development. However, they had underestimated the strength of local feeling against their proposals, and the passing of the 1887 Metropolitan Open Space Act did not offer much in the way of comfort to the intentions of the Ecclesiastical Commission. The Act promoted the growth of public parks and strengthened the powers of local authorities in relation to the plans being promoted by the potential developers.

In 1887 two local members of Stoke Newington parish vestry – Joseph Beck and John Runtz – joined the newly formed Commons Preservation Society, while the Metropolitan Gardens Public Association also enlisted in the campaign. Beck was employed by the Council of the City of London and Runtz worked for the Metropolitan Board of Works, which would shortly become the London County Council (LCC), and these two men were instrumental in the battle to retain the estate as a public park. Working night and day, and securing a petition from 12,000 local objectors to the commercial development of the park, they succeeded in their aims.

Having secured sizeable donations from the local parish vestry, and with funding from the Charities Commission, South Hornsey, Islington and Hackney, Runtz persuaded the Metropolitan Board to buy the park, under the 1887 Clissold Park (Stoke Newington) Act, thereby ensuring that the land would be opened in perpetuity for free public access. On 10 January 1889 Beck paid in to the Bank of England a cheque for £96,000, and saved the land from commercial development. The chairman of the newly formed LCC, the Earl of Roseberry, opened Clissold Park at a well-attended ceremony on 24 July 1889, and Stoke Newington now had its own public space.

As the original estate had been planned by local horticulturalists and botanists, there was already in existence an abundant variety of rare and admired trees, shrubs and plants, and it was one of the first parks in London to provide space for animals, with the deer pen – which exists to this day – being the first-ever animal enclosure in a British urban park. The press hailed Clissold Park as 'the finest of London's open spaces' and observed that 'for beauty, it cannot be matched for miles around'.

The Hackney Brook, by the 1860s an underground sewer, had formed the northern edge of the Common and, in the years prior to the park's opening, the two adjacent northern lakes had been filled in with clay from the construction of the filter beds for the New River. They had then been more or less abandoned. These lakes were re-excavated for the opening of Clissold Park, were refilled with water and were christened Beckmere and Runtzmere to acknowledge the two men who had fought with such vigour to retain the land for local use. The lakes remain today, providing a home for swans, geese and wildfowl, with the larger lake having been a popular boating pond.

As further recognition of Beck's and Runtz's commitment to saving the park in the face of strong competition for the land, a public subscription was raised in 1890 to erect a water fountain immortalising their names. This imposing fountain, renovated and restored for the park's 125th anniversary in 2014, can be found along the pathway to the House that begins at the park's two entrances on Church Street near Old St Mary's.

Having passed the Grade II–listed boundary stone dated 1790 that marked the boundary between South Hornsey and Stoke Newington parishes, the avenue heads westward over the cast-iron footbridge, passes the 1930s paddling pool, the deer enclosure, the bowling green and pavilion, and the fountain, and terminates at Green Lanes. The text on the fountain concludes, 'In grateful recognition of the united efforts of Joseph Beck and John Runtz: As leaders of the movement by which the use of the park was secured to the public for ever.'

Clissold House is today a Grade II★ building constructed of yellow brick, and is two-storeyed to the west and three-storeyed to the east. Its main entrance is via steps to a six-column Doric verandah, while its south side has a curved copper verandah, under which are cafe seats and a flower garden. To its north-west is a wide tarmac area that was the site of a bandstand, now replaced by a wooden stage. Its northern aspect faces another memorial stone water fountain, this one from 1893, the avenue leading to the lakes, and to the north-east are the children's playground, sports area and tennis courts.

In 2007 the park was granted £4.5 million by Hackney Council for purposes of upgrading the house and parkland. The Clissold Park and House Restoration Project was completed two years later at a cost of £8.9 million, the extra money coming from the Heritage Lottery Fund and the Big Lottery Fund.

Clissold Park now attracts over 2 million visitors a year, and its current success is in no small measure due to the efforts of Joseph Beck and John Runtz, whose commitment, in the spirit of all true dissenters, arose from the unwavering belief that they were working in the interests and for the betterment of the people. In this case, their unceasing toil was for the benefit of all residents of Stoke Newington, both then and for generations to come. We should be grateful for the communal spirit of both these men.

◆ ◆ ◆

The opening of this spacious new park could hardly have been more timely. The quiet, secluded little village of a century ago, with its wide fields, rural meadows and market gardens crossed by gravel paths and peaceful country lanes was, by the late nineteenth century, being gradually transformed, at least on the surface, into a busy metropolitan suburb. In Chapter Four I describe the arrival of the railway and the expansion of London as the propelling factors in this process.

Despite the conformist attitudes of many, but far from all, of the newcomers, there remained in the parish a good many people who continued to regard Stoke Newington as an escape from the suffocating norm of externally imposed beliefs. These were people who continued to admire this still attractive, historically important little place as a rare area in which they could ease themselves away from the constraints of normal suburban life and in which they could express themselves intellectually and spiritually to a depth and in a manner that was difficult, if not impossible, elsewhere. To this extent, dissent continued to flourish in Stoke Newington.

However, what was increasingly required above all else in Stoke Newington was housing and, with the acres of open land in the parish and beyond, by the late nineteenth century new homes were beginning to appear at an unprecedented rate in the area. Builders had been arriving here since the 1820s, and the first builder to develop Stoke Newington in an appropriate and sympathetic manner was Thomas Cubitt.

EMPEROR OF THE BUILDING TRADE

One could argue that Thomas Cubitt, the man who built Albion Road, was Stoke Newington's first Marxist dissenter.

Perhaps I should qualify this statement, particularly as Karl Marx was only 3 years old when Cubitt began his project. Marxist political and economic theory is based on the primacy of those who own and control the means of production. Control of the means of production is the *sine qua non* of Marxist theory. Cubitt was the first British builder of any real size to have on his payroll, and answering to him alone, all the necessary tradesmen – the means of production – he required from the start to the conclusion of all his construction projects. To this extent (but admittedly in few other respects) he could therefore be described as a Marxist, and he was a dissenter because he resolutely followed his beliefs, obviously for his own financial good health but also for the benefit of many others, irrespective of the prevailing, dominant practices of his time.

The son of a Norfolk carpenter, he established his building company – which still exists today – in 1810 in London. He gained his reputation with the construction of the London Institute in 1819 and, as well as Albion Road, he was responsible for building a good many of the streets, squares and houses in Belgravia, Pimlico and Bloomsbury, as well as the Albert Memorial in South Kensington. In so doing, he acquired fame as an outstanding master builder, and he was hailed as 'the emperor of the building trade'.

His well-planned, handsome and solid houses were highly regarded in the building trade and by their inhabitants, and every last brick, tile and toilet seat was put in place by his full-time staff of eventually 1,000 tradesmen who included civil engineers, masons, carpenters, bricklayers, plumbers, roofers and all the other specialists involved in house building.

Before Cubitt had put everyone 'under one roof', house construction was then normally an *ad hoc* affair where craftsmen helped each other out as they proceeded, resulting in the inevitable disagreements, time-wasting, duplication of effort, personal feuds and all the rest of it. This frequently led to buildings being over budget and not being completed on time, if at all.

Under Cubitt, materials were bought in bulk to exacting specifications, many doors and windows were mass-produced, and there was no sub-contracting. In these respects Cubitt was well ahead of his time, and the quality and reliability of his men's work were of an obvious high standard. Later in his career he directed his various projects from his 11-acre site headquarters in Pimlico. However, his building career, and his subsequent rise to national eminence, began in Stoke Newington.

Prior to the early years of the nineteenth century it was difficult to persuade any building company to invest in house construction and development in Stoke Newington, mainly because the land was 'copyhold'. This feudal system of land ownership meant that the lords of the manor, and the Prebendary of St Paul's that ultimately owned the land, could not grant leases for longer than twenty-one years unless specifically agreed otherwise. This was an insufficient time period for commercial, speculative builders to realise a profit on the sale and resale of newly constructed homes. Also, the lord of the manor was not legally able to grant building leases without approval from the owner of the land.

Under pressure from the Eade family who had acquired the Abney Park estate, in 1814 the Prebendary obtained an Act of Parliament that permitted St Paul's and the lord of the manor to lease land for ninety-nine years, and which also allowed the possibility that the leaseholder could grant sub-leases. Furthermore, the Act empowered 'enfranchisement', so that 'demesne' land, and all its copyholdings, were also now amended to ninety-nine-year leases. This Act was responsible for converting the late-Georgian, rural village of Stoke Newington into the populous, multi-street suburb that we know today, as the builders wasted little time in moving into the parish.

The new legislation changed everything. Local historian W.F. Baxter described it as 'a turning point in the annals of Stoke Newington'. He also wrote thus of the Act's impact: 'the demolition of the old and picturesque houses was commenced to allow new streets composed of villas, terraces, places and cottages to be formed so as to house the ever increasing population which was concentrating in the Metropolis'. Cubitt was not slow to react to this potentially lucrative opportunity.

Although his work on the London Institute had gained Cubitt plaudits as a reliable, innovative young builder, Stoke Newington was his first big opportunity to demonstrate his credentials and to make serious money. In May 1821, at a land sale at the Three Crowns on the corner of Church Street, Cubitt acquired seven lots of 2-acre plots of almost completely undeveloped land, which began across the road from St Mary's Church, avoiding the parish glebe land, and headed south in the direction of Newington Green.

By the following year he owned both sides of today's Albion Road down as far as the shopping arcade known as Albion Parade, and much of the east side down to the border of South Hornsey parish. He had also bought, and sold on to various other developers, plots of land stretching south of the west end of Church Street, on which other builders created Clissold Crescent, Burma Road and other streets in that area. In 1837, his brother William acquired from the parish vestry two further plots of land that then connected Albion Road with Newington Green. Cubitt moved away from Stoke Newington in the late 1830s, having constructed over seventy houses on and around Albion Road.

In Stoke Newington, Cubitt's houses were simply but attractively designed villas and terraces. They contained little in the way of unnecessary ornamentation, were constructed within their time limits and were built to last. Many have now been demolished to make way for 'modern' housing, as one can tell today when travelling along Albion Road, but this has been dictated as much by changing architectural fashions and population pressures as by the durability of Cubitt's construction methods. Several of his houses remain on this, the most important major new road to have been constructed in the parish since Church Street, and then Ermine Street almost a couple of thousand years previously.

Cubitt died in 1855 and, on his death, Queen Victoria (no less) eulogised him as 'a real national loss … a better, kind-hearted or more simple, unassuming man never breathed'. A fulsome tribute indeed, but he certainly regenerated this part of Stoke Newington and, after he had finished Albion Road, new houses and roads were already proliferating across this parish.

In 1814, there were 379 houses in the parish of Stoke Newington. By 1831, the number had increased to 670. Forty years later in 1871, Stoke Newington contained 1,816 houses, and its sister parish of South Hornsey had grown rapidly to 1,087. Thomas Cubitt may have been the first large-scale builder in Stoke Newington, but he was far from being the last.

♦ ♦ ♦

When one compares a map of Stoke Newington in 1848 with the Ordnance Survey map of 1868, it is interesting to observe that most of the parish land south of Church Street – with the exceptions of Cubitt's streets to the south-west, the High Street to the east, and the Palatine estate and Shacklewell to the south – remained undeveloped brickfield, nurseries and pasture, with little evidence of new housing over these twenty years. It was a similar story on the West Hackney side of the London Road.

However, the transformation in the mid-nineteenth century of the two areas of South Hornsey (or 'Hornsey Detached') – called 'Victoria Town' and 'Albert Town' and named from a sense of patriotism created by the Napoleonic Wars – was remarkable. The former (bordered by Victoria Road, Nevill Road, Brighton Road and the High Street) was clearly undergoing early housing development in 1848 but, in the same year, the latter (whose boundaries were Allen Road, Albion Road, Matthias Road and Wordsworth Road) appears virtually devoid of housing. In the 1868 map both of these areas were fully developed, and Albert Town, in particular, contained little if any room for more houses. How did this happen?

HOUSING IN ALBERT TOWN

Also known as 'Poets' Roads', the area that was called Albert Town sits in the south-west corner of Stoke Newington and was previously in South Hornsey parish. (Since 1900 South Hornsey has been a fully paid-up member of Stoke Newington.)

Most of the roads in this area are named after Milton, Shakespeare, Spenser, Cowper and Wordsworth – which explains the nickname – while Howard and Allen Roads honour two famous Stoke Newington residents: John Howard (*see* box, p.63), after whom is named The Howard League for Penal Reform, and William Allen, the Quaker chemist and abolitionist. Matthias Road, once Coach and Horses Lane, forms Albert Town's southern boundary and reflects the presence of St Matthias School (1849) and St Matthias Church (1853) in this area. South Hornsey Town Hall was located in Milton Grove, and is the focus of the redundant sign on Albion Road that today indicates 'Town Hall Approach'. The area was developed in the 1850s as a direct result of the Repeal of the Corn Laws in 1852.

By as late as the 1840s in England, land ownership was an essential require-ment for a male individual to be able to vote. The requirement laid down by Parliament for obtaining a vote was to own land, whether or not in use, and to pay a minimum of £1 per year in ground rent. If an individual was a freeholder, he could vote. Otherwise, he could not.

The 1832 Reform Act had widened the franchise, abolished 'rotten boroughs' and established more parliamentary seats in larger cities. But the
Reform Act did not change the necessity for an individual to be a landowner
in order to vote. Although it widened the franchise (except, of course, for
women) it did not repeal the Corn Laws, which kept wheat and grain at an
artificially high price, thereby damaging the living standards of the majority
of the population while enhancing the power and profit of landowners.

In 1849, the Corn Laws were abolished by Sir Robert Peel, against the
wishes of his own Tory party, and this repeal significantly diminished the
rights of landlords in England. The opposition Liberals, who wished to
increase their share of the vote, could do so by increasing the number of
voting small landholders, who tended to favour Liberals. Therefore, they supported the establishment of the Freehold Land Society, an organisation that
did not sell land on leases but in small freehold plots. Houses built on these
plots would then become freeholds, and the occupiers could then vote, preferably for the Liberals.

When Cubitt was acquiring the land on Albion Road, he could then only
buy ninety-nine-year leases and then sublease to the house buyers on a similar term lease. The Church owned the freehold. Now times had changed.
The FLS bought up fields, divided them into small 'twenty-bob' lots and sold
them to builders and individuals, who could then acquire homes on freehold
and become voters.

One of the first areas that the FLS selected was in Stoke Newington,
namely 'Foy's estate', which later became known as Albert Town. Because
house building was a risky financial business, most small builders took on
small plots for development. This being so, a total of fifty-three builders
bought the Albert Town land and, by 1852, all the roads and homes in the
area had been built. It became known as 'an island of voters in a sea of
freeholders'.

The Freehold Land Society, which gradually evolved into today's Abbey
National Building Society, did indeed increase the Liberal vote in Albert
Town but, as they moved out to today's 'stockbroker belt', they also increased
the Tory vote. And within a few years, the landholding requirement for
voting was abolished. Albert Town was, in the longer term, an unnecessary
experiment but, at the time, it worked.

The abundance of builders in the area helps to explain why the houses in
Albert Town were a variety of styles and sizes, often next door to each other

in the same street, unlike most of the rest of Stoke Newington, which was designed by larger builders working to roughly similar requirements. Milton Gardens is a good example of a street of contrasting and often intriguing architectural styles.

◆ ◆ ◆

Elsewhere in the parish, and particularly to the north of Church Street, by 1868 new streets and housing had also appeared. However, the fact that much of the northern area was 'demesne land' meant that a far greater degree of unified planning – both architecturally and spatially – was possible than had been the case in Albert Town. Development in this northern part of Stoke Newington reflected the more elegant style and coherence of the manorial vision, and the new streets and buildings displayed a visual congruence that, aside from Cubitt's Albion Road, was absent from the necessarily piecemeal patchwork that existed to the south of the parish.

Prior to the early nineteenth century, Lordship Road, the drovers' path leading north from Church Street, was undeveloped, but by the 1840s there were three large detached houses standing on the west side of the road between Church Street and Manor Road. The first two – with their gardens extending back to Queen Elizabeth Walk, and situated slightly north of Grayling Road – were Linton and Willow Lodges. The third villa – St Mary's Lodge – was built in 1843 on the corner of Manor Road and opposite the Presbyterian Church. St Mary's Lodge has had a colourful, if depressing, history (*see* box).

ST MARY'S LODGE

Sitting forlornly on the western side of Lordship Road, at the junction with Manor Road, is St Mary's Lodge, one of the last remaining early Victorian detached villas in Stoke Newington. It was built in the late 1830s, and named after St Mary's Parish, as one of three grand houses on what was then Lordship Lane, between Lordship Terrace and Manor Road, but the building is today in a sorry state of repair.

The house, with its once-elegant garden of $1/3$ acre, was designed by architect John Young, who lived there until his death in 1877. It was acquired in 1878 by the Crabb family, one of the sons being Lionel 'Buster' Crabb, a diver in the Second World War and a recipient of the George Medal for bravery. Crabb's wartime exploits were portrayed by actor Lawrence Harvey in the 1956 film *Silent Enemy*. (Buster's headless and handless body was discovered in 1957 on the coast near Portsmouth after he had gone missing on a secret mission to examine the hull of a Soviet warship that had brought Nikita Khrushchev on a trip to the UK.)

Several other residents occupied the villa, until the Hyde family in the late 1950s sold the house to the LCC, at below market value, on the express understanding it would be used 'for charitable purposes'. From early 1960 until the mid-1990s it was run by nuns as a home for unmarried young mothers, and after the departure of the nuns the building and grounds became a derelict, squatted eyesore.

The Lodge was put up for sale by Hackney Council in 2000 but it was withdrawn from auction when the nearby Torah Etz Chaim Synagogue bought the property. Although the Council specified St Mary's was to be used for 'community and educational purposes', there was no similar requirement for maintenance of the structure. In 2004 Lordship Road became a Conservation Area, so demolition was not an option, and over the following ten years this precious reminder of an older era became increasingly dilapidated and suffered further damage from a serious fire in 2005.

With little sign then of refurbishment, its grounds even became a used tyre dump in 2008. In 2014 St Mary's Lodge was bought, after discussions with the Council about compulsory purchase, by a Hasidic group, Keren Habinyan, whose intentions remain unclear. The building and its grounds urgently require restoration, and it is heartening to observe the recent appearance of scaffolding and indications of imminent refurbishment. If this is not carried out, yet another monument to Stoke Newington's history will disappear.

Manor Road had been laid out and developed in the 1820s. Although plans had been proposed in the mid-1850s to connect the road with Green Lanes, this new thoroughfare, under the name Lordship Park and along with associated housing development, was not achieved until the late 1860s. Meanwhile, Queen Elizabeth Walk, to the west, had also extended northwards to the new Lordship Park.

East of Lordship Road on Church Street, Park Street (Yoakley Road) had connected with the recently completed Grayling Road, and an adjacent new street was taking shape. Bouverie Road, at the junction with the Clarence Tavern on Church Street, was begun in the late 1850s and soon extended north to Manor Road. One of the road's earliest buildings was the Particular Baptists chapel (today a Scout hut) not far from the Roman Catholic church, Our Lady of Good Counsel. At the southern end of Bouverie Road was and is the 'Cobbled Yard', once a livery stables for local residents' animals.

Only a two-minute eastward stroll from Bouverie Road is the Church Street entrance to one of London's most unusual burial grounds: Abney Park Cemetery. Today, Abney Park may appear simply a somewhat neglected, run-down old burial ground, but it is also an enigmatic, mysterious place and is one of London's most intriguing open spaces.

ABNEY PARK: A DISSENTERS' RESTING PLACE

By the early years of the nineteenth century, London had become one of the world's largest cities. The wealth accumulated during the Industrial Revolution, Britain's imperial expansion and exploitation, and London's position as a major trading and financial centre had led to the development of imposing and elegant squares, streets and buildings, and many of the richer inhabitants were flaunting their wealth on luxurious homes, extravagant lifestyles and other forms of conspicuous consumption.

The city's population was also dramatically expanding and, as a result, so too were slum areas of growing poverty and urban squalor. This was becoming a matter of serious concern for a number of influential reformers, many of whom had been schooled in the principles of the Enlightenment and social justice. The growing incidences of disease, such as cholera, and premature death were being monitored and recorded by these observers, who were searching for ways to improve the public good and, although these problems were mainly found in poorer areas of the city, ill health, lack of sanitation and low levels of hygiene impacted on all strata of society.

One of these sanitary problems to which reformers were devoting their research was the disgraceful state of human burials in London. Despite the city's accumulation of wealth, the dead were consigned to eternity in small, scandalously overcrowded and neglected churchyards, where infilling and burial on top of existing graves were common practices. The filthy state of these churchyards, and the disgusting smells that they frequently emitted, were being regarded as growing contributors to ill health and disease, and this was seen as a serious issue for all residents of the city.

By the late 1820s, London still possessed no sizeable and maintained public cemeteries. A few other British cities had taken steps towards the establishment of public cemeteries, inspired perhaps by the magnificently laid-out Père Lachaise in 1804 in Paris. For instance, Norwich had the Rosary, Liverpool had the St James and Glasgow had the Necropolis, but, although certainly an improvement on London, these were modest, small-scale attempts to deal with the problem. Something had to be done about this unacceptable situation.

Writing in the early 1830s, Sir Edwin Chadwick, a social reformer in public health and urban sanitation and a disciple of the utilitarian philosopher Jeremy Bentham, commented on the graveyards in London: 'On spaces of ground which do not exceed 203 acres, closely surrounded by the abodes of the living, 20,000 adults and nearly 30,000 youths and children are every year imperfectly interred.'

Chadwick cited a woman who had seen four green, putrefying heads sticking up from St Olave's churchyard in Bermondsey, and there was also a burial ground off Drury Lane that was raised several feet by constant use and was 'a mass of corruption'. He described other examples of churchyard mismanagement and neglect, caused primarily by the lack of available space in the inner city. He called for new cemeteries to be created, and these should be well-drained, enclosed, professionally managed and appropriately landscaped. In 1830, John Claudius Loudon, a renowned and influential Scottish botanist and landscape gardener, proposed the construction and establishment of a number of cemeteries and accompanying botanical gardens around the outer suburbs of London.

These and other voices of protest and reform could no longer be ignored by the authorities, and an Act of Parliament was passed in 1832 that opened the door for joint-stock companies to bid for these cemeteries along the lines proposed by Loudon. Meanwhile, George Frederick Carden, a London barrister who had for several years been another proponent of burial reform, had formulated a plan and had established a company – the General Cemetery Company – whose efforts would result in what would later become known as the 'Magnificent Seven', in accordance with Loudon's vision.

Within the following decade, these seven new cemeteries – unprecedented in their scale and the quality of their landscaped design – were built
around the outer suburbs of London. These were, in order of their construction, Kensal Green (1831–33), Norwood (1836–37), Highgate (1836–39),
Brompton (1838–40), Abney Park (1839–40), Nunhead (1839–40) and,
bringing up the rear, Tower Hamlets (1840–41). The fact that all these
unprecedentedly spacious and, as the years passed, enduring cemeteries were
designed, built and in operation was a remarkable achievement, and their
existence much diminished the hygienic and offensive problems that had
been posed by London's overcrowded churchyards.

Six of these necropolist landmarks were each allied to specific Acts
of Parliament. The seventh – Abney Park Cemetery – did not receive
parliamentary sanction, for two main reasons. The first was that this meant
there was no imperative to pay fees to the clergy of the parishes in which
had lived the dead. This saved the Abney management a significant sum
of money, as they would retain all income from the burial rights. Second,
and the defining reason for the decision not to seek formal parliamentary
approval, was that there was now no need for the cemetery grounds to be
consecrated by a bishop of the established Anglican Church, as at that time all
'dissenters', including Roman Catholics and Jews, were banned from burial
in consecrated ground.

Although the six other cemeteries were content with, and in some cases
insisted on, consecration, the guiding principle of Abney Park Cemetery
was that, in order to reflect the variety and sincerity of the religious views
of many inhabitants of the Stoke Newington area, the new cemetery was
to be the final resting place for dissenters, and therefore had to remain as
unconsecrated ground.

'IN MY TIME OF DYIN''

George Collison was a London solicitor and the son of the Rev. George
Collison, President of Hackney Congregational Theological College. He was
also the man ultimately responsible for the acquisition and establishment of
Abney Park Cemetery in Stoke Newington.

Aware of the increasing death rate in north-east London, and of the
pressing social necessity for, and the potential profitability of, a new public

cemetery in the area, he had been paying close attention to the London Cemetery Company who were then laying out Highgate Cemetery. In order to pre-empt the Company from moving into this part of London, in 1838 he contacted nine gentlemen of his acquaintance and suggested the possibility of forming a joint-stock company, acquiring the land formerly belonging to the Abney and Fleetwood estates, and establishing Abney Park Cemetery on the old mansions' grounds. In early 1839, as Secretary and Register of the Abney Park Cemetery Company, having received the consent of his nine colleagues and having acquired the land on the basis of enfranchisement, i.e. the recently available freehold, Collison and his men set to work on planning and designing the new cemetery.

The members of the new Company were hard-headed, mainly local businessmen, a breed from whom it is normally difficult to secure a unified agreement, particularly on such a potentially speculative commercial venture. However, it seems that the internal bickering and disagreement that one might expect from such a grouping was relatively minor, as they shared one overriding characteristic: they were all Congregationalists.

Congregationalists were descended from the seventeenth-century Independent Puritans, and they believed that every local church congregation had to be self-supporting and autonomous. As was the case with Baptists, they differed from the Presbyterians, in that they eschewed 'elders' and similar authority figures, and from the established Anglican Church, as they disdained the hierarchy of bishops. In other words, a couple of centuries earlier they would have been religious 'dissenters'. This unanimity helped in securing Collison's vision of creating London's seamless sequel to Bunhill Fields burial ground, the permanent home in Clerkenwell of General Fleetwood, Daniel Defoe and Isaac Watts, which was seriously overcrowded and would close in 1854. It also meant that one could guarantee a steady stream of dead Congregationalists to Abney Park, which is what happened.

The Abney Park Company enlisted the professional guidance of William Hosking in laying out the cemetery. Also a nonconformist (and related to one of the members), Hosking was later to become Professor of Architecture and Civil Engineering at King's College London. The avenues and paths totalled 3 miles in length, were planned to offer the widest possible frontage for each grave, and all areas within the cemetery were ideally to be easily and equally accessible. These stipulations were not always easy to achieve due to the necessarily asymmetric space available, so there was an element of compromise in the layout.

All the main avenues were to converge on a central chapel, which had to be strictly non-denominational, and with an interior appropriate for all Christian sects. A fair amount of discussion took place, and it was eventually agreed that there would be one entrance and a single main room to be used only for funerals and not worship. There would be no catacombs – subsidiary galleries with side recesses for coffins – as this equated with religious conformity, so any of these would be placed outside. For the chapel's exterior, Hosking settled on an early-fourteenth-century English Gothic style with an unmissable 120ft steeple. Today, the structure, which has been refunded and is undergoing refurbishment, is the oldest surviving non-denominational chapel in Europe.

From the outset of the project, it was agreed that the overall appearance of Abney Park Cemetery would not be perceived by visitors as a dour and forbidding space but rather would be seen as an ornamental, attractive and pleasant environment through which to stroll, while retaining an air of dignity appropriate to its permanent residents. The company was fortunate in this respect to have inherited a good many mature trees from the old estates, and could offer elms and yews to sit alongside and afford shade to the main avenues, and rarer specimens, including seventeenth-century tulip trees and other American exotica from the Fleetwood grounds.

As well as the new cemetery's spacious, arboreal and carefully maintained sense of peaceful contemplation, Abney Park possessed another attraction that well complemented its sophisticated yet rural surrounds. In the mid-1770s, Conrad Loddiges, a botanist and landscape gardener, had initiated a plant nursery in neighbouring Hackney, just off Mare Street, and he and his family had subsequently enjoyed wide respect and a deserved reputation for their large-scale floral and plant creations and multi-shrub landscapes. The Abney company had spoken to Conrad's sons, George and William, about contributing their horticultural skills to the new cemetery, and they happily accepted the commission. The fact that the Loddiges family were staunch Lutherans and fellow nonconformists made the proposed arrangement even more amenable to both parties, and George Loddiges became a shareholder in the company.

When the German horticulturalists eventually completed their task, Abney Park could rightly boast that the new cemetery was the first in Europe to contain an arboretum, and one that was specially designed for the grounds and substantial in its scope. There was also a rosarium that contained 1,000 types of roses. When the arboretum opened to the public, over 2,000 different tree and shrub species were in place, with only autumn-growing plants and a few American varieties yet to be planted. Outside of the Loddiges' nursery in Hackney, it was the largest collection of named trees and shrubs in Britain.

John Loudon, who had earlier proposed just such an idea, was fulsome in his praise and described the innovative project as 'a complete arboretum, including all the hardy kinds of rhododendrons, azaleas and roses … and in which also dahlias, geraniums, fuchsias, verbenas, petunias etc are planted out in paths in the summer season'. He later commented that Abney Park was 'the most highly ornamented cemetery in the neighbourhood of London'.

There was already in place on Church Street an entrance to the cemetery, which consisted of the original wrought-iron railings and curlicued iron gate that once led to Abney House. However, the main entrance on the High Street, just south of the Hackney Brook, was grander in its concept and appropriately captured the company's optimism and high aspirations for the cemetery.

Hosking had called in an expert on Egyptian symbolic decoration, Joseph Bonomi junior, as the designer. Bonomi produced a wide forecourt, stretching to a length of almost 120ft with, at each extreme, the cemetery keeper's lodge and the company's local office. The gates were tall railings with four 17ft-high gate pillars constructed of white Portland stone. Above these, surrounded by lotus flower and leaf motifs, were ancient Egyptian hieroglyphics that translated as 'The Gates of the Abode of the Mortal Part of Man'. The design was extraordinary and, for the time, unique. This much-heralded burial ground was formally opened to the public on 20 May 1840, with speeches from various dissenting divines and with over 1,500 people attending the ceremony.

'SEE THAT MY GRAVE IS KEPT CLEAN'

The first burial in the 32-acre Abney Park Cemetery took place on 3 June that year and was, unsurprisingly, that of a Congregationalist minister from Upper Clapton. By the end of the first decade there had been a total of 5,000 burials.

Throughout the nineteenth century, the cemetery proved a popular final resting place for Protestant dissenters, but local conformist families had also found it an attractive and appropriate site for loved ones. However, even in such a supposedly egalitarian cemetery the Victorian class system was evidenced by the location of the 'common' graves close to and abutting the boundary walls, while the higher-status internees generally enjoyed more central exposure. Nevertheless, in 1860 with the positioning underground of the Hackney Brook, Abney Park remained the nonconformist cemetery of choice, and its area expanded beyond the old Brook and the walls were rebuilt further to the north.

However, almost inevitably, given its finite available space, the cemetery entered a slow process of decline. By the end of the nineteenth century the mortal remains of 100,000 people lay in Abney Park. An observer noted: 'The tombstones are crowded together as closely knit as seems possible and yet they are constantly being added to.' Infilling (building new plots between existing graves) and replanting was gradually reducing the cemetery's capacity and its spectacular visual appeal.

By the 1920s, old plots were being dug up for new burials, leading to accusations of neglect and overcrowding, and repair work was hasty and piecemeal. By the 1950s, there was insufficient revenue to cover the cost of repair and maintenance, and an atmosphere of decay hung over this once celebrated nonconformist graveyard. In early 1973, in the context of not only financial problems but also vandalism and desecration of the tombs and chapel, the owner, Chingford Mount Cemetery Company, declared itself in a state of bankruptcy.

The following year saw the formation of 'Save Abney Park Cemetery', led by playwright and local resident Nemone Lethbridge, who warned that the space was becoming a 'graveyard jungle'. This organisation of volunteers comprised local people, tree and plant specialists, stone masons and others who wished to preserve and refurbish the original ethos of the disgracefully neglected old place.

In 1979 Hackney Council paid £1 to take over the cemetery, although a council spokesman warned that 'the council have no authority at this stage to maintain the cemetery'. The volunteers began to tackle this unkempt urban 'jungle', with its toppled and collapsed gravestones, crumbling walls, cracked and dangerous pathways, previously uncontrolled undergrowth and plant life – such as brambles, ivy and Japanese Knotweed – and much else. Groups such as the Tree Musketeers worked on saving the trees, although some had to be felled and some had already fallen. The chapel was graded A status by English Heritage as an 'at risk' building and was closed for purposes of reconstruction.

As a result of the care and attention paid to restoring Abney Park, in 1993 it was officially declared Hackney's first local Nature Reserve, and in early 2019 it was included in English Heritage's 'Best Places To See' listing. Today, the cemetery is frequently used as a live music venue, a pop video and film backdrop, hosts tours – including bird and ecology walks, historical talks and a veteran tree trail – and offers classes in stone masonry and 'bodging', green woodworking and stone carving. It also runs forest schools and courses in environmental management, and a good deal more.

Although there is no room for new burial plots (other than a few family graves), Abney Park Cemetery today is a tribute to the dedication of the people who have helped in bringing back into existence what is undeniably Stoke Newington's most famous landmark and also a unique ecological habitat.

'DEATH DON'T HAVE NO MERCY'

In today's Abney Park Cemetery are interred the mortal remains of around 200,000 men, women and children, the great majority of whom lived and worked in, or had a close connection with, Stoke Newington and the surrounding area. Their graves are marked by commemorative masonry – Gothic sculptures, ornate granite columns, domed pedestals, symbolic stone vignettes, urn-capped decorative monuments, plain and occasionally legibly lettered headstones and much more – which are as varied and different as were the lives of the people buried in this necropolis.

These memorials are surrounded by numerous species of trees, some rare (swamp cyprus, Turkey oak, Indian bean), some not, while there is a matching profusion of shrubs and plants, as well as a thick carpet of woodland and garden flowers. The bird life is more diverse and omnipresent than anywhere else of a similar nature in Britain, which one would expect from a 32-acre area as densely wooded, shaded and quiet as is Abney Park. There can be few urban cemeteries anywhere that contain as varied and uplifting a wildlife backdrop as does Abney Park.

It seems invidious to select just a few of the people whose remains populate this vast underground tomb but, to offer a flavour of the inhabitants, I have selected some of those who are here interred and have included brief accounts of their deeds and achievements before they entered 'the life eternal'.

These include a few of the many Protestant 'dissenters'. Aside from the numerous Congregationalists whom I earlier mention, there are the resting places of Baptist, Presbyterians, Independents, Wesleyans and other nonconformist preachers and divines, as well as Anglicans and others whose religious affiliations were unknown. There are also political radicals, contrarians, social reformers, political figures, immigrants, and even a fireman and a policeman, both of whom died in service, and general 'In Memoriam' sites for those who died in devastating conflagrations.

I do not here allude to the numerous music-hall stars, sportsmen, civic figures and others more reflective of 'normal' lives, but fuller details, including locations, can be obtained from more specific publications and by attending the various illuminating talks and tours on offer at the cemetery.

Before mentioning anyone else, it is perhaps appropriate to acknowledge that this is the burial place of **Rev. Dr Thomas Archer** (1806–64), Pastor of the United Presbyterian Church in Westminster. Archer was a renowned, eloquent preacher, and he spoke at the opening ceremony of Abney Park Cemetery in May 1840. Almost twenty-five years later, he too entered 'the gates of the abode'.

When entering Abney Park Cemetery from the old mansion gates on Church Street, one arrives at Watts Walk, which heads northward to the publicly funded memorial to Isaac Watts, whose remains lie in Bunhill Fields, and then to the cemetery chapel. 'Dr Watts' Mound' – where the dissenting divine would sit in contemplation under a spreading horse chestnut tree when he was resident at Abney House – is today a somewhat derelict spot at the extreme north-east of the cemetery, close to the Listria Park/Montalban Road area south of Manor Road.

The stone steps from Church Street up to the Walk lead to the large slab memorials to **William Booth** (1829–1912), his wife Catherine and eldest son, and the first commissioner of the organisation that Booth had founded: the Salvation Army. The Army had a long association with the area. The Booths had lived on nearby Clapton Common, then a leafy, rural hamlet, since 1880, and in 1882 they had converted the London Orphan Asylum into a meeting hall – renamed Congress Hall – capable of accommodating almost 5,000 adherents to their Christian work and beliefs, as well as providing space for a training barracks. By the opening years of the twentieth century, the Salvation Army had grown into the most successful and popular Protestant group in the Stoke Newington and Hackney area.

When Booth died in 1912, his body was initially taken to Congress Hall in Clapton, where it lay in a glass-topped coffin for four days as the mourners filed past. Booth's body was then taken to Olympia for the funeral service and, on 29 August, his funeral procession passed through central London to Abney Park Cemetery. His funeral attracted an estimated 150,000 people, the highest number of mourners to have attended a funeral at Abney Park Cemetery.

Also to be found in the southern part of the cemetery are the graves of other people of dissenting distinction, including the following:

♦ **Nathaniel Rogers** (1806–94). Doctor of medicine. This is Abney Park's only mausoleum (a grand architectural tomb usually reserved for a person of distinction) and it is located on the spot once occupied by the Abney House front door.

♦ **Andrew Reed** (1874–62). A Congregationalist minister, hymn writer and philanthropist, Reed was the son of a London watchmaker. Diligent and hard-working, he raised funds for chapels and founded in 1813 the London Orphan Asylum in Lower Clapton ('no catechism shall be imposed on any child … without respect to sex, creed, place or country'), the Royal Hospital for Incurables and other non-denominational institutions. He was also active in supporting the Repeal of the Corn Laws and was an abolitionist.

♦ **Sir Charles Reed** (1819–81). Second son of Andrew Reed, educated in Hackney, lay Congregationalist, trustee and director of Abney Park Cemetery, printer and Liberal politician. Reed was elected in 1868 as the newly created parliamentary borough of Hackney's first MP, and was chairman of the London School Board from 1873 until his death.

♦ **Alexander Fletcher** (1787–1860). Scottish-born Presbyterian divine, known as 'The Prince of Preachers to Children' and 'The Children's Friend' for his children's books and his talents in preaching to youngsters. As an Independent, Fletcher was the founder of London's Finsbury Chapel in 1825 and he stayed there as preacher all his life. He was also Director of the London Missionary Society and a slavery abolitionist who arranged for the American ex-slave Frederick Douglass to talk at the Chapel in 1846.

- **James Braidwood** (1800–61). Edinburgh-born founder of the modern municipal fire service, Braidwood took over London Fire Engine Establishment in 1833. He often visited firefighters and families on behalf of London City Mission. He died in June 1861 when crushed by a falling wall during the Tooley Street Fire, and such was the ferocity of the conflagration that it was two days before his body was recovered. A statue was erected in his honour in 2008 in Parliament Square in Edinburgh. Fittingly, Braidwood is buried only a few yards away from Stoke Newington fire station.

- **Stoke Newington municipal war memorial**. Commemorates those civilians who died in the Second World War, mainly in the area's worst incident in the Blitz when, in October 1940, an air-raid shelter at Coronation Avenue was bombed (*see* Chapter Six).

- **Samuel Morley** (1809–86). Liberal MP for Nottingham and Bristol, woollen manufacturer, Congregationalist dissenter, philanthropist, abolitionist, political radical and publisher of Liberal paper *Daily News*. In the 1880s he endowed the foundation of Morley College of adult education on London's South Bank, whose staff have included Gustav Holst, Virginia Woolf, Michael Tippett and Ralph Vaughan Williams. Morley lived in Stoke Newington.

- **Joanna Vassa** (1795–1857). Daughter of Olaudah Equiano (died 1797) – former African slave, slavery abolitionist campaigner and author of *The Interesting Narrative of the Life of Olaudah Equiano* (described as 'the most important single literary contribution to the campaign for abolition') – Joanna's mother, Susannah, died in 1796. In 1821 in Clerkenwell, Joanna married Congregationalist minister Henry Bromley, who is buried beside her. She lived in Devon, Essex and Suffolk, and moved to Hackney, where she died. Her crumbling headstone was discovered by an American academic in 2004 in Abney Park, and it was re-erected in 2007, the bicentenary of the Act that abolished slavery in the British Empire. The grave is today Grade II listed.

- **William Tyler** (1877–1909). A police constable who was murdered when trying to arrest anarchists in the Tottenham area, an event then known in the national press as the 'Tottenham Outrage'. On his body's flag-draped

2½-mile journey to Abney Park, the streets were lined by 2,000 police officers and a crowd of 500,000. PC Tyler's grave is marked by a stone representation of a policeman's cape and helmet, inscribed with Tyler's official number, and is also Grade II listed.

♦ **Servicemen's memorial.** Once the original catacombs, they were converted in 1922 into a war memorial for servicemen buried in the cemetery but without named headstones, and added to after 1945. A parapet walk is over the roof and carries a Great War Cross.

Elsewhere in Abney Park Cemetery are numerous other graves with interesting stories attached to their dissenting occupants. These include the following:

♦ **William Hone** (1780–1842). Born in 1780, William Hone was an English writer, satirist, publisher and bookseller, and is regarded as one of the fathers of the modern media.

A socialist from an early age, in 1796 he joined the London Corresponding Society, one of whose main aims was to secure votes for working men. Some of its members were tried for treason and sedition, although Hone avoided this fate. In 1800 he married Sarah, and the pair produced twelve children. He also set up a circulating library and then tried bookselling, both without success.

He made his name as an investigative journalist when in 1817 he published the 'Reformists' Register', with illustrations by George Cruikshank, which lambasted abuses of state power, and he was taken to court by the Attorney-General on three charges of 'blasphemy and libel'. He was acquitted on all charges over three successive days, and he became a much-admired public hero. The trial was a resounding victory over state censorship and a landmark in the battle for press freedom and free public expression. He continued his satirical writing in this manner and, with the assistance of his friend Charles Lamb, over the years 1826–29 he wrote the *Every-Day Book*, the *Table-Book* and the *Year-Book*, works that were highly successful and which remain his best known.

However, his personal financial management skills were poor, and he ended up in prison for debt. He was freed due to his many friends' financial assistance, and he then discovered religion. He became a follower of the **Rev. Thomas Binney** (1798–1874, also buried in Abney

Park), an English Congregationalist divine known as the 'Archbishop of Nonconformity' and a popular orator, and Hone converted to nonconformist Christianity. Hone died in nearby Tottenham in 1842, and his interment at Abney Park was attended by, among others, his old friends Cruikshank and Charles Dickens.

♦ **James Bronterre O'Brien** (1805–64). James O'Brien was a Chartist leader, organiser and journalist. Irish-born, he attended Trinity College and in 1829 he moved to London. He became involved in the struggle for universal suffrage and joined the London Working Men's Association. He wrote for *Poor Man's Guardian* under the pen name 'Bronterre', which he adopted as his middle name, and in 1837 he established a magazine, *Bronterre's National Reformer*. Also a member of the militant London Democratic Association, he nonetheless advocated a middle way between the Moral Force and Physical Force wings of the Chartist movement.

He then wrote for the Chartist newspaper *The Northern Star*, was arrested for 'seditious speech' in 1840 and jailed for eighteen months. After his release, he organised Chartists to stand as electoral candidates, particularly against Lord Palmerston, and he continued to write and publish on universal suffrage. His poverty and relentless work for the Chartist cause led to his poor health in the 1850s, and he died from bronchitis.

Abney Park contains the grave of another leading Chartist, **Harry Vincent** (1813–78), who established a radical paper, *The Western Vindicator*, and who was also jailed, for 'inflammatory remarks'. A Quaker sympathiser, he was a lay nonconformist preacher and charismatic orator who was described, after his speech as chief speaker at the great Chartist meeting of 1838 in London, as the 'Demosthenes of the new movement'. Like O'Brien, he was also an abstaining teetotaller, saying that alcohol is 'the serpent in the bowl'.

During **Black History Month** – an event celebrated in venues across Stoke Newington every October – the lives of other cemetery residents are remembered. Here are three of these:

♦ **Joseph Jackson Fuller** (1825–1908). Born to a slave, and one of the earliest slaves to be freed in Jamaica, Fuller became a traveller, translator and preacher. In 1840 he joined the Baptist Missionary Society and condemned slavery in the traditional kingdoms of West Africa. Ordained in 1859, he carried out similar work in Cameroon for the following thirty years. He came to London in 1888, lived in Sydner Road in south-east Stoke Newington and, until his death, he attended Devonshire Square Baptist church.

♦ **Thomas Caulker** (1846–59). Son of the king of Bompey in Sierra Leone, he was sent by his father – 'Canrey Bey' Caulker from a slave-trading family but who had been converted to evangelical Christianity by British abolitionists – to England for a Christian education. Young Caulker lived with two separate Methodist families, but debilitating blindness and ill health resulted in his death at the age of 13 in Canonbury, Islington.

♦ **Eric Walrond** (1898–1966). Born in Georgetown, British Guyana, Walrond moved to New York City in 1920 in order to further his writing aspirations. He became part of the Afro-Caribbean 'Harlem Renaissance' movement and he published in 1928 his best-known book, *Tropic Death*, still in print today. He knew Marcus Garvey – the black nationalist and pan-Africanist, Jamaican national hero and sometime resident of Stamford Hill – and Walrond was awarded a Guggenheim Fellowship for Fiction two years in succession. He moved to England in the 1930s, continued to write short stories, and died here.

The people I describe above are only a few of the many thousands whose remains are to be found at Abney Park Cemetery. Their stones, graves and tombs are a continual reminder of the cemetery's and the area's diverse, complex and historically renowned dissenting heritage.

THE ANGLICAN CHURCH REVIVAL

Towards the middle of the nineteenth century, the Anglican authorities in the parishes of Stoke Newington, South Hornsey and West Hackney were concerned about the continuing growth of religious dissent in the Stoke Newington area and the possible damaging impact on Anglican worship. The increasing population of the parishes, and the consequent growth in the number of nonconformist chapels, meeting rooms and halls, was a source of concern to the established Church.

Many of these incomers preferred to worship in a different manner to that of the Anglicans, and in smaller, more personal chapels than were provided by the Church. The Anglican Church perceived these 'dissenting' sects as challenges to their authority and to their dominance as the one true religion. These nonconformists in Stoke Newington included Quakers, Methodists, Baptists, Congregationalists, Presbyterians and several other smaller groups, whose spiritual teachings and more intimate surroundings appealed to many of the new arrivals to a greater degree than did the orthodox preaching of the Anglicans.

One of the solutions to this perceived decline in the Anglican status was to commission and build substantial new churches that, by their grandeur and innovative layout, would decrease the influence of nonconformism in the area. By the mid-nineteenth century, Stoke Newington was home to several major new Anglican churches.

◆ ◆ ◆

Hackney was in 1823 divided into three separate parishes, the new parish being West Hackney, which began across the London Road from Stoke Newington. The 1818 Church Building Act was designed to combat the effects of nonconformism by re-establishing the Church of England as and where necessary, and it was certainly needed in the neighbouring parish of Stoke Newington, where nonconformist chapels proliferated.

The first new Anglican Church to be built was the **West Hackney Church** on Stoke Newington Road, which was located at the confluence of today's Evering Road and Amhurst Road and which opened in 1824. Designed in Classical Greek style, it could accommodate up to 2,000 worshippers and it loomed imperiously over its surrounding area. To its rear was an impressively extensive burial ground, occupying a hectare of land, overlooked to the south by the large rectory, which stretched back in the direction of Rectory Road. Known locally as St James's, the church endured for well over a century but it suffered badly from bomb damage during the Second World War and had to be demolished.

(Around this time there were several, mainly private, schools in Stoke Newington. Directly across the road from the West Hackney Church burial ground, which is now known as West Hackney Recreation Ground, on the junction of today's Evering Road and Leswin Road there stands a typical example. Sombre and severe in its appearance, it displays a large stone address: 'West Hackney National School. 1837'. This has been recently refurbished as the sign wasn't there ten years ago when my office was nearby, and today it is a recently converted block of flats.)

On the site of the demolished West Hackney Church today is **St Paul's Church**, a rather more architecturally modest but popular church, particularly with the Saturday shoppers at the weekly Farmers' Market and also with homeless people, as the North London Action on the Homeless charity is based there and provides regular meals, support and much else. The burial area remains a green public space, and it's pleasant enough, although the park is rendered rather melancholic by the fading and virtually illegible details on the curved tombstones lined against and close to the southern wall.

Not far away from St Paul's and close to the Newington Green end of Albert Town sits **St Matthias Church** on Wordsworth Road, overlooking the Poets' Roads. In terms of its size and location, it is an unmissable structure and its dark, stern appearance is hardly its most attractive feature. However, as I discovered at a recent funeral service, the interior design is more inviting and, today at least, the atmosphere is more relaxed and informal than the exterior might suggest. The church was built in 1849 to serve worshippers in south-east Stoke Newington, and it was the first 'daughter church' of St Mary's.

However, unlike the old St Mary's, St Matthias was established as a Tractarian 'High Church' and 'Anglo-Catholic' in its religious views. This being so, and as the years progressed, although St Matthias' preachers normally attracted large congregations, these worshippers on occasion had to be protected by the police from angry Protestant crowds, as the social composition of the area was changing and 'dissenters' were now numerous. Indeed, by the end of the nineteenth century there were almost twenty nonconformist chapels and meeting places in the Albert Town area, and over half the residents were 'dissenters'.

During that period, the area was 'overrun with dissent' and nonconformism was 'vigorously in the ascendant'. Gradually, however, as Albert Town and its surrounds became a predominantly working-class, immigrant and Jewish area, dissent withered away. St Matthias remains today, its appearance as enigmatic as ever.

Up on Church Street, the old **St Mary's Church** was becoming increasingly dilapidated, and its structure, despite the restoration work it had undergone over the centuries, was deteriorating. In 1826, after several coffins had been discovered floating in water under the floor, the vestry decided again to refurbish the building, restoring both the spire and windows, repairing its rotting roof and increasing its capacity from 500 to over 700 worshippers. However, there was a limit to the numbers it could accommodate as the building was too small to cope with the area's rise in population, so a new church was required.

Sir George Gilbert Scott was commissioned to build a new church directly opposite Old St Mary's and on the site of the Old Church's Rectory. The much larger **New St Mary's Church**, designed in thirteenth-century English Gothic style, with rich stained-glass windows, a wooden roof and capacity for 1,300 Anglican worshippers, was consecrated in 1858, although funds were then limited and a spire – then the tallest spire in London – was not added until 1890. This omission gave rise to a local ditty:

Stoke Newington is a funny place, with lots of funny people.
Now they've built a funny church which hasn't got a steeple.

The last laugh lay with the vestry, however, as when the steeple was eventually erected it was, at 250ft, then the tallest church steeple in London. By 1900 the New Church could boast a full house for its services, a Sunday School attended by 1,000 children, and a wide range of popular church-linked societies.

When the new church was proposed, concern had been expressed about the future of the 'Old Church' (as it now became), amid fears that this historically important building might be demolished. However, the vestry decided to retain the building and to continue with its maintenance when necessary, describing it as providing an 'old-fashioned service to old-fashioned worshippers'. Despite damage to both churches during the Second World War, today they remain very much involved in local communities. Old St Mary's proved its worth during the War as, given the extent of the damage to the newcomer, it held most of the services during the conflict. The New Church was repaired after the War and was re-dedicated in 1957. It continues to attract sizeable congregations, occupies itself with various local groups, and is still the focus of Anglican worship in the area.

The Old Church is increasingly used as a venue for artistic events of all kinds and, although its graveyard was closed to non-family burials in 1855, this 700-year-old, distinctive and locally cherished building and grounds are well maintained as a memorial to internees such as Anna Laetitia Barbauld, Presbyterian Divine Thomas Manton, Lady Mary Abney, slavery abolitionist James Stephen, the brewer and builder Henry Sandford, and the Eade family, once lords of the Stoke Newington manor.

As I discovered several years ago when promoting musical evenings during the 'N16 Fringe', the historical importance, intimacy and vibrant acoustics of the Old Church create a magnetic atmosphere for audiences and musicians alike. In particular, two internationally renowned singer/guitarists, who have played in major concert halls and famed music clubs across the world, each told me after their gigs here that this had been their favourite venue, a sentiment echoed by many in the audience. Such an accolade may not have been on William Patten's agenda when he refurbished the church in 1563 but, had he been around today, he would probably have shared the audience's enjoyment. It's a remarkable little place, and it's heartening to see that the Old Church remains in use.

There were a number of other Anglican churches established or being planned in the Stoke Newington area, including St Andrew's (to the north), St Olave's (Woodberry Down) and St Michael's and All Angels (Stoke Newington Common). However, substantial nonconformist places of worship were also appearing or would be in place by the end of the nineteenth century.

As well as the various chapels and meeting halls to the south of the parish – and not including Quakers and Unitarians whom I have previously mentioned – there were Methodists (Stoke Newington High Street, Northwold Road and Green Lanes), Congregationalists (Church Street, Rectory Road, Albion Road), Baptists (the main Baptist church, Devonshire Square, facing West Hackney Church on Stoke Newington Road), Presbyterians (Manor Road) and other dissenting groups whose meeting rooms and small churches variously arrived, moved and disappeared across the Stoke Newington area.

By the early years of the twentieth century, religious antagonisms of this nature were declining in their relative importance, particularly as divisive forces. Not only was 'dissent' being expressed in other terms and through channels more closely linked to social and urban modernity, but also the arrival in the area of immigrant groups and alternative belief systems – in particular, Islam and Judaism – stressed the increasingly communal, multicultural nature of Stoke Newington and the corresponding requirement for a greater tolerance of other beliefs, activities and cultures.

In the chapter that follows, I will be examining in Stoke Newington the revolutions in transport, communications, local government and the early years of immigration, all of which combined to create what, spatially and functionally, appeared to be a typical inner-city suburb. Under this apparent facade of conformity, however, the spirit of dissent was far from absent.

CHAPTER FOUR

A VILLAGE NO MORE: 1870 TO THE FIRST WORLD WAR

Many factors, not just the railways, had got the suburban ball rolling and, once started, the centrifugal tendency would not stop, for it was propelled by the pressure of private capital seeking profitable outlets. It afforded new business opportunities —for landowners, railway and tram promoters, shareholders in utilities, land companies, speculative builders, property dealers, solicitors, house agents, shopkeepers and publicans. With abundant supplies of cheap labour, land and capital, suburban development became a bonanza, especially for the petty capitalists who dominated the building trade.

London: A Social History, Roy Porter

The process and impact of suburbanisation was, to a greater or lesser degree, replicated across the London area during the latter half of the nineteenth century and, in this respect, Stoke Newington was no exception.

The geographical expansion of London was hardly surprising. In 1800, the city's population had been around 1 million. By 1881 it had risen to 4.5 million, and by 1911 it was estimated that 7 million people were inhabitants of the metropolis. There were many reasons for this remarkable increase, but the principal cause was immigration, internal and external: from the disastrous Irish Famine, from the enclosure movements and the crisis in English agriculture, from overseas and from people seeking opportunities or security elsewhere unavailable. London was a magnet for the marginalised and displaced, the careerist and opportunist, and the exploiter and the exploited. The city was again becoming intolerably overcrowded, and outward expansion was inevitable and essential.

Before the establishment of the London County Council in 1888, there had been little or no central authority, direction or representative government in the capital. Urban planning and housing development had generally been left to private capital and speculative builders. This resulted in such glaring contrasts as the wide avenues and extravagant mansions of Belgravia and the poverty-stricken slums and crumbling tenements of much of the East End.

Such shameful polarities had yet to be addressed but, for some of the less advantaged London residents – clerks, small shopkeepers, skilled craftsmen and others from what one could then describe as the lower middle classes – a move to the healthy, spacious, affordable and yet easily accessible surrounding countryside seemed a sensible decision. This opportunity for rural relocation, however, was available only to those who could afford the transition. Many poorer urban dwellers could not raise the money, and had to remain in some of the most wretched environments of the City. Proximity to these much-deprived urban districts, and their frequent outbreaks of disease, was often another reason for these new commuters to leave London.

Although the arrival of the railway had, in the short term, adversely affected many of the social, architectural and ecological environments in which trains were established and through which they passed, this new mode of transport was of crucial importance to the creation and economic development of the beckoning new inner and outer London suburbs. The proliferation of local train services, and the consequent financial opportunities offered by the emerging suburbs, was also welcomed by house builders and by the entrepreneurs and chancers who would follow in their wake.

TRAMS AND TRAINS

In 1872, the Great Eastern Railway company opened Stoke Newington railway station as part of the branch line that ran from Enfield to Shoreditch.

Around the same time, the first tramlines appeared on the main streets of the area. Horse-drawn commercial omnibuses had operated on these roads since the early years of the nineteenth century, but their lack of regulation, the number of small companies jostling for space in a crowded market, and the drivers' unpredictability led to frequent accidents as they raced along the congested streets, such as London Road towards the City.

In 1870 the North Metropolitan Tramways Company introduced horse-drawn trams, which were not only more comfortable and safer for the passengers but also more profitable for the operator, as the same number of horses could transport twice as many passengers. By 1875 the trams operated regular services, including Upper Clapton to the City, up the Kingsland Road to Stoke Newington and Newington Green to Clissold Park.

CLAPTON TRAM DEPOT

A ghost sign across the Upper Clapton Road from its junction with Brooke Road reads 'Tram Depot'. It's a fair bet that most drivers and passers-by don't see it, and they probably don't notice the grey-bricked, crumbling wall that bears the sign. Even fewer will be aware that this is one of London's last remaining Victorian horse-drawn tram depots.

The Lea Bridge Tram Depot, as it was originally known, was opened in 1873 by the North Metropolitan Tramways Company. Upper Clapton was then home to some of the finest and most expensive houses in the capital, and between 1872 and 1907 the new horse-tram service offered its wealthy residents regular and reliable journeys into the City and West End. One of the trams that serviced this route is preserved today in the London Transport Museum in Covent Garden.

Although its exterior may appear less than promising, a stroll today around the depot yard and buildings reveals a mini-complex of shops, artists' and photographer's studios, a popular restaurant – the Clapton Country Club, no less – and several other outlets, all maintained by enthusiastic and committed small businesses, artisans and artists. The depot's original features have, as far as possible, been carefully and lovingly retained: the granite setts remain on the uneven cobbled yard close to the U-shaped tram sheds and stables, the tramlines run through or under the central shed, and the cast-iron colonnades and stable flooring on the first floor are still there. The original buildings, constructed from local bricks, also remain. The depot today is a fine example of co-operative

STOKE NEWINGTON: THE STORY OF A DISSENTING VILLAGE

endeavour by the businesses on the site, and of how most appropriately to maintain an important historical site while earning a livelihood.

Demolition by Hackney Council, although averted, has been a prospect in the recent past, and the current owner's plans for the depot's future are, it appears, uncertain. Brooke House across the road was demolished by Hackney Council in the 1950s, and Clapton Federation Synagogue, just round the corner on Lea Bridge roundabout, was torn down by the same council in 2006. It would be another major scar on Upper Clapton's history if the depot was allowed to disappear, although there are plenty of potential objectors and dissenters in the area should this proposal be suggested.

The tramlines were electrified from 1906, and the same decade saw the introduction of motor buses, so the horses gradually disappeared from the streets. The new railway line, with its convenient station in Clapton, 100 yards up the road from the depot, and the line through Stoke Newington and Rectory Road (as the northern section of Shacklewell Lane was now named), were speedy and dependable. The completion of Liverpool Street station in 1874 ensured that the train became the travellers' preferred route into the City.

Stay-at-home Stoke Newington residents were less enthusiastic, as the GER line drove directly through the open public space of Stoke Newington Common (unlike the train from Clapton, which local protest had forced into a tunnel under Hackney Downs), it introduced intrusive railside development and blighted residential areas, and it created jerry-built pockets of sub-standard housing, such as 'Navvies' Island' bounded by the railway line, Rendlesham Road and Ottoway Street, which was home to many of the railway labourers and which remained a run-down area until its demolition in the 1970s. The 'Island' is currently being redeveloped.

These negative side-effects, however, mattered little to the incoming inhabitants of the parish. Stoke Newington was a pleasant place in which to live, the railway transported them to and from their places of employment and on trips to the countryside, and the 'speculative builders' provided them with affordable, pleasant enough homes. In *Life and Labour of the People of London*, Charles Booth wrote in 1902 of Stoke Newington, 'the district is residential rather than manufacturing. People sleep here but work elsewhere', so the railway was a convenient arrangement for all concerned.

♦ ♦ ♦

Although Roy Porter observed that across London 'many factors, not just the railways, had got the suburban ball rolling', in the case of Stoke Newington the railway does appear to have been the crucial stimulus for the unprecedented growth and spread of housing that occurred after its arrival.

However, without the co-operation of local landowners, the railways may as well have remained in their urban sidings. The large landlords, such as the Tyssen family – originally of Flemish descent and who had for generations owned most of the available land across Clapton and West Hackney – quickly realised that the financial returns from building development would dwarf the profits from nurseries and brickfields, and they were happy to negotiate with developers. Likewise, many smaller estates and owners of larger gardens were aware of the advantages in selling these acres as building plots. Special services – 'workingmen's trains' – were laid on by GER for areas that required such assistance, and houses began to appear across the Stoke Newington area.

By the end of the nineteenth century, Stoke Newington had become, in terms of its housing stock, local economy and population size, virtually unrecognisable from the upper-middle-class, rural village of thirty years earlier. Although lying barely 3 miles north of the City of London, it had previously been regarded as a peaceful hamlet that was slowly and tentatively expanding in size and in the number of its inhabitants. Horse-drawn buses, short-stage coaches and carriages had for a number of years transported local businessman, bankers and government officials from their substantial garden villas in Stoke Newington to the City and West End.

With the exception of a few small areas and the recent development of Albert Town to the south of the parish, Stoke Newington had been, until as late as 1870, a wealthy middle-class, pastoral retreat from the rigours of city life. The establishment of the two reservoirs in the 1830s had stimulated the development of villa housing around their edges, as well as the construction of carefully laid-out roads and houses to the north of the parish. Cubitt's construction of Albion Road, and the associated development on and along the western end of Church Street, had also been designed with the well-off in mind, and Church Street itself remained a desirable address.

Within these thirty or so years, however, the Stoke Newington area underwent the deeply transformative experience of suburbanisation. Its comfortable elitism, with a few exceptions, was largely to disappear along with its wealthier residents to the outer suburbs, and the impact of urban life significantly changed Stoke Newington in terms of its architecture, its open spaces and the social composition of many of the newcomers.

THE HOUSING BOOM

The Ordnance Survey map of 1894 clearly reveals the astonishing growth in the number of roads and houses in Stoke Newington and the surrounding area over the previous twenty-five years. The economic depressions of the late 1840s and '50s had deferred the impact of the 1814 land 'enfranchisement', but thereafter the more opportune economic environment, combined with the new railway, led to a housebuilding boom. The number of houses in Stoke Newington surged from 1,800 in 1871 to just under 8,000 in 1901 – a fourfold increase within only thirty years – and the empty brickfields, nurseries and many of the longer back gardens on the 1868 OS map had succumbed to the financial inducements of the builders.

The ribbon development along the main roads – London Road, Green Lanes and Church Street – that had for so long characterised the parish had been extended back to the extent that, south of Church Street, there was little room remaining on which to build. The process began in 1874 when the old Pawnbroker Lane (now, in a nod to gentrification, retitled Kynaston Lane) was developed into Kynaston Road, leading to Nevill and Oldfield Roads, and then onward. By the end of the decade other roads – from Dynevor Road in the east to Hawksley Road in the west, and to the south immediately above the previously developed South Hornsey parish – had been laid out with streets, schools, shops and terraced houses.

Also, the land to the west of Park Lane (Clissold Crescent), including Burma Road, Aden Grove and further down Green Lanes to Newington Green, were now built up, and homes on the Palatine estate extended to Crossway, the old parish boundary. St Mary's, a large, newly built primary school, also occupied much of the land on the London Road north of Barrett's Grove.

Although north of Church Street the various builders worked to a more leisurely timescale, the development of the fields and nursery gardens from Lordship Park to the reservoirs was also completed by the end of the nineteenth century. Several of the larger houses abutting the reservoirs were left relatively unscathed but new roads – Bethune, Fairholt, St Kilda, Allerton and others – were created and, like the housing to the south, they were generally terraced homes designed for family use and not, with a few exceptions, built as flats.

One of these exceptions was the Allen estate, started in 1873 and named after its developer Matthew Allen (a member of the local Allen Quaker family), which began on Manor Road and stretched north up Bethune Road. Aimed at the middle- and upper-middle classes (there were live-in servants' rooms included in several larger flats), these were tenement blocks of flats, a radical architectural concept for the times. Each block contained a rear garden, behind which was a communal area with tennis courts and greenhouses.

On Church Street there were also significant changes occurring as the nineteenth century drew to a close. Whenever the remaining older mansions and villas with gardens were sold, there was a rush by builders to replace them, usually with terraced side streets. For instance, when Daniel Defoe's house was demolished in 1870, within five years his mansion and small estate had been replaced by Defoe Road, St Mary's Assembly Rooms and more than fifty terraced homes. In the same year as the demolition of Fleetwood House in 1872, sixteen terraced houses had been built on the new Fleetwood Street.

In 1877, sixteen terraced houses were built on Summerhouse Street on the site of James Stephen's old family home. Where once had stood Newington Hall at the junction with Green Lanes, virtually overnight Statham Grove and thirty-two terraced houses had appeared. Paradise Row and its wealthy, City-based residents remained, although Paradise House had become a school. As well as the villas around the reservoirs, these were one of the few untouched remnants of the old parish, although the new housing terraces were slowly encroaching on their still-extensive gardens.

As well as housing, small industrial concerns and shops were taking over the sites of many older buildings. There were estimated in 1914 to be over twenty manufacturing firms and outlets on and immediately around Church Street.

However, not all development on Church Street was connected to terraced houses and commerce. In keeping with Church Street's literary heritage, and under the provisions of the 1892 Libraries Act, a public library was opened at the corner of the street and Edwards Lane, partially funded by Andrew Carnegie and other philanthropists, and another public library would soon open at the Upper Clapton end of Northwold Road. But from the end of the nineteenth century until the early 1930s there was very little building development, mainly due to available land on Church Street being at a minimum.

In contrast to the north of the parish, the buildings to the south of Church Street were more densely populated and smaller than those to the north, and they were all terraced. They were described, patronisingly but with a basis in truth, as 'suffering from a fearful eruption of bricks and mortar of a very low type'. Albert Town and the south-east of the parish generally were already showing signs of 'social decline', due mainly to serious overcrowding.

At the southern tip of the parish, the fervid atmosphere of religious dissent in Newington Green had cooled down over the nineteenth century, and the conurbation of London was edging closer to the Green, still a rural area but not for much longer. The Unitarian Church had been refurbished but its congregation was decreasing. The China Inland Mission building to the west of the Green, which today is a student hall of residence, had been founded by James Hudson Taylor, who claimed 18,000 converts. The Mission had certainly generated sufficient funds to pay for its imposing curved stone entrance.

Also, the Radical Society, formed in Mildmay in 1886, had relocated next to the Unitarian building, and it had been primly denounced by a vicar at the nearby St Matthias Church as 'a pernicious influence among the young'. The club changed its name in the 1930s to the Mildmay Club and Institute, and claimed it had become 'non-political'. Still there today, it is also one of the few places in north London to have full-size billiard tables available for members to hire by the hour so, along with its decent-sized dance and live music hall, it has a good many local supporters.

Despite all the to-ing and fro-ing of the late nineteenth century, Stoke Newington remained, at least in the eyes of its residents, a middle-class 'well established and reputable' inner-London suburb.

EAST OF LONDON ROAD

On the eastern side of the London Road in West Hackney, the 'speculative builders' had been, if possible, even harder at work. The land to the south of the parish, from Shacklewell to Rectory Road, including the laying out of Amhurst and Farleigh Roads, was under development before the rail and tram lines were in place, and the coming of the railway served only to expedite this process.

However, there was a wide expanse of open brickland, commercial nurseries, large gardens and pasture land that stretched from Lower Stamford Hill to the south of Stoke Newington Common and west almost to Upper Clapton Road, land that offered the builders ample scope for profitable investments.

During the 1870s and '80s four main roads were completed that linked the London Road with Upper Clapton Road. Starting at the north, these were Cazenove, Northwold (previously Keats Lane, then Brook Road), Brooke and Evering Roads, which provided the lateral framework for the other north–south roads close to the Common. Again, these were mainly neat, middle-class terraces (such as Alkham, Kyverdale, Osbaldeston and Fountayne Roads), which came down from Lower Stamford Hill and Cazenove Road. Similar streets (Jenner, Benthal, Maury and Norcott Roads) travelled up to the Common from Evering Road. The presence of Rectory Road station (on the western end of Evering Road) on the GER line stimulated demand for these new homes, as did Clapton station, only a few minutes' walk away at the eastern end of Northwold Road.

VARIETY IN TERRACES

As one today walks along these streets around Stoke Newington Common, it's interesting to note that, although the houses in the terraces seem to possess the same facades, one occasionally notices small discrepancies in their individual appearances.

There are, of course, certain obvious differences – such as the number of storeys, type of brick and the distance back from the road – and these have clearly been erected by a single builder. However, as with Albert Town, although nothing like the same variety of style, these streets have mainly been built by a few large companies but also by various individuals who have left their own 'calling cards'. So, in an otherwise identical terrace, one discovers slightly differently shaped or smaller windows, a roof that is a foot below the others, the occasional absence of a stone column by the door, a guttering of a different design and shape to the others, an oval rather than rectangular window above the door, and so on.

These could be constructional errors or more recent additions but are more likely to be a one-off builder attempting to impress his individuality on an anonymous row of identical houses. If so, good for him. Have a look for yourself.

Further north from Brooke Road, up the High Street, was the newly created Garnham Street, once a run-down and deprived part of the parish but converted in the 1890s into fourteen blocks of walk-up flats. Still heading north, before reaching Northwold Road on its route past the Common, sits a large, gloomy building that, before being converted into flats, housed Fleetwood school, an early example of 'elementary' schooling and which was built in 1876 by the London School Board, the first all-London body to have enjoyed direct elections.

On the northern side of Northwold Road, as it leaves the High Street, is located **Gibson Gardens** (originally **Gibson Buildings**), a large complex of flats and cottages set back from the main road. Gibson Buildings was another example of late-Victorian, purpose-built flats and typical of the work of the 'model dwellings' movement. Unlike Matthew's Allen estate in Bethune Road, these 'dwellings' were not aimed at the middle classes, although Allen designed several buildings across London for a 'model dwellings' concern, the Improved Industrial Dwellings Company.

Gibson Gardens was designed, funded and built in 1892 by the Metropolitan Association for Improving the Dwellings of the Industrious Classes (MAIDIC), one of the earliest and largest 'model dwellings' companies and was, in the words of the company, 'formed for the purpose of providing the labouring man with an increase of the comforts and conveniences of life, with full return to the capitalist'. Before it was obliterated in the 1980s – another attempt at gentrification – the company's name was proudly emblazoned on an eight-chimneyed roof structure high above the twin stone-pillar entrance to the flats.

MAIDIC was one of almost thirty 'model dwelling' companies in late-Victorian Britain that built houses for the working classes while enjoying profitable returns on their investments: 'five per cent philanthropy', as it became known. Perhaps the best-known such company was the Four Per Cent Industrial Dwellings Company, which originally focused on poverty-stricken Jewish immigrants in the East End, although it was also responsible in 1902 for the construction of Coronation and Imperial Avenues in Victorian Avenue, just off Stoke Newington Road.

As the nineteenth century progressed, sanitary problems in urban areas – including the possible spread of cholera and typhus from poorer districts – had been a growing concern among reformers. In 1875 Disraeli's government passed the Public Health Act, which provided local authorities with the powers to create and maintain sewers, control water supplies and buildings and, if necessary, demolish slums. When criticised by MPs for allocating precious parliamentary time to this legislation, Disraeli replied *'sanitas sanitatum, omnia sanitas'* ('health above all'), and he was praised by the emerging trades unions for 'humanising the toil of the working man'.

The provisions of the Act enabled the 'model dwelling' companies briefly to flourish as, although the Act was permissive and not compulsory, a number of local authorities in larger cities commissioned them to build new or replacement accommodation for 'the working man'. It has even been claimed that these companies were largely responsible for demonstrating to the local authorities the social benefits of creating the subsequent council estates, which today proliferate across the capital.

The companies, however, were also criticised. They were accused of exploiting the workers purely in the interests of self-aggrandisement and profit. They also came under attack by, among others, Friedrich Engels, for attempting to ensure the continuance of capitalism through 'embourgeoisement': the process of luring away affluent members of the working class into the middle class to dilute the power of organised labour. The nineteenth century in Britain had witnessed the combined power of organised workers, social reformers and leftist intellectuals, most notably with the Chartist movement, and there were a good many employers and public officials who feared a recurrence of another such alliance. Others objected to the companies' concentration on the upper levels of the working class while not providing for the needs of the poorest sections of society who desperately needed 'model dwellings', or indeed anywhere that wasn't a rat-infested slum.

Whatever the merits of these views, in the early years of the twentieth century the London County Council (LCC) embarked on the provision of social housing and moved on to the development of large council housing estates. The 'model dwelling' movement was unable or unwilling to compete with the LCC, and it gradually withered away. Gibson Gardens stands today as a reminder of the Victorian and Edwardian era of philanthropic capitalism.

FIRE STATION

Just off the High Street — heading towards the Common at the junction with Brooke and Leswin Roads — was established in 1886 the new home for the fire station, which had suffered a peripatetic existence since the 1780s, when

Stoke Newington possessed a pump-powered fire engine based at St Mary's Church. The station then moved to near Barn Street and, in 1820, to behind the Red Lion. It moved again in 1858 to the High Street, opposite today's Dynevor Road. Within ten years the service was merged with the Metropolitan Fire Brigade.

The station's new Leswin Road depot was built at a cost of £5,500, and it remained in this central location for over eighty years. At the turn of the twentieth century – now renamed the London Fire Brigade and under the control of the LCC – the service had two fire escape stations in the area, which consisted of two-wheeled carts manhandled by volunteers to control local fires. The heavy German bombing the during the Second World War kept the Brigade fully occupied, and the destruction by fire of the J.J. Hibberd depository in Church Street in 1954 required the attention of 150 firemen and fifty pumps, and was described as 'the biggest catastrophe since the War'.

By the early 1970s, the Leswin Road station was outdated, and in 1976 a new station was built on Church Street – on the site of the western side of Fleetwood House – with a two-engine, two-storey capacity and a separate practice tower station, and it remains there today. The Leswin Road site was not, however, forgotten and is today a restored and much-used community centre, under the prominent wooden painted sign 'The Old Fire Station'.

As well as housing, the religious impulse remained strong in the Stoke Newington Common area. The Anglican church St Michael and All Angels was built in 1885 at the foot of Fountayne Road, and this tall red-brick structure still faces the Common. This was followed in 1911 by St Barnabas Church, also Anglican, which is tucked away in Shacklewell. St Barnabas, the daughter church of St Paul's on Stoke Newington Road, was created to serve the Merchant Taylors' School missionary work in the area. This attractive building was designed in an unusually round, basilica architectural style and is largely hidden from public view by higher buildings, which is a pity. St Barnabas is a building that deserves closer scrutiny and appreciation.

Heading back north, the 'dissenting' Trinity Congregationalist church relocated from South Hornsey to Rectory Road, opposite the station, in 1882. On the east of the High Street, between Tyssen and Brooke Roads, was rebuilt the impressive Methodist church and school, which backed onto Leswin Road. Further down Stoke Newington Road sat the larger

Devonshire Square Baptist church, and other smaller nonconformist chapels were not too far away. Religious dissent, although now more institutional-ised and less theologically belligerent than it had been in previous centuries, continued to flourish in West Hackney and Stoke Newington.

However, there remained in the area isolated examples of what one might politely term 'idiosyncratic' nonconformism, a good example being located a bit further north on the Upper Clapton Road where Rookwood Road meets Clapton Common. Here is to be found John Betjeman's favourite Hackney building (he described the interior as 'a blaze of glory'), today's Cathedral Church of the Good Shepherd. This distinctive neo-Gothic struc-ture, with its four stone statuettes representing each of the early evangelists, was once known as the Church of the Ark of the Covenant, the house of worship of the Agapemonites (*see* box).

A DISSENTING CULT ...

Deriving their name from the Greek 'agapemone' ('the abode of love'), the Agapemonites were a religious sect founded in the 1840s in Brighton by Henry James Prince, a defrocked Anglican priest and a charismatic preacher, particularly when it came to wealthy, gullible women, preferably widows. His teachings – based loosely on German mysticism, the 'spirituality' of marriage, the imminent arrival of the Messiah, an unconventional view of the role of women (he had numerous 'brides') and the certainty of immortality – per-suaded his followers to fund the sect's acquisition of 200 acres in Somerset for a self-supporting community, and then the construction in 1892 of the church in Upper Clapton.

Seven years later, the immortal Prince died, and was buried standing up, ready for the Resurrection. His successor, John Hugh Smyth-Piggot – a plausible Irish womaniser – immediately announced that he was the new Messiah: 'God, not man'. However, he was unable to fulfil his promise to walk across Clapton Pond, and he quickly retreated to Somerset, where his 'spiritual brides' num-bered up to seven per week. However, his claim to immortality lasted only until his death in 1927.

Having lost two immortal Messiahs in succession, the surviving community fell into decline and eventually disbanded. In the late 1920s, the Agapemonites abandoned the Clapton church, which was acquired in 1957 by the Ancient Catholic Church. Today it stands as an architectural footnote to a bizarre 're-ligious' cult whose leaders, it appears, were inspired less by principled dissent than they were by promiscuous deception.

... AND A DISSENTING BULLOCK

In 1911, a *Hackney Gazette* report was eye-catchingly headlined: 'Bullock Runs Amok In Stoke Newington'. A Devon bullock was in a stall next to the Brooke Road slaughterhouse, when he spotted an opportunity. He sidled out from an unlocked door, smashed through a glass window, and began to lumber up the High Street towards Stamford Hill. On reaching the Jolly Butchers public house, he hesitated – 'as if between the devil and the deep sea' – then turned right down Garnham Street and sauntered onto Stoke Newington Common.

Resisting inducements by irritated slaughterhouse workers to return to his place of impending dispatch, and enjoying the attention of the swelling crowd and a growing number of children, he seemed in no hurry to get there and kept them all at bay for over an hour. The Common, reported the *Gazette*, 'was like a bull ring', with increasingly excited children being prevented by newly arrived local policemen from provoking the bullock.

However, the bullock eventually conceded to the butchers' pleadings and suffered its inevitable fate. This lingering folk memory could perhaps explain the unusually high number of people in Brooke Road today who are vegetarians.

STOKE NEWINGTON: A METROPOLITAN BOROUGH

Stoke Newington parish had long been under the control of the local vestry of St Mary's Church, which had possessed or assumed similar powers to those of today's local authorities, and then by the largely ineffective Metropolitan Board of Works in the 1850s.

However, in 1899 the London Government Act changed fundamentally the management of London parishes, whose vestry systems were deemed inappropriate to the rapid transition to modernity that had been experienced during the late nineteenth century. They were also considered excessively complicated, over-elaborate, and seen to be in need of streamlining, and they had to be kept at a distance from future local decision-making.

The year 1900, therefore, saw the creation in London of Metropolitan Boroughs, which entailed the subordination of the parish vestries mainly to matters ecclesiastic while responsibility for local government would be under the control of new mayors, aldermen and councillors. Under the 1899 Act, all boundaries were to be simplified and the Metropolitan Boroughs would contain minimum populations of 100,000 residents.

The neighbouring new boroughs of Shoreditch and Hackney possessed populations significantly in excess of this figure but Stoke Newington could lay claim to only 50,000 people, which would have made it the smallest borough in London. As a merger with Hackney was unthinkable to Stoke Newington – 'a great ill-feeling and mutual ill-will' existed between the parishes – it decided to merge with South Hornsey. Although this union still resulted in well under 100,000, it was assumed that population growth would quickly correct the shortfall. The eastern boundary was to extend to the GER railway line, so Stoke Newington Common, or the western section thereof, was included in the new borough.

The Metropolitan Borough of Stoke Newington was divided into six wards and proclaimed its councillors to be 'Non-Party', although the majority of them were 'Conservative in character', and the Town Hall was to be located in Milton Grove. The first Mayor was John Johnson Runtz, son of one of the two men behind the creation of Clissold Park and a resident of one of the exclusive villas north of Lordship Park, an area in which lived many of the more prosperous inhabitants of the borough.

However, it was a different story to the south of the borough in St Matthias parish, and particularly in Albert Town. In the late 1880s, the population was 'increasing at extraordinary speed' and the area's character 'had much degenerated'. By the first decade of the twentieth century, St Matthias parish was almost entirely working class, with many residents close to or below poverty levels.

In the north the population level was a comfortable 28 to the acre, while in Albert and Victoria Town it was, in places, well over 150 to the acre. The well-off merchants, local government officials and businessmen from the lands near the reservoirs generally remained close allies of St Mary's vestry, while southern residents were increasingly nonconformist, a situation exacerbated by the growing number of Jewish immigrants arriving from the East End. The poverty and destitution of these people were in stark contrast to the middle-class respectability of those who lived in the large houses and gardens of Lordship and Bethune Roads, only a mile or so to the north of the parish.

BEYOND 'THE PALE': JEWISH IMMIGRATION

Many of the Jewish people who had been invited back to England during the Cromwellian Protectorate had remained here, and several Jewish families – Rothschilds, Montagus, Montefiores and others – had become some of the wealthiest people in the country. The Rothschild and Goldsmid families owned large houses in Stamford Hill, in the early nineteenth century one of the wealthiest areas within easy reach of central London.

These Sephardic Jewish people normally worshipped at the Bevis Marks Synagogue (the name in Hebrew meaning 'Holy Congregation Gate of Heaven') in the City, founded in 1701 and which is the oldest, continuously used synagogue in the UK. The aforementioned Benjamin D'Israeli, who resided at Stoke Newington's Church Row, certainly attended the synagogue, as did a few other Sephardic Jews in this area. One such was Solomon de Medina, who married a Christian and had his children baptised in the Christian faith but, when he was elected to become St Mary's churchwarden, his oath was refused by St Paul's Prebendary. Another Jewish resident was Isaac Furtado, whose children were also baptised and who is buried in St Mary's churchyard, the only Jewish internee in this old burial ground.

These settled Jewish residents of the Stoke Newington area were middle class, English speaking, and fitted well into the Gentile neighbourhood. From the 1880s onwards, Ashkenazi Jews began to arrive in the UK, particularly in London and, more particularly, in the East End. This trickle of incomers soon turned into a mass immigration, and initially this created a number of problems.

While Anglo-Sephardic Jews originated in Spain and Portugal, the Ashkenazi Jews were another part of the Diaspora (from the Greek word for 'dispersal') who had made their homes in the Holy Roman Empire almost 1,000 years previously, and who spoke Hebrew at ceremonial occasions while their day-to-day language was Yiddish, a derivative of medieval Germanic. The majority of the population lived in or close to 'The Pale of Settlement', an area in Poland, Ukraine, Russia and Lithuania, to the south of Central Europe.

These people had suffered from anti-Semitism for centuries and, when a few Ashkenazi were accused of implication in the assassination of Russia's Tsar Alexander II, this hatred became violently expressed in the vicious 'pogroms' (from a Russian word loosely meaning 'attacks on Jews', but which was renamed by suffering Jews as the 'Storms in the South'). Between the years 1880 and 1914 – especially during 1903–06 – tens of thousands of Jews were killed and millions made homeless. More than 2 million Jews emigrated to escape these horrors.

The USA was most emigrants' preferred destination, but in many cases unscrupulous ships' captains dropped many of them only as far as London, informing them that they had reached 'the land of the free'. At the beginning of the twentieth century there were over 120,000 Ashkenazi Jews living in London, with the majority crammed into the East End. The existing Anglo-Jewish community and other sympathetic reformers did what they could to help these often working-class, non-English-speaking immigrants find homes and food in this strange land. Some found employment in the Whitechapel and Spitalfields clothing and furniture workshops and factories, although there was often resistance from English workers who were worried about threats to their livelihoods. Other immigrants had to resort to soup kitchens and other charitable outlets.

The established Anglo-Jews, concerned about their own 'respectable' image and the public's possibly negative perception of Jews in London, had warned as far back as 1871 that 'the decentralisation of the East End is most urgently demanded'. However, it was not until the start of the twentieth century that they established a Dispersion Committee, which would remove the perception of the East End as a Jewish 'ghetto'. One of the most expedient means of achieving this was to build synagogues outside the area, as these new places of worship would attract the immigrants, who would be encouraged to find work and accommodation outside the East End.

The Jewish immigrants began to move from the crowded East End to such neighbouring areas as Hackney, Dalston and Stoke Newington, where synagogues were beginning to appear. Their relocation was assisted in Stoke Newington by the Four Per Cent Industrial Dwellings Company, which had been founded by Nathaniel Mayer Rothschild in the late nineteenth century and which had built Coronation and Imperial Avenues, as well as Navarino Mansions in neighbouring Dalston Lane, with the Jewish immigrants in mind. These were designed to be comfortable, affordable and close to the synagogues.

There were also plenty of work opportunities in these areas, given the speed of recent housing development and the arrival of factories in which the early Jewish occupants could make profitable use of the skills learned and practised in their homelands. Some of the better-off incomers moved to the more spacious acres of Stamford Hill, an area that by the end of the nineteenth century (as was also the case with Stoke Newington) had become a less exclusive, upper-middle-class suburb and more a combination of new terraced roads alongside the few remaining large villas and mansions of yesteryear.

The first new synagogue in the Stoke Newington area was established on the junction of Green Lanes and Burma Road in 1911, and then a house was converted to a synagogue on today's Belgrade Road in 1912. Both buildings belonged to the ultra-orthodox Adath Yisroel Hassidic Jewish sect. The Hassidim synagogues were originally based on rabbis from the central European 'Pale of Settlement' although, as more Hassidic Jews arrived in the area, each new synagogue tended to be located in individual private houses.

By 1912, the Jewish immigrants had moved in significant numbers to the Stoke Newington and, in particular, Stamford Hill areas, and they had been joined there by many other relatively affluent Ashkenazi Jews who had arrived in England earlier in the nineteenth century and been worshippers at the New Synagogue in Bishopsgate, opened in 1838 and one of London's three main Ashkenazi synagogues. Stamford Hill was gradually becoming the heart of this community, so the United Synagogue Council agreed to move the New Synagogue, or a replica thereof, closer to the worshippers.

Originally, this was going to be built further into the outer suburbs, but the thousands of working-class Jews who remained in the East End argued for a more accessible location. It was, therefore, constructed in Egerton Road, on the Tottenham side of Amhurst Park but still close to the expanding new community. The spectacular New Synagogue was opened to its public in 1915, and it rapidly became a well-attended place of worship. Its funding had come largely from the sale of the Bishopsgate synagogue and its site, and it was similar in appearance to the older building, retained its Edwardian Baroque style and was described as being less a new building and more a 're-erection' of the original.

Today, Stamford Hill is home to around 30,000 Hassidim Jewish residents, and many of the Jewish families who attended the Egerton Road synagogue have moved away from the area. I will discuss in Chapter Seven the development of the Stamford Hill Jewish community, for much has changed in the area since the arrival of the New Synagogue.

The mass arrival of Jewish people – in particular, the settlement in Stamford Hill in more recent years of ultra-orthodox Jews – was another important factor in the maintenance of Stoke Newington's 'dissenting' (in the sense of 'different') tradition. As the twentieth century progressed, the appearance of other groups of overseas peoples and cultures, along with the area's ever-changing social composition, its shifting urban landscape and economic fortunes, and its contrarian history, served only to solidify and strengthen the unique atmosphere and the defiantly rebellious appeal of Stoke Newington.

♦ ♦ ♦

Between the Edwardian years and the onset of the Second World War – a hiatus that lasted for around thirty years – the metropolitan borough of Stoke Newington, although continuing to nurse contrarian attitudes, experienced a relatively serene period. Aside from the depredations of the First World War (with which I begin the next chapter), the area continued to expand, although at a more leisurely pace than the frantic urban development of the late nineteenth century.

These years were largely ones of internal consolidation: the adoption of appropriate measures to satisfy the needs of its new and existing inhabitants, the growth and complexity of local small manufacturing, the accommodation within its boundaries of both wealthy and economically deprived, the requirements to assist in popular leisure and entertainment initiatives, the early stages of local and LCC involvement in social welfare and provision, particularly in housing and the early council estates, and a good deal more. Stoke Newington was kept busy in adapting itself to this new world of the twentieth century, but it was doing so with a certain aplomb and assurance.

It was not until the end of the Second World War – a much more damaging conflict than its predecessor in terms of civilian mortalities and infrastructural damage in the area – that the borough again found itself in a position of having to deal with structural dislocation and to contain the re-emergence of dissent. This experience – combined with renewed external immigration, increased political and social disagreements and emerging cultural conflicts – resulted in profound changes to the physical landscape and the complexity of the rapidly changing population and residents of Stoke Newington and its surrounding area.

CHAPTER FIVE

THE INTER-WAR YEARS: 1918 TO 1939

The reduction of the proportion of persons in poverty in the forty years (1890–1930) is enormous, whatever figures we take.

The New Survey of London Life and Labour: The Eastern Area, Sir Hubert Llewellyn

Respice Proscipe (Look to the past and the future)

Stoke Newington Metropolitan Borough motto

Alkham Road is a pleasant enough little street, which curves its way up from Stoke Newington Common, crosses Cazenove Road, passes Clapton Hall – once a Plymouth Brethren chapel and today a block of flats named Ark Court where lived a woman who supposedly was the last person in the area to employ a butler – then sidles past Windus Road before coming to an abrupt halt.

However, when you begin this unremarkable trip from the Common, look to your right – opposite the George Downing Estate – and you will see 16 Alkham Road. Look more closely, and you will notice that, although part of a terrace, the brickwork appears significantly younger than its neighbours. It also bears a small memorial plaque above its front door.

The reason? On the night of 31 May 1915, 16 Alkham Road was the first house in London to be bombed by a German Zeppelin during the First World War. The bomb – which was probably 11kg in weight, filled with thermite and wrapped in tarred rope – went straight through the roof and must have caused considerable damage, as much of the house was rebuilt.

The Zeppelin then flew over Stoke Newington Common and dropped another bomb, which failed to explode. Next, it lumbered over the High Street and released further similar missiles on, respectively, Dynevor Road, Nevill Road and Cowper Road. The Cowper Road house was gutted by fire and a small girl was killed. The Zeppelin's assault on Stoke Newington terminated when it dropped a bomb in the front garden of St Matthias vicarage. Two of these bombs failed to explode, and they were taken away from the scene in the arms of a local policeman, but there is no record as to their fate. ('What's this, then?' 'An unexploded German bomb, Sarge.' 'I don't want it. Chuck it in the bin.')

This was Germany's – or, indeed, anyone's – first aerial assault on London. No. 16 may have been specifically targeted, but this is unlikely. Either the bomb fell out or was accidentally launched by the flying behemoth, as the Kaiser had forbidden this clumsy and, in a strong wind, uncontrollable monster that possessed, to say the least, an errant target-seeking facility, to drop bombs elsewhere other than the area around the docks. Three months later, the Kaiser expanded the target to include anywhere in London. This flying machine, incidentally, was identical to the Zeppelin that had earlier in the war dropped a bomb on what the pilot thought was the London Docks but which was, in fact, a factory in Hull.

These Zeppelins were not reliable masters of aerial carpet bombing. In their fifty sorties over London from May 1915 to March 1917, they did kill a good number of civilians, including several in the Stoke Newington area, which was on the aircrafts' flight paths, but as many people would probably have died in domestic and road accidents. Zeppelins were eventually replaced by more reliable German Gotha bombers and, although the total number of people who died or were injured in London from German air raids in four years was around 5,000, this was a small proportion of the millions who lived in the capital.

Nevertheless, although the chances of being hit by these flying balloons was minimal, the public reaction was one of outrage, and these airborne bombers were labelled 'baby killers'. However, it could be argued that what was learned from these 'air raids' – the need for lighting restrictions, blackouts, air-raid warnings and air-raid shelters – compensated to some extent for the damage and civilian deaths they caused, as these were immediately put into effect when the awesome and massively more destructive 'Blitz' hit London in 1940.

During the Blitz, however, 16 Alkham Road remained intact: the fortunes of war, I guess.

◆ ◆ ◆

The First World War was a horrifying bloodbath. Of the 6.2 million British men who enlisted during this four-year war, 745,000 were killed in the brutal conflict.

Several British towns and cities were damaged but, as well as a collective grief at the slaughter, the main effect was the psychological impact of being attacked with little or no personal means of retaliation. There was enormous relief, particularly in London, when hostilities ceased in November 1918 with the German surrender.

Throughout the war, most of the people of London could only watch as hundreds of thousands of soldiers and a vast range of weaponry and machinery passed through, but others did what they could to help the many wounded and maimed men who had returned from the front for medical and hospital care.

Before the war, Germans had been the largest single European national group in London. They had managed shops, restaurants and manufacturing businesses in the capital, and worked as merchants, bankers and financiers in the City. The German presence was particularly noticeable in the East End, traditionally the home of immigrants and the residence of most of the German citizens.

The website British History Online observes that in Stoke Newington 'a certain cosmopolitanism, present in the upper reaches of Stoke Newington society at the old settlements, spread to the newly built up areas in the north. German "gentlemen" from the City came to live in Lordship Park in 1878, 1881, 1887 and 1896.' I imagine that the British merchants, financiers and businessmen in this area maintained a discreet silence about the presence of their German neighbours during the war. In other parts of the borough, the prevailing attitude of generally peaceful co-operation with German people, which had previously been displayed by most residents, changed after war had been declared, and it was replaced by a hostility to anything Germanic. For instance, the name of Wiesbaden Road was quickly changed to Belgrade Road.

Elsewhere, the royal family decided that 'Windsor' was a safer name than was their 'Saxe-Coburg and Gotha' surname, particularly as Gotha was the same name as the new German bombers. Across London, similar renaming was widespread, including the Wimbledon-born writer Ford Hermann Hueffer changing his name to Ford Madox Ford (which was probably also a wise career move). Also, although Hackney's German Hospital had been established in Dalston in 1845 on the site of the Infant Orphan Asylum and had subsequently treated patients from across Britain and Europe, it was periodically under threat from anti-German vigilantes, and the building was perhaps fortunate to survive the war.

The anti-German mood intensified in May 1915 when the SS *Lusitania* was sunk by a German submarine and many lives were lost. This action led to riots and wholesale damage to German-owned ships in the docks, and violence increased against London's Germans, many of whom, voluntarily or otherwise, left for Holland. Those who stayed in East London, particularly small retailers who had their German names displayed on their shops, frequently suffered from mob violence. As an instance, the *Hackney Gazette* reported that a German baker's shop in Clapton, owned by Henry Lunken, 'was the object of an anti-German demonstration last night which assumed such serious proportions that a heavy force of police of the J Division with truncheons drawn were drafted from head quarters to the spot'.

The policemen managed to quell the riot, but such mob behaviour was far from untypical in this area. Major incidents of this nature also occurred in Kingsland and Chatsworth Roads, among a number of other Hackney streets. These anti-Germanic feelings gradually evaporated after German citizens adopted low profiles or left the country, and especially when British victory in the war was in sight.

In the First World War, it was common for enlisted men who had been born and brought up in the same towns, villages and rural areas within Britain to be installed in the same regiments, perhaps in order to ensure a greater unity and comradeship when in battle. In accordance with this policy, the Stoke Newington Territorials was formed, and its first encounter with the Germans was at the First Battle of Ypres in 1914, where many thousands of fighting men were killed and wounded. This policy was discontinued after the war, as the authorities had slowly realised the devastating psychological trauma of witnessing old school friends and neighbours being blown to pieces, and the crippling effect of this on the smooth functioning of these local regiments.

In June 1923 there was unveiled in the entrance lobby to Stoke Newington Library a memorial and a plaque – today Grade II listed – to the servicemen from Stoke Newington who lost their lives in the First World War. It reads: 'All ye who pass in quest of happy hours, behold the price at which these hours were bought.'

◆ ◆ ◆

However, despite the carnage and horror of the war, it did result in lasting benefits for the people of the East End and the Hackney/Shoreditch/Stoke Newington area.

One of these benefits was the positive economic changes it introduced, particularly for the working class. The continuing demand for labour in the proliferating weapon, armament and aircraft factories dramatically reduced unemployment, which in the immediate pre-war years had often been at a high level and work had been sporadic. These industries' requirements diminished significantly the queues for jobs, left homeless hostels virtually empty, and did much the same for mental hospitals and prisons, which released numbers of petty criminals for the sake of the 'war effort'.

This surge in available jobs – similar, in a way, to the increasingly advantageous positions of feudal farm labourers after the devastating fourteenth-century Black Plague had led to an acute labour shortage across Europe – was not only of short-term economic benefit to workers but also led to a less supine and more assertive working-class consciousness. In turn, this shift in attitude strongly influenced the growing powers of trades unions as well as contributing to the consolidation and rise of the Labour Party.

Another enduring legacy of the war was the empowerment of women. Although women had to wait until the 1928 Representation of the People (Equal Franchise) Act in order to achieve the full franchise, which added 8.4 million to the UK's voting population, the fact that many men were serving overseas created work opportunities for many thousands of women in offices and in large factories, and these opportunities, and this precedent, were grasped eagerly.

Another unforeseen but welcome outcome of the First World War was the steep decline in poverty levels in the East End of London and the surrounding area (as was noted by Hubert Llewellyn in this chapter's opening quote). Indeed, the conflict was a factor that led to the end of poverty as the scourge of the East End, with the evidence pointing to a decline from 38 per cent in 1890 to 6 per cent in 1930. The war was not the only determinant of this relatively rising affluence but, in its immediate aftermath, it was the major one.

Likewise, the impact of the First World War may not have been the principal reason for the focus on perhaps the most urgent social problem of the post-war years as, given the demographic and economic changes taking place across the country, it was something that, in time, would have been impossible to ignore. However, the conflict certainly hastened the state's willingness to address the issue. This growing problem was housing.

THE HOUSING CRISIS

From the early 1920s, there was gradually increasing intervention by local authorities and the state into social welfare, health, education and other areas of social concern. However, as accommodation was urgently required for the UK's fast-expanding workforce, house construction headed the agenda of state concern. The first-ever Labour government elected in the UK was in power for only one year but, in that brief period, its major and enduring achievement was the passing of the 1924 Housing (Financial Provisions) Act. This legislation provided local authorities with substantial grants to build municipal housing, at affordable rents, for low-paid workers. As a result of this enlightened policy, 500,000 homes were built in the UK over the following three years.

The second Labour government, which lasted eighteen months, passed in 1930 another Housing Act, which not only increased the grants to local authorities but also allowed them, and granted them further subsidies, to demolish their slum areas. These Acts finally allowed poorer working-class people to move away from these crumbling, unhealthy inner-city slums into decent, affordable and well-maintained accommodation in the council estates that were slowly become visible across the country.

The first such development in the Stoke Newington area was the **Lordship Estate**, to the north of Church Street and bounded by Lordship Terrace, Lordship Grove and Lordship Road, with Queen Elizabeth Walk and Clissold Park to the west. The first three blocks in the estate were completed in 1934 and new flats were added in 1937. However, it remained the only pre-war council estate of any appreciable size in Stoke Newington and, by 1939, the borough still contained little more than 300 local authority dwellings, mainly on this site.

Meanwhile, to the south of Church Street some of the housing was manifestly sub-standard, and it was a poverty-stricken and disease-prone area of Stoke Newington. The principal reasons for these problems, particularly evident in Albert Town, were that many of the houses had been sublet and were multiple-occupancy, that they were being used as small businesses and that some landlords had not carried out essential repairs.

The death rate from disease in Stoke Newington had risen to well above the average for London, and Albert Town was described as 'a mass of unskilled labourers below the poverty line'. The council, therefore, in 1934 and under the terms of the 1930 Act, designated seven areas in the borough for slum clearance and, by the end of the decade, the worst of them had been replaced by council houses.

The north of Church Street, although now built over, remained by contrast a middle-class, well-housed part of the borough and contained 'skilled workers and similar'. Also, the area between Seven Sisters Road, Manor Road, and the large houses around the reservoirs, was a wealthy one.

Although in the early 1930s there was little council housing in Stoke Newington, only a couple of hundred yards north of the borough boundary there was the growing **Stamford Hill Estate**, which, although compared to other London estates was atypical in its appearance and in its modest facilities, paved the way in the Stoke Newington area for the development of the larger and more innovative housing estates – such as Woodberry Down, Somerford Grove and The Beckers – which were built in the post-Second World War period (*see* later in this chapter). These later developments were not only architecturally more experimental but they also more appropriately matched the requirements of their tenants.

The Stamford Hill Estate, between Lynmouth Road and Portland Avenue on the eastern side of Stamford Hill, was built by the LCC, with work beginning in 1930 and completed by 1939, on an area that until the late nineteenth century had been occupied by large Georgian houses and extensive gardens. Although much of the existing land and houses had already been replaced by terraced houses and now contained a higher density of population, several of these larger houses remained in place in the late 1920s. Those houses that were on the site earmarked for the new estate were peremptorily acquired by the LCC under Compulsory Purchase Orders (CPO).

The area chosen for the estate lay close to Stoke Newington railway station, and it was also on the route of buses heading into Central London, thereby providing speedy and inexpensive transport networks. The LCC had learned from its previous experience in estate construction, when they had built estates in the more isolated outer-London suburbs. Stamford Hill was accessible for prospective tenants, who were not the earlier wealthy traders and merchants but rather working-class people who relied on inexpensive public transport for reaching their places of employment.

By 1933 there were in place eight, mainly five-storey blocks, which sat alongside the old Ermine Street. By 1936 there were a further five blocks added to the north and east, and CPOs again had to be enforced, particularly for the acquisition of a large tennis court. By 1939, the estate spread over 11 acres, which contained more than 500 flats, but there were then few facilities, such as community centres and play areas, for the residents.

In 1965, the GLC took over the estate from the LCC and, in 1986, it became the property of the London Borough of Hackney. The rooms and buildings by now required expensive refurbishment, and the estate was sold to a housing association. As with a number of other estates, in the earlier years Stamford Hill tenants had enjoyed the relative spaciousness of their flats but gradually the rents became excessive, the blocks lacked lifts, the buildings were uncomfortable and the atmosphere was oppressive.

The LCC, architects and builders, however, had again learnt from Stamford Hill Estate, and would apply this knowledge to the later estates, notably the controversial Woodberry Down estate.

♦ ♦ ♦

To complement this growing awareness of the need for decent and affordable social housing in Stoke Newington, the 1930s witnessed the construction of, in particular, two grand buildings that in their different ways continue today to serve the residents of Stoke Newington. These are the Simpson factory on Stoke Newington Road and the Stoke Newington Civic Centre on Church Street.

TAILORING IN STOKE NEWINGTON

There have been numerous activities in which Stoke Newington has taken justifiable pride, but it would be difficult to find manufacturing industry on any such list.

Although Manor House underground tube station had opened in 1932 on the Piccadilly line, and its arrival had assisted the development of new factories and industry to the north-west of Woodberry Down, these initiatives were relatively small-scale. Stoke Newington had for centuries produced skilled artisans – such as shoemakers, roof tilers, cotton weavers, market gardeners and the like – but it had never embraced the demands of mass production. The parish had always preferred intellectual rigour to industrial toil, aside, that is, from one remarkable exception.

When one walks north from Kingsland Road, one soon observes on the eastern side of Stoke Newington Road, close to its junction with Somerford Grove, a giant, three-storeyed building that at first glance looks as if it was designed by Stalin. Looking down Somerford Grove, this building, which then sports a fourth storey, seems to extend as far down as Shacklewell Lane.

On its front facade on Stoke Newington Road there is a carved sign that says: 'Established 1894. Built 1929. The House of …'. Unaccountably, the name is missing, but if you ask a local passer-by, you will be told that this was, from 1930 until 1981, the principal manufacturing premises of the internationally known Simpson clothing and retailing company, the developer of DAKS trousers and for many years the largest manufacturing company in Hackney.

The company's founder, Simeone Simpson, learnt his trade in the late 1890s as a small tailor in the City, and by the 1920s he owned several workshops, manufacturing units and retail outlets in London. Wishing to consolidate his business into one unit, Simpson bought the houses at 92–100 Stoke Newington Road, demolished them and commissioned a building in art deco style. During the 1920s, he lived in Stoke Newington's Bethune Road, and was briefly a local councillor, so he kept a close eye on his building works. The factory was completed in 1929. The three-storey facade, with double-height windows from the ground to the first floor, was fronted with artificial stone and held together by steel frames and reinforced concrete floors. Each floor was a completely undivided space and open plan, allowing in as much light as possible and, in this respect, was revolutionary for the time.

The main entrance was a grand affair, with imposing teak doorways. The ground floor contained the offices, packing and dispatch facilities, and was the administrative and retail space. The first floor was reserved for making the trousers and a range of clothing, and the second floor was where these were cut to various sizes. On a recent visit, I noticed that the original large ventilation and heating pipes on the ground floor, which kept the employees comfortable, remained in place. Many of these specialist workers were Turkish and Jewish immigrants, and they had received earlier training in the clothing business.

By 1933 Simpson had added the extension down Somerford Grove (after lengthy discussions about 'ancient lights' with the Metropolitan Police who owned St John's House next door) and he had also acquired a few houses on Somerford Grove. The extension was made from red brick with bands of faience (moulded terracotta blocks) between each floor. At its operational peak, the building covered around 200,000 sq ft, employed over 3,000 people and was producing 11,000 garments every day. In 1935 Simpson developed and launched DAKS casual trousers, which were an instant international success. The revenue generated by these trousers, and by the company's adroit marketing and sales strategies, helped him to fund and open the main Simpson shop in Piccadilly in 1936.

The Simpson building was acclaimed in the clothing and other industries as a model factory in terms of its architecture, internal layout, productivity and its relations with its staff, and it remained here until 1981. The building then became for a number of years a Turkish/Kurdish Halkevi Community Centre, with a section of the Somerford Grove extension used by another company for document storage.

Today, the upper floors are apartments while the ground floor is occupied by two large vintage/retro clothing shops, which seems somehow appropriate. On my visit I dropped into one of these shops, but I couldn't see any DAKS trousers. Maybe they're temporarily out of stock, but I can't think of a better place to sell them.

CIVIC CENTRE AND ASSEMBLY ROOMS

In recent years I have attended a number of gigs at the Assembly Rooms. These have included the rock band Dodgy (drummer Mathew Priest was *N16 Magazine*'s music critic) and a five-piece Baroque music concert from Battuta. I have also enjoyed an evening with the one-time geography teacher who then became Dr Feelgood's manic-eyed lead guitarist, Wilko Johnson, the last being as part of the Stoke Newington Literary Festival.

I found these and other evenings enthralling – as obviously did the sell-out audiences – and the auditorium is spacious, with its contemporary design, its adjacent bar, the second-largest glitter ball in Europe (how do they know this?) hanging from its ceiling, its sprung dance floor of Canadian maple and its excellent acoustics well complementing the outstanding performers. The venue – which can hold 400 people comfortably seated – is a match for any other similarly sized concert hall in London.

The Assembly Rooms were part of the original Stoke Newington Civic Centre, which was officially opened in September 1937 by the Lord Mayor of London. The Centre was built in the mid-1930s on the site of the early-eighteenth-century Church Row, which, sadly, was demolished to make way for it. Its facade, an art deco combination of Portland stone and handmade brick, faces Albion Road, the Rose and Crown and Church Street, as it curves along between the library and Old St Mary's Church.

In 2009, Hackney Council spent £8 million on refurbishing the exterior and interior of the building, both of which had become faded, unsightly and no longer fit for use. This timely restoration has rejuvenated the building.

On the facade were, until recently, the painted designs used as camouflage during the Second World War. A perhaps apocryphal story is that, during the war, the entire roof of the Civic Centre was painted to resemble, as seen from a bomber aircraft's height, a field with cows grazing contentedly. This was done so that the German bombers would assume it was simply a continuation of next door's Clissold Park and wouldn't bother wasting their bombs on it. Whatever the truth, the Civic Centre was unscathed during the Blitz, while a number of other nearby buildings (except 16 Alkham Road) suffered badly from bomb damage.

Prior to the reconstruction of this grand Civic Centre, Stoke Newington Metropolitan Borough Council often had to meet in a vestry room in Milton Grove, so the newly restored Council Chamber, on the first floor, must have come as a welcome surprise to the councillors. The Chamber is reached by a handsome teak staircase, balustraded in bronze and wrought iron, and it is a grand circular space with a domed roof and wooden galleries to the sides.

The ground floor contains offices to the rear and the revamped Assembly Rooms. This rectangular space offers a gallery (with room for another 100 people) on the Church Street side and a stage overlooked by a proscenium arch. In the entrance hall, with its glass ceiling, there is a preserved 1m section of the wall of the original Manor House, on which was built Church Row.

The Rooms were used during the war for various variety shows, while the Centre also acted as a gas-mask dispensary. From the end of the war until it became dilapidated and then closed in the 1990s, the Rooms featured dances and concerts, latterly featuring such then-popular names as Eartha Kitt and George Melly. It was, and is, also a popular venue for weddings and other celebrations, particularly with the local Turkish, Orthodox Jewish and Asian communities.

The Civic Centre is an impressive modernist building – although architecturally something of an anomaly in a street of mainly Victorian and late-Georgian buildings – which represents and is much used by the various peoples who inhabit Stoke Newington. Its recent refurbishment has served only to increase its local appeal.

ENTERTAINING STOKE NEWINGTON

The people in this parish have always known how best to enjoy their leisure hours, and the dancing and musical evenings at the new Assembly Rooms were only the latest manifestation of this.

Earlier in this book I mention the dismay expressed in the early seventeenth century by the abstaining Puritan dissenters at the number of taverns in the Stoke Newington area. On Church Street there were at least five of these – Le Bell on the Hoop, Rose and Crown, The Falcon, Red Lion and Three Crowns – and on the High Street there were a few more. The influence of the Puritans ensured that, by the early eighteenth century, there were no more than ten licensed victuallers in the parish.

Despite their efforts, it is hardly surprising that the number of taverns was high, as Stoke Newington's location on the main north road from the City of London did little to discourage their growth. One can fancifully describe the parish during these earlier years as a late-medieval version of the old Watford

Gap motorway service station. Travellers heading north on the main road from London faced an arduous journey and required fortification, while those heading south felt they deserved a beer or several before entering the City. The local workers in the brickfields, market gardens and other trades also believed that they deserved relaxation when their arduous efforts were over for the day.

If the objecting dissenters had still been around Stoke Newington in 1870, they would have been furious that the number of beer houses had increased to twenty-five, and their fury would have turned to apoplexy when discovering, in 1918, that the borough was home to thirty-seven public houses. The growth in bars paralleled the increased population, with several of these new taverns occupying the corners of the new street terraces, of which there were many.

The consumption of alcohol, and the social enjoyment thereof, was far from being the only form of leisure in the area, although taverns were also providers of skittles, billiards and darts, among other pastimes. As the nineteenth century developed, they also often offered rooms for musical concerts and the many Friendly Societies, Literary and Debating Clubs and the varied political discussion groupings that then flourished in Stoke Newington.

The equally numerous churches and chapels also involved themselves in an array of activities, although these were, naturally, less 'frivolous' than those found in public houses. These included library services and lectures on worthy subjects, and they gave advice on civic and religious matters. In the mid-nineteenth century they also hosted the Stoke Newington Book Society and the monthly meetings of the Literary and Scientific Association, which was shared with Clissold House.

The churches also assumed important social functions, principally helping the poor, unemployed and generally deprived residents of the parish. These included Sick Clubs, Visiting Societies and a range of Working Men's Clubs (whether or not these men were in work). These church initiatives, though admirable in their charitable spirit, also contained more than a hint of missionary zeal, but that was to be expected.

During the nineteenth and early twentieth centuries, there were also many physical leisure activities available, and inter-district competitions were popular. These activities included boxing, wrestling, cricket, tennis, cycling, athletics, bowls (there were several bowling clubs in the area) and rifle ranges, among others. By 1929 the Clissold Swimming Pool had been built on the previous Glebe grounds, and this was an attractive leisure option, as were gardening and photography, both popular pastimes in Stoke Newington.

The replacement of the swimming pool by the Clissold Leisure Centre in the early years of the new millennium was a project that went well over budget, and created big problems for the builders and for Hackney Council. Its construction was also the subject of strongly critical articles by Ken Worpole over several issues of *N16 Magazine*, and with good reason. However, the heated arguments and the initial aggravation have now dissipated. It is today a well-run, well-attended and popular swimming and health centre.

The most popular sport in the world – association football – was also one of the most recently formed (the FA rules date from 1863). Although English public schools had effectively kept the game alive in the earlier nineteenth century, the newly codified form of football was speedily adopted by workers and middle classes, and it was played on several parks on the area, particularly on what were now the public open spaces of Hackney Marshes, only a couple of miles east of Stoke Newington, as well as on Clissold Park, Stoke Newington Common or any other open and available space.

Professional football clubs – including Clapton Orient, Tottenham Hotspur and Royal Arsenal (who moved from Woolwich to Highbury just before the First World War, and then changed their name to simply 'Arsenal') – also attracted thousands of supporters to their games. Although not based in Stoke Newington parish, these clubs were not far away. In the case of Arsenal, it required a fifteen-minute stroll across Clissold Park, along Riversdale Road to the junction with Blackstock Road, and five minutes away stood the 'marble halls' of Highbury Stadium. However, if one began at the Red Lion, dropped into the Rose and Crown, visited the White House on Green Lanes and then had a final couple of pints at the Bank of Friendship on Blackstock Road before entering the North Bank at Highbury, it took quite a bit longer …

◆ ◆ ◆

'Entertainment' today is, for many people, a more sedentary means of passing one's leisure time than are the activity-based pursuits I mention above. The constantly emerging new technologies have permitted viewers of films and movies, for instance, the opportunity to stay at home while watching the latest cinema releases, something that was not available to Stoke Newington residents throughout the first half of the twentieth century.

The passing of the Cinematograph Act in 1909, followed inevitably by the establishment of the Board of Film Censors in 1912, led to the arrival of 'cinemas'. When these moving pictures were released for public consumption they were a sensational success, and people queued to watch them. During the first fifty years of the last century, cinemas were omnipresent across Britain, but the arrival of television, videos for hire and, eventually, the internet contributed to the disappearance of many local ones, including those in Stoke Newington.

Consider this comparison. Between Stamford Hill and the southern end of Stoke Newington Road at Shacklewell Lane (where Stoke Newington formally ends), at the height of the twentieth century's cinema mania there existed nine large, busy cinemas on or close to that 2-mile stretch of Ermine Street. Today there are none. The nearest cinema today is the Rio, which is in the borough of Hackney and not in Stoke Newington.

There are no doubt other reasons than those I have mentioned for the decline of local cinemas in the later twentieth century. However, for the sake of nostalgia, what follows is a listing and brief description of Stoke Newington's cinemas, whose owners and whose names frequently changed but whose presences enthralled and charmed audiences across the borough, until the arrival of the TV anyway.

THE RISE AND FALL OF 'THE FLICKS'

Albion Cinema. 4 Albion Parade. This was the only Stoke Newington cinema that was not on Ermine Street. It opened for business in 1911 in the middle of the shopping parade on Albion Road, and was thereafter opened and closed on at least three occasions. It shut for good in 1952 due to structural damage. The auditorium then became a Turkish Islamic Centre.

Alexandra Theatre. 65–67 Stoke Newington Road. Designed by Frank Matcham, who also designed the Hackney Empire, the Alexandra opened as theatre in 1897, its first performance being *Dick Whittington*. A cinema from 1917, it again became a theatre from 1920 to 1945 and was used for amateur boxing competitions during the Second World War. In 1947–50 it was the New Yiddish Theatre but a dangerous roof sealed its fate. It was demolished and replaced by the Alexandra Court block of flats.

Cinema. 117 Stoke Newington Road. Opened 1914 as the Apollo Cinema, it was located virtually next door to the Baptist chapel and was considered sacrilegious by some in the congregation, It contained seating for over 1,000 people and boasted two large external domes. Reopened as the Ambassador in 1933, it closed in 1963 and opened as a bingo hall. It was reborn as a cinema – the Astra – in 1974 and screened mainly martial arts and softcore sex movies until its final closure in 1983, and it then lay derelict. The building eventually became the Aziziye Turkish Mosque (*see* box).

Biograph. 181 Stoke Newington High Street. This was opened 1910, just around the corner from Three Crowns, and occupied a converted corn merchant's shop. With 350 seats, it closed in 1919 to become a billiard hall, then a retail unit.

Coliseum Cinema. 31–33 Stoke Newington Road. The Coliseum started life as the Electric Coliseum in 1913, located close to the Classic and Savoy cinemas. Seating for 600. It closed between 1940 and 1946 ('enemy action'), and the lights were finally extinguished in 1972. The building was then demolished and replaced by shops/flats.

Majestic Picture Palace. 34 Stoke Newington High Street. Began as the Electric Palace in 1910, then the Majestic in 1913 and the Vogue in 1938. It seated 490, and was London's only non-smoking cinema in 1953. Closed in 1958, then derelict. The foyer today is a revamped Turkish restaurant.

Savoy Cinema. 11–15 Stoke Newington Road (corner of Truman's Road). Opened in 1936 with 1,900 seats, this luxurious and comfortable movie house had a state-of-the-art organ and sound system. Renamed the ABC Cinema in 1962, it closed in 1977, becoming the independent Konac Cinema in 1977 and Ace Cinema in 1982 until final closure in 1984. It was thereafter a large snooker club, and today is a recently opened, popular, spacious live music venue.

There were also two grand cinemas in Stamford Hill:

Regent Cinema. 1A Amhurst Park Road. Opened in 1929 with an elaborate facade, glass-canopied swing doors, large dome-dominated auditorium, elaborate full stage and Wurlitzer organ, and it could comfortably seat 2,200 people. It was the largest and plushest cinema in the area, and was renamed Gaumont in 1960 and Odeon in 1962. In 1969 it became the only cinema in the area in which a man was stabbed to death. It closed 1972, it then hosted a Top Rank bingo hall but, despite a 'Save the Odeon' local campaign and an attempt to turn it into a sports centre, the building was demolished in 1981. Since then, the site has been home to supermarkets.

Stamford Hill Cinema. 152–158 Clapton Common. Opened in 1925 with room for 1,800 seats. It was closed in 1959 and converted into a fourteen-lane bowling alley, the first such conversion in the UK. The alley was opened by Everest mountaineer Sir John Hunt. Demolished in early 1970s, a supermarket (yet again) was built on the site.

THE AZIZIYE MOSQUE

According to the 2011 Census, Turkish people represent 4.5 per cent of the population of Hackney. The community's presence in Stoke Newington can be seen simply by strolling up the High Street and observing the number of Turkish retail outlets, cafes, clubs and restaurants. I also well recall sitting in The Magpie and Stump (today's Red Lion) in the summer of 2008, when Turkey knocked out Croatia in the Euros quarter-final. That evening, Church Street was taken over by local Turks singing, chanting, hooting car horns and celebrating in a delirious cacophony of uncontained exuberance. I could have been in Istanbul.

Cypriot Turks first arrived here, as British subjects, in the 1950s, seeking employment and an escape from the continuing Greek/Turkish tension on the island. A second wave arrived in the 1970s from the Turkish mainland and were soon much in demand for their expertise in the clothing industry. Gradually, these people diversified into other sectors of the local economy, and today Turks are an integral part of the Stoke Newington area.

Many are Sunni Muslims, and the first Turkish mosque in the area, opened in 1977 and seating up to 600, was a converted synagogue on Shacklewell Lane. In 1983 the UK Turkish Islamic Association bought what was then the Astra Cinema (the old Ambassador) on Stoke Newington Road, and the organisation spent the following fifteen years raising the necessary funding and converting the old cinema into a mosque.

The Aziziye Mosque finally opened to worshippers in 1999. The mosque is eye-catchingly colourful and a splendid building, with its exterior – twin dark-green domes, multi-coloured tiles and columns and bronze window frames – bringing a dash of Middle-Eastern exoticism into what is otherwise an historically interesting if visually unexciting main street. The interior of the pre-existing cinema was gutted and redecorated throughout in neo-Ottoman style, and the foyer contains a halal butcher and restaurant.

Today, over a century after its arrival as a cinema, the building has been turned into one of London's largest Turkish-speaking mosques.

In recent years there has been a resurgence of interest in cinemas at a local level, as evidenced by the growing number of film clubs, and specialist local cinemas. But these older Stoke Newington cinemas had the misfortune to coincide, in their later years, with a downturn of interest in film-going generally, mainly caused by the arrival of TV and with the rise to dominance of the major high street movie chains. A pity, though, that the show had to stop.

♦ ♦ ♦

By the end of the 1930s, the relative serenity of the inter-war years was fast becoming a fading memory, as the menacing threat of a re-energised, expansionist Germany was increasingly occupying the minds and disturbing the suburban cosiness of the inhabitants of Stoke Newington.

Although entertainment was still available, on a sporadic basis, in local bars and meeting places such as the new Assembly Rooms, over the coming few years the strident wail of distant air-raid sirens was to interrupt the reveries and halt the proceedings quicker than did the obligatory 'God save the King' at the end of the evenings.

As the audiences ran from the buildings into the dark streets in search of public shelters, and gazed at the reddening skies to the south, the need for fun-filled escapism was quickly replaced by a desperate scramble for security and personal safety as the ominous drone of the enemy bombers drew ever closer.

CHAPTER SIX

SECOND WORLD WAR TO 1965

The course of the Thames was a great help to the German navigators. Londoners came to expect particularly heavy raids during full-moon periods, and these were known as 'bombers' moons'. Once over the target area, the raiders dropped heavy, high-explosive bombs and small but effective incendiary bombs. In later weeks land-mines also caused great devastation ... a total of 18,800 tons of high explosive was dropped in night attacks between 7 September 1940 and 11 May 1941.

The London Encyclopedia, Ben Weinreb and Christopher Hibbert

The Blitz, though short lived, became the defining event of London's war. Dubbed the second Great Fire of London, its civilian death toll was roughly 30,000 ... some 300,000 houses were flattened and ten times that number damaged. Parts of the East End saw half their properties rendered uninhabitable.

A Short History of London, Simon Jenkins

Over the early summer of 1939 there were several influential members of the British government who clung to the hope that a combination of astute diplomacy and Germany's concentration on mainland Europe would restrict Britain's involvement in the imminent war in Europe. However, Hitler's invasion of Poland, whose security had been guaranteed by Britain, nullified any further possibility of appeasement, and the British government declared war on Germany on 3 September 1939.

Contingency plans for the impact of such a conflict in London had already been made, and these were quickly enacted. Machine-gun nests and pill-boxes soon ringed the city, trenches were dug in public parks, gas masks and Anderson shelters for gardens (although the majority of Londoners had no back gardens) were distributed, air-raid training was offered to thousands of volunteers, and much else in the way of wartime defence was made available to the citizens. Perhaps the activity that initially affected most Londoners was the mass evacuation of several hundred thousand women and children to places outside London perceived as potentially safer environments.

However, by the end of the 'Phoney War' – an initial eight-month period of relative inactivity – most of these evacuees had already returned to their London homes when the full impact of the Second World War on London was realised. On 7 September 1940 ('Black Saturday'), massed ranks of Luftwaffe bombers arrived in the skies over the River Thames. The Blitz had begun.

During the following nine months, the Luftwaffe dropped almost 20,000 tons of bombs on the capital, killing and injuring thousands of the city's residents and devastating many of the capital's buildings and its infrastructure, particularly in the dockside region and the surrounding East End. In May 1941, the aerial assault came to a temporary halt while Hitler turned his attention eastward to Operation Barbarossa, the invasion of the Soviet Union.

The German bombardment of London returned in June 1944, this time with V1 flying bombs and then the hugely destructive V2 rockets, with the latter ascending up to 60 miles in height before plunging into the heart of the city. It is estimated that a further one and a quarter million houses suffered serious damage, and these terrifying attacks continued through the winter of 1944–45. It is unsurprising that on VE Day, 8 May 1945, the residents of a bomb-shattered London greeted the Allied victory with jubilant celebration.

Prior to the Blitz, with memories of German bombing tactics in the Spanish Civil War and particularly the destruction of Guernica fresh in people's minds, alarming views had been expressed across the political spectrum concerning the dire consequences of a German aerial attack on London. Philosopher Bertrand Russell had warned that London would be 'levelled to the ground on the outbreak of war', military historian J.F.C. Fuller foresaw a 'vast raving bedlam … an avalanche of terror', the Air Ministry predicted almost 20,000 casualties after only one week of bombing raids, the Home Office calculated that 20 million sq ft of seasoned wood per month would be needed for coffins, and Winston Churchill had anticipated that 'several million' of London's 9 million residents would flee the savage pounding by flooding into the surrounding countryside.

The reality was that, although the death toll was high, none of these neo-apocalyptic visions occurred and most Londoners did not succumb to the panic and hysteria that had been forecast. Hitler's attempts to cow the population into abject submission, and their government into resigned acceptance or even alliance, achieved the opposite result, with residents, although in continual fear of their lives, generally uniting in a determination to resist and survive the onslaught.

However, the invocation of the defiant 'Blitz spirit' was largely propaganda designed to raise the national spirit, as most people were nervous and terrified in equal measure throughout the bombing. During the Blitz, King George VI had proclaimed that 'the walls of London may be battered but the spirit of the Londoner stands resolute and undismayed'. The King, however, did not live in Stepney, Whitechapel or Poplar.

The persona of the 'cheerful Cockney' was also widely propagated but, while containing an element of truth, it was largely another government-inspired fiction. As John Marriott notes in his history of East London, *Beyond The Tower*:

> At a time of great peril, this image may have served well to boost morale, but it was partial, for amongst the acts of extraordinary courage, selflessness and stoicism displayed in the East End were less public stories of how panic and terror were fuelling a profound social discontent … no matter how determined the attempts to maintain a semblance of normality, people were ever closer to breaking point.

As with the impact of the First World War, but on a far greater scale, the immediate post-war years both created and revealed many wider social and economic problems, to some degree the most crucial being the desperate lack of housing, and yet again this was most apparent in London's East End and the nearby boroughs.

◆ ◆ ◆

In relation to the London boroughs that lay to its south-east and which were closer to the docks, Stoke Newington during the Second World War was far enough north of the city to suffer less bomb damage than its neighbours.

Hackney, for instance, lost 730 residents and over 2,300 people were injured during the war, while the flying bombs alone had destroyed over 24,000 houses. The 1950 *Stoke Newington Official Guide*, on the other hand, lists just over 200 killed and 1,000 injured in the borough, with 474 buildings destroyed as a result of the conflict. For readers who wish a detailed listing of where the bombs fell – by date, street name and number and type of bomb – over the course of the Second World War, I recommend Jennifer Golden's book *Hackney at War*, which provides this information, as well as offering a concise summary of the conflict's local impact.

I mention in Chapter Three the Municipal War Memorial in Abney Park Cemetery that commemorates Stoke Newington's civilian war dead. It is apparent from this memorial that the greatest disaster in the borough was the bombing of the Coronation Avenue block of flats. This block, situated at 157–161 Stoke Newingon Road, had been built and was owned by the Four Per Cent Industrial Dwellings Society and was inhabited mainly by Jewish people. On the night of 13/14 October 1940, a heavy German high-explosive bomb dropped on the building, destroyed all of its five floors and blocked all the exits from the shelter in the basement. The bomb also burst a water main, the shelter was quickly flooded and a fire then broke out. One hundred and seventy-one people died in the tragedy, the single greatest loss of life in the Hackney area during the war.

The *Hackney Gazette* reported thus: 'There were some pitiful scenes. Generally, however, the community is bravely facing the catastrophe.' A few days later, the King and Queen turned up at the scene to offer their 'heartfelt sympathy' and the *Gazette* noticed that 'Her Majesty wore a costume of dove grey'. Given the constraints of censorship, the demands of propaganda and the necessity to remain silent about such horrors as Coronation Avenue, what else could the *Gazette* say?

When the war finally came to an end, the July 1945 general election resulted in a nationwide landslide victory for Clement Attlee's Labour, which ended with the party holding twice as many parliamentary seats as Churchill's Conservatives. Labour's campaign slogan of 'winning the peace' – with its promised programme of nationalised health care, state-funded education, national insurance, social reform, new housing policies and other social welfare provisions outlined in the 1943 Beveridge Report – had convinced the British voters.

In Stoke Newington, Labour claimed over 50 per cent of the vote, the first time that the Tories had not represented the borough in Parliament. The constituency's new MP's main priority was social housing, and the borough's first Housing Department was established in 1948. However, the LCC had already moved in this direction with the creation of the Woodberry Down estate, sitting to the north of Stoke Newington and overlooking the East and West reservoirs.

WOODBERRY DOWN ESTATE

Surrounded by an exhilarating natural waterside environment and just 15 minutes from the city, Woodberry Down is the perfect place to appreciate an unrivalled living experience in Britain.

Berkeley Homes

Clearly, although the authority had little choice financially – public funding for large-scale housing development is simply not available – there are issues arising from the private sector-led nature of the new development.

'Woodberry Down Reborn' in *Hackney: Portrait of a Community, 1967– 2017*, Ray Rogers

LOOKING NORTH

I recall four years ago sitting wet and bedraggled on a 106 bus that was weaving its way along Manor Road towards Stoke Newington Common and my home.

Half an hour earlier I'd been balancing on a dinghy on the middle of the West reservoir. I'd been gazing to the north at a new high-rise apartment block in what was now 'picturesque' Woodberry Down, when I was told by a shipmate that its 'penthouse flat' was priced at well over £1 million. In my astonishment, I jerked round, knocked against the rudder, and, wallop, into the freezing dark water I went.

I was rescued and tidied up by the helpful staff at the Sailing Centre, and advised to cut short my visit for the day. As I dripped my way homeward on the 106, I reflected on two of the areas in the Stoke Newington neighbourhood that, in the late 1980s and '90s, were considered 'no-go' night-time districts, particularly for recent arrivals and the emerging middle classes.

One was the Kingsland Road and its surrounding streets in Dalston. The other was the forbidding environs of the Woodberry Down estate. The former today, with its cafes, clubs and late-night crowded pavements, gives every appearance of being a twenty-four-hour holiday camp for hipsters and other young people. But, in common with many other arrivals to Stoke Newington, I knew less about the recent changes at Woodberry Down, a large post-war development once regarded as a model for the 'cradle-to-grave' new welfare state.

As a general observation, I believe that the longer people live in an area, the less they know about it. Following the initial enthusiasm of settling into a new area, people form mental maps of what drew them to the place and, through habit and preference, tend not to deviate from these self-imposed cartographic constraints. This tendency is more pronounced in a large city like London, where friends and familiar attractions are spread across the metropolis, and given extra emphasis in an area such as Stoke Newington, where most of the people who live here do not work in the parish.

In recent years, stimulated by the Olympics-related development of Shoreditch, Hoxton and Stratford, the eastern perspective has become relatively more favoured. However, the tendency for newcomers to Stoke Newington was, and largely remains, to look first at Church Street and its immediate surrounds, west towards Islington and Highbury, and south towards Clerkenwell, Covent Garden and the West End. The east and particularly the north were not regarded as attractive destinations, which is one of the reasons why, although I frequently travelled through Woodberry Down on Lordship Road, I had seldom visited the estate.

Woodberry Down is as much part of Stoke Newington as are Abney and Clissold Parks, and its story is an intriguing one, particularly in recent years as controversy and polarised opinions over 'social housing' and 'gentrification' within it have become increasingly and bitterly evident.

The election in 1934 of a Labour majority, led by Herbert Morrison, on the London County Council had been unexpected, although the party's domination of the Council remained until the LCC's dissolution in 1965 and its replacement by the Greater London Council. Under Morrison, Labour had been given the mandate to progress both its wide-ranging East End slum clearance programme and its equally ambitious plans for rehousing these people by building new social housing estates within the capital.

Morrison's party had already identified a suitable area for a major North London new council housing estate. Woodberry Down was 64 acres in extent, lay to the north and south of Seven Sisters Road, was close to frequent public bus, underground and railway services, and it neighboured the large public spaces of Finsbury and Clissold Parks as well as facing onto the two New River reservoirs. Much of the land had for centuries been part of the Stoke Newington demesne, and it was owned by the Church Commissioners.

The LCC moved quickly and, armed with Compulsory Purchase Orders, it acquired the land from the uncomplaining Commissioners, but there was considerable opposition from many locals. Since the opening of the reservoirs and the northward spread of Stoke Newington, the area had increasingly been home to wealthy villa owners, many of whose extensive gardens stretched to the reservoir banks. Resistance from these privileged people was predictably vocal – supported by local newspapers carrying such headlines as 'Slum dwellers' paradise' and 'Morrison drives out mansion owners' – but ultimately futile. Their reaction to the mass arrival of the working classes can be illustrated by one resident who objected to 'all these urchins from the East End coming round my drinking water'. There were also worries about this staunchly Conservative area turning Labour.

Planning for the new Woodberry Down estate began immediately, but there were problems with legal actions, compensation claims and planning schemes that, along with the onset and duration of the Second World War, delayed the start of this massive project. Even at this early stage it was clear that a 'cottage estate' would be insufficient to accommodate the number of scheduled arrivals and that higher-density European public housing schemes would be the required models.

In 1943, J.H. Forshaw (co-author with Patrick Abercrombie of the then-recently published *County of London Plan*, or 'Abercrombie Plan') proposed a scheme for Woodberry Down based on the German Zeilenbau ('row-building') principle of aligned five- to eight-storey blocks of flats set in parallel and running north–south to achieve optimal sunlight, as well as two-storey houses and maisonettes. The new estate would deliver 1,790 dwellings. Also located on the estate would be open public spaces, a community centre, schools, a library, a health clinic, an old people's centre and a shopping arcade. Such a scheme was described in the *County Plan* as 'mixed development', and work along these lines began in 1946.

Two years later, four of the eight-storey blocks – Nicholl, Needwood, Ashdale and Burtonwood – were completed and the first residents moved in. These were the highest blocks that the LCC had built so far and they were revolutionary, due partly to their lifts, cantilevered cream and blue balconies and their reinforced concrete structures (mixed, because of post-war materials shortages, with recycled air raid shelters). Several more conventional five-storey blocks then followed. Although regarded by many in the architectural profession as dull and unimaginative buildings – they were used in the 1993 movie *Schindler's List* to represent the Warsaw Ghetto – these new homes and modern facilities were nonetheless welcomed by their new residents, who had been used to inhabiting some of the country's worst slums.

Britain's first purpose-built NHS health centre (today, the John Scott Health Centre) was opened in 1952 on the estate, followed three years later by one of the country's first purpose-built comprehensive schools. By the mid-1950s, 6,500 people lived in 1,796 homes on Woodberry Down, with over 1,000 being members of the tenants' committee, which was then an effective and determined pressure group and a counterweight to bureaucratic interference. At that time, Woodberry Down was hailed as the 'Estate of the Future', and there were then few who would have disagreed with this description.

However, over the following decades, and particularly by the late 1980s, much of the estate had begun to deteriorate, both physically and socially. There were a number for reasons for this: inevitably, the original pioneering residents died away and were replaced by more diverse, less community-oriented populations; the cheap post-war building materials used by the LCC were showing their age in the growing dilapidation and decay of the original blocks of flats, both externally and internally, revealing damp, drainage problems, crumbling walls and other structural defects; and the necessary funding for general repair and maintenance of the flats was now becoming more difficult to obtain.

Also, because of the estate's proximity to the reservoirs with their large volumes of water, ground subsidence became a serious issue, and this was a major reason for the closure of the comprehensive school in 1981 and its merger with Clissold School to become Stoke Newington School; relations between the tenants and the administrative staff were becoming increasingly strained; and the Thatcherite 'Right to Buy' legislation of the early 1980s was creating social divisions among residents.

For these reasons and others, in the 1980s some of the empty flats were being occupied by young punk squatters whose presence, although the squatters normally co-existed with tenants with a mutual lack of hostility, helped to generate a perception from residents and observers alike that crime and violence were becoming prevalent on Woodberry Down. This was when the estate was being described as a 'no-go' area, a situation to which I earlier refer. Meanwhile, Hackney Council, who ran what was now officially 'Britain's poorest borough', were reportedly ignoring residents' complaints and generally neglecting the estate.

Matters reached a critical point in the late 1990s when a report commissioned by Hackney Council revealed that thirty-one of the fifty-seven blocks of flats on Woodberry Down were 'beyond economic repair', and that it would be more costly to repair them than to demolish them. At this point, given the lack of state funding, Hackney Council had little choice other than to enter into 'self-funded regeneration', a relationship that inevitably would result in private housing subsidising 'affordable' housing and the community infrastructure.

Hackney Council teamed up with commercial developers Berkeley Homes and, with another private company, Genesis, assuming the role of a housing association, announced a public/private partnership plan that it was claimed would see, by the year 2032, 2,700 new homes built on the estate, of which 59 per cent would be privately owned and 41 per cent would be social housing (compared with the existing ratio of 61 per cent social housing and the remainder leased). The new development was also to be re-christened 'Woodberry Park', in an unsubtle attempt to distance itself from the old 'problem' estate.

The option available to leaseholders – those who had exercised their right to buy and who may have lived for decades on the estate – was to sell to the Council and buy a leasehold on a new home on the estate. However, so dramatic had been the rise in house prices in the area that this would effectively have disbarred them from purchase, and they would have to move to a cheaper area.

Although the figure of 41 per cent 'affordable housing' is markedly higher than several other London councils' similar arrangements – 'affordable' being defined as 'up to 80 per cent of existing market rates' – this was soon labelled as 'state-sponsored gentrification', and even 'social cleansing', by critics, who also likened the estate and its future to David Harvey's concept of 'accumulation by dispossession': 'the capture of valuable land from low-income populations that may have lived there for many years'.

The Guardian, in a special report on May 2014, described Woodberry Down as 'an increasingly rare example of inner-London belonging to working poor, elderly and unemployed … now being broken up to sell to the well-off'. It appears that many of the private flats are today being acquired by wealthy overseas buyers for the purposes of letting at high rentals and as long-term investments, a situation not unknown elsewhere in London.

Meanwhile, the newspaper's interviews with the long-term tenants revealed that the new gym and swimming pool were reserved for private owners, discovered that private tenants often crossed the road to avoid council residents, and that the old shops – cheap Chinese takeaway, off-licence, chip shop and so on – had been removed to make way for upmarket boutiques, a shop 'selling £85 Japanese kettles' and an expensive hairdressing salon: 'It's like a fucking club, not a barber's,' said one old-timer.

Given the size and social complexity of the site, and the necessarily limited extent of the newspaper's sample, it is quite possible that other longer-term residents – particularly those inhabiting the flats to the north of Seven Sisters Road – would have continued to express more favourable views of Woodberry Down. But the fact that the former opinions were being increasingly aired does indicate that the impact of the new privatisation was far from welcomed by a sizeable number of residents.

The *Guardian* headline was 'The truth about gentrification: rejuvenation or con trick?', and it concluded its report with the ironic phrase: 'welcome to the brave new world of social housing'. And it seems that the penthouse flat was indeed for sale at a price of over £1 million.

POST-WAR HOUSING: SOUTH STOKE NEWINGTON

The principal housing development in the Stoke Newington area in the immediate post-war years was the change from private to public construction of new homes by both the council and the LCC. Having sold the land for Woodberry Down, the Church Commissioners then divested itself of several other old Victorian houses and terraces north of Church Street, including parts of Bethune, Fairholt and Bouverie Roads, for purposes of new housing or commercial development.

The south of the borough – in particular, the 'Poets' Roads' area of Albert Town – had long possessed the highest density of population and had also been the area most heavily bombed. The new borough housing department had built almost eighty council flats on Milton Gardens by 1949, and within the following decade many other blocks of flats were appearing in the south. During the 1950s and early 1960s, Shelley House, Browning House and other mid-rise council blocks were replacing the older houses, to the extent that today Albert Town contains a variety of mid-rise council blocks and dwellings, intermingled with unusual and historically interesting Victorian houses and terraces.

Demolition spared many of southern Stoke Newington's older, more distinctive dwellings, including the early-nineteenth-century Albion Villas on Victorian Grove, several 1850s houses in Milton Grove and Shakespeare Walk, and the architect James Brooks' detached Grange in Clissold Crescent, where he lived and died. These preservations maintained to a degree the communally cosmopolitan and historical nature of the area.

The creation of **Butterfield Green** provided an open and friendly green space for the residents of the area. The Green has its northern boundary on Allen Road, and stretches from Milton Grove to Wordsworth Road. Named after the architect who designed St Matthias Church in the 1840s, the Green has received 'Green Flag' status and its volunteer-run community orchard has won a British Urban Regeneration Award. Another interesting sight in this cheery, unusual setting is that of a stream (artificial, but you'd never guess) flowing under a small wooden bridge and banked by large granite boulders.

Butterfield Green and the nearby Shakespeare Walk Adventure Playground are fine examples of what human ingenuity and a bit of effort can produce from what was, until recently, an inner-city bombsite, hemmed in between medium-rise blocks of flats and some genuinely interesting early Victorian houses.

ALLEN ROAD

Church Street has for centuries been the street at the heart of Stoke Newington, and recently the High Street has been showing encouraging signs of recovering its Edwardian eminence. However, in the 1960s and early '70s, and in terms of retailing and local popularity, Allen Road could have rivalled either of these busy roads. Located towards the south-west of the borough, and linking Milton Road with Wordsworth/Nevill Roads, Allen Road formed the northern end of South Hornsey and the roads south to Matthias Road that were, in the 1850s, christened 'Albert Town'.

Fifty years ago, the area remained the poorest in the borough, and its shabby housing – much of which was due for replacement – reflected this. Nevertheless, its main street was far from idle. In an article in **N16 Magazine**, Ken Worpole recalled its role as the district's shopping centre:

> Poor though the surrounding streets appeared, Allen Road had nearly forty shops and three pubs. In many ways it was a rival to Stoke Newington Church Street for chemists, doctors' surgery, grocery shops, bookmakers, wireless repair shops, butchers, tailors, wool shop, newsagents, dry cleaners, cafe, hairdressers, scrap merchants, second-hand shops and various other small traders. Today, hardly any shops survive, and just one pub, The Shakespeare.

In the light of Ken's reflections, it's interesting to note how quickly local neighbourhoods can change, even in such a relatively small area as Stoke Newington, when confronted with external forces such as gentrification and imposed housing development.

By 1951, Stoke Newington contained around 10,500 dwellings, a quarter more than had existed before the war, and social housing construction continued as a priority across the borough throughout this decade, although in the 1960s the twin processes of gentrification and conservation began to slow down the construction of new council tower blocks in Stoke Newington.

Considered to be a pioneering example of post-war social housing, the 9-acre **Somerford Grove** estate lies on the eastern side of Stoke Newington Road. Influenced by Le Corbusier, Mies van der Rohe and Scandinavian 'new humanism', the architect and landscape designer Frederick Gibberd created and built the estate in 1948 as a 'mixed development'.

With its three- and four-storey modern flats, terraced houses and bungalows with gardens and pitched roofs, the absence of long straight roads, a series of varied courtyards and closes, and intimate public spaces and play spaces throughout, Somerford was designed to be visually interesting and appealing to residents.

An open and attractively landscaped estate, which was far removed from the pre-war concept of 'council housing', Somerford Grove was described in *The Times* as 'encouraging proof that even dense housing need not be inhuman', and it received an Award for Merit from the 1951 Festival of Britain's architectural committee.

However, over the next few years the designers of estates such as Somerford were finding that local and London councils were increasingly sceptical about the virtues of low-rise, spread-out schemes. The growing cost of urban land, its encroachment into agricultural space and the spread of estates beyond cities were all becoming problems. These, combined with such social factors as the higher number of single households caused partly by longer life expectancies and by the growth of the divorce rate, indicated the need for higher-rise blocks of flats. Indeed, the 1956 Housing Subsidies Act encouraged councils to move in the direction of high-rise by offering funding for extra storeys.

Gibberd's next scheme in Stoke Newington was **The Beckers** estate, close by Somerford Grove on the eastern side of Rectory Road and along Downs Road as far as the railway bridge. Although this estate, finished in 1955, was another mixed development – with three-bed house terraces, low-rise blocks of two-bed flats, and blocks of single-bed flats and bedsitters – it also contained two eleven-storey blocks of flats that, oddly enough, in this generally low-rise context, seem to fit almost unobtrusively into the surrounding environment.

Between the eastern side of the railway bridge up to Rendlesham Road lies the triangular space of 'Navvies' Island' that, as I write, is currently a building site with large cranes towering over the continuing renovation of this residential area. Then, after a terrace of Victorian and more recent houses on Downs Road, is the frontage of the once-oppressive **Nightingale** estate that looks over Hackney Downs and which is also undergoing rehabilitation. This estate, when built by the Greater London Council in its early swashbuckling years between 1967 and 1972, possessed six twenty-two-storey blocks of flats. The estate was taken over by Hackney

Council in 1982 but the numerous alleys, skywalks and dark passageways encouraged criminal activity, and gradually mugging, burglary, drug-dealing and violence became endemic. With the Council subject to funding cuts and itself in some disarray at the time, the estate was improperly maintained and fell into serious disrepair.

In the late 1980s, the government's 'Action for Cities' programme selected the Nightingale estate as one of its financing and refurbishment targets. With the support and assistance of an effective tenants' association, by 1993 five of the six towers had been demolished – the last tower was retained for those who enjoyed high-rise living – with more lower-rise housing currently under construction and absorbing the existing space as far north as Kenninghall Road. Nightingale is no longer perceived as a threatening, crime-ridden estate.

This south-eastern area of Stoke Newington – including the aforementioned estates, the Simpsons building, the nineteenth-century Shacklewell developments around the Seal Street area and the streets leading off Evering Road – are all close to a stretch of public land that may formally be part of Hackney but which a good many Stoke Newington residents consider as part of their borough: Hackney Downs.

HACKNEY DOWNS

A wide expanse of seemingly well-tended public parkland raises the spirits of most inner-city dwellers. The 40 acres of Hackney Downs – the largest such open space south of Church Street – is, on a fine day, popular with walkers, cyclists, joggers, dog-walkers, sport enthusiasts and lovers of peace and quiet who live in south-east Stoke Newington.

For several centuries the Downs was 'lammas land' that was owned and harvested by the Tyssen family – the lords of the manor – and which, between early August to early April every year, was handed over to the labouring poor of the parish as grazing land for their animals. This relic of the feudal system operated smoothly until the nineteenth century when, with land enclosure movements sweeping across England, the Tyssens attempted to erect fences and dig trenches on the Downs. In 1875, a crowd reported to have been around 50,000 people, aided by the Commons Preservation Society, assembled on Hackney Downs in protest at the Tyssens' actions, set fire to the fences and filled in the trenches. In 1884 the Metropolitan Board of Works acquired Hackney Downs and declared it common land and a public park, which it remains to the present day.

Having walked along the pathway in the Downs running parallel to Nightingale, at the north-east corner of the Downs – on the junction of Downs Road and Queensdown Road – sits the impressive Downs Baptist Church, built in 1869 and today re-baptised the Open Door Baptist Church. Downs Road continues on to Clapton Pond, which also borders the seemingly ever more complicated Lea Bridge Road roundabout, where begins Upper Clapton Road to the north.

Queensdown Road, a terrace of Victorian houses, runs along the eastern side of the Downs, and it would be difficult to find an architecturally less compatible neighbour to the Nightingale estate. Earlier in this book I mention the stylistic complexity of the seemingly similar terraced streets in the area round Stoke Newington Common. In *The Victorian Villas of Hackney*, Michael Hunter observes of other terraces in the borough: 'Even when firms built more than a couple of houses at a time, they were frequently scattered rather than being bunched in the same road. The variety in the design of houses within the same street is more marked in some cases than others. An extreme example is Queensdown Road.' The houses in Queensdown Road were constructed in the late 1860s and early '70s, and the terrace is as fascinating in its diverse, haphazard nature as it is appealing in its overall absence of rigid symmetry.

The business end of the Downs is along its southern rim. Strolling from the south-east corner towards the centre of the park, one crosses over the underground railway tunnel from Clapton to Liverpool Street, passes the Lodge, four tennis courts, several bowling greens, two basketball courts, a football pitch, pavilion, and ends up in the centre of the Downs. On the southern edge sits the Stormont House School, an older building that today is a centre for children with special educational needs. Walking back down to the south-western corner, close by another railway line from Stoke Newington to Liverpool Street, sprawls Mossbourne Academy.

The academy is still known as 'Grocers', as Mossbourne was originally a formidably neo-Gothic building and a day school for middle-class boys, which was established in 1876 by the Worshipful Company of Grocers. It became Hackney Downs School, and was converted into a comprehensive school in 1974. As an illustration of the changing social complexity of the area, in 1950 the number of pupils was 50 per cent Jewish and by 1970 it was 50 per cent Afro-Caribbean. Through a combination of various unfortunate circumstances, 'Grocer's' achieved in the national press the dubious honour of being branded 'the worst school in Britain'.

The school was closed in 1995, then redesigned and substantially rebuilt, and it was opened in 1999 by Tony Blair as one of the earliest 'academies' in England. Since then, it has won back the plaudits it routinely received in the days when its graduates included such luminaries as Harold Pinter and Steven Berkoff, the novelist Alexander Baron and (briefly) Maurice Micklewhite Jr, the last-mentioned borrowing his thespian name from the movie *The Caine Mutiny* and becoming actor Michael Caine.

On the western edge of the Downs is a raised railway line, which not only reveals the garish yellow and light-blue rear walls of the academy but which also acts as a barrier between the rolling acres of the Downs and the council estates on Amhurst Road. In particular, the architecturally acclaimed Evelyn Court, which was built by the Four Per Cent Industrial Dwellings Company and completed in the 1930s, faces onto the main road, with the Downs as its backdrop. From here, it is but a few minutes' walk north to the junction of Shacklewell Road and Rectory Road, and to what was the Amhurst Arms, once my local and the only bar in the area that could lay claim to possessing a full-size billiard table, which fitted neatly into the bar's upstairs room. Just before this junction, a narrow lane on the right brings one to a recently built series of artists' studios and an equally new bar/restaurant, before a bridge under the railway line curves back to the Downs and The Beckers estate.

As well as being a splendid area for a bracing walk, and an ideal location for appreciating the eccentrics and eccentricities of the area, until about fifteen years ago the Downs was the venue for the Hackney Show, held every summer and hosted by Hackney Council, as well as providing space for a spectacular Guy Fawkes fireworks display that was best seen from my flat's back window. The Show featured music (rock, African sounds, folk, reggae, etc. in individual tents), a funfair with helter skelter and dodgems, stalls selling all sorts of useful and unusual stuff and food from across the world, a real beer tent provided by the Workers' Beer Company … and local people having a great day out. However, Council cuts put an end to both these events, much to the disappointment of regular show-goers. Nevertheless, Hackney Downs remains one of Stoke Newington's and Hackney's most popular open spaces.

◆ ◆ ◆

During the 1950s, Stoke Newington underwent a restructuring and consolidation that, although it had not experienced the onslaught of two world wars
to the extent that had deeply scarred several of its neighbours, was a necessary,
and perhaps even therapeutic, period of reflection.

For most people, the 1950s were years of relative austerity, rationing and
attempting to plan for the months to come rather than to expect change in the
immediate future. The new Welfare State, in all its aspects, was certainly a great
benefit to the average citizen, but these were relatively colourless years that,
although not lacking in entertainment and camaraderie, were to be accepted
rather than celebrated. Despite the Labour victory of 1945, social attitudes –
to, for instance, sexual matters, the importance of class structure, the role of
women and the relevance of religion – remained generally conservative and, in
this respect, little appeared to have changed since Edwardian times.

This being Stoke Newington, however, debate and disagreement continued, albeit in a less spiritual and modified form. As an example, David
Mander's collection of newspaper reports from the area, *Late Extra!*, contains
a letter written by a Presbyterian minister in 1911 to the now-defunct *Stoke
Newington Recorder*. An excerpt from the letter reads:

> There is a plague spot. It is called Hackney Downs … On the wide spaces of
> the grass at night scores, if not hundreds, of couples resort, lying about shame-
> lessly in attitudes suggesting nothing save unworthy and corrupting conduct.
> This is flagrant and increasing.

The letter continues in this vein, and it receives various replies, including one
from the Mayor of Hackney who replies: 'Hackney Downs is an open space
dedicated to the use of the public, and there is no power to prevent persons
from lying on the grass if they desire to do so.' Rigid (perhaps tongue-in-
cheek) bureaucracy meets outraged accusations of immorality, and one can
imagine similarly parochial exchanges of such views even as late as the 1950s.

However, by the early years of the 1960s social attitudes were becoming
more relaxed and enlightened, and this new atmosphere was regenerating
'dissent', but in a significantly more varied and in a wider cultural and ethnic
sense than had been the previous disputes over religious preferences and
public fornication.

A recharged spirit of defiance, together with a restless post-war younger generation, was emerging in Stoke Newington, and this was about to challenge many of the preconceptions that had long existed in the area. Dissent would shortly be making a reappearance in its home parish.

CHAPTER SEVEN

THE RETURN OF DISSENT: 1965 TO THE PRESENT DAY

Bliss was it in that dawn to be alive
But to be young was very heaven

The Prelude, William Wordsworth

Kick out the jams, motherfuckers

MC5, Detroit 1960s band

On the first day of April 1965, the Metropolitan Borough of Stoke Newington formally joined Shoreditch and Hackney as part of newly constituted London Borough, one of the thirty-two boroughs that were formed under the administration of the new Greater London Council in a major restructuring of the capital's governance. The GLC replaced the LCC, a body that had become excessively narrow in its scope and ultimately incapable of representing Greater London, a city that had much expanded over the LCC's seventy-six-year existence.

The London Government Act of 1963 was proposed by the Tory government, which had been in power since 1951. The Tories also had their eyes on the Conservative votes now potentially available in the outer suburbs. Elections for the new GLC were held in April 1964, and the two organisations ran in parallel for a year until the LCC was finally abolished. Ironically, the GLC began its existence with a Labour majority and under Harold Wilson's Labour government, which had won the previous year's general election.

In the discussions prior to the GLC's establishment, representatives of Stoke Newington – which had long prided itself on its independence and had resisted attempts to be 'absorbed' into Hackney – had favoured naming the proposed new borough Amherst, Kingsland or Dalston: anything but 'Hackney'. However, the larger and more populous south-east borough had its way, and the 'London Borough of Hackney' it became.

The GLC's powers were 'strategic', and it had no control over London's policing, transport or education. Its specific responsibilities included the preparation of a Greater London Development Plan, the management of existing LCC estates and deciding on the future of high-rise and historic buildings in the capital. The role of running and administering the city – its social services, housing, planning and development, local roads, refuse collection and other day-to-day aspects of urban life – was devolved to the new boroughs, who were each described by Sir Edwin Herbert, author of the 1960 report that paved the way for the GLC, as the 'primary unit of local government'.

Effectively, power had been decentralised and responsibility had been granted to those localised bodies who, theoretically at least, were best equipped to allocate their resources in what they considered to be the most efficient, equitable and socially beneficial manner.

GLC AND 'GENTRIFICATION'

Undeterred by its essentially administrative powers, but influenced by such books as Jane Jacobs' *The Death and Life of Great American Cities* and her vision of reintroducing the concept of 'community' into the social geography of a city's estates and streets, the GLC began its efforts to revive the decaying Victorian structure and the alienating tower-block-ridden council estates of the capital.

Aided by the 1956 Clean Air Act and the 1967 Civic Amenities Act – which Simon Jenkins has described as 'the two most beneficial innovations in late-twentieth-century London' – the authority began to initiate sweeping changes to the built environment of the inner city, whose population had decreased by over 15 per cent between 1950 and 1970.

Although the GLC was opposed to the indiscriminate construction of council tower blocks, and was to abolish the Tory 1956 subsidy that encouraged this policy, high-rise mega-estates were still appearing across London. In poorer boroughs such as Hackney, the erection of these blocks of flats had often required the demolition of shabby but eminently serviceable Victorian houses and even entire streets. Today in Stoke Newington, a few high-rise blocks – such as in the otherwise mixed housing of the George Downing estate overlooking Stoke Newington Common and the oppressive Hugh Gaitskell House opposite the railway station – remain as reminders of those 'build 'em high' days.

The Civic Amenities Act, however, empowered the GLC, after consultation with borough councils, to introduce 'conservation acts', which meant that local neighbourhoods of historical or architectural importance could be preserved as 'conservation areas' and that, if necessary, development permission could be legally denied.

Within ten years of the passing of this Act, over 250 conservation areas existed in the metropolis. Landowners, who had been concerned about falls in the value of urban land due to the Act, discovered that land prices began to rise in and around conservation areas. This increase, particularly in formerly run-down areas such as Hackney, was mainly initiated by the investment of private rather than public money, as the middle classes began to buy and renovate these Victorian homes.

Although council guidelines had been established as to the type and extent of the refurbishment, these were mainly sturdy houses that usually required not much more than cosmetic repair. The existing residents of these homes, which had become valuable assets, often sold to newcomers. Old neighbourhoods were attracting new residents, the retailers, restaurants and bars that remained were now serving wealthier customers, and previously waning local communities were becoming fashionable.

In Stoke Newington, for instance, in 1983 Church Street was declared one of Hackney Borough's first conservation areas. Grants and assistance suddenly became available to repair the peeling, dilapidated fabric of houses and to cover the cost of necessary repairs, particularly to older listed buildings and those at a higher risk of decay. Other parts of Stoke Newington soon followed the conservation path and, despite the initial reservations expressed by a number of retailers and older property owners, the increase in house prices and the new money being spent by incomers on local services and in the immediate area was the main factor that led to the revival of Church Street.

'Gentrification' had arrived in Stoke Newington.

POST-WAR IMMIGRATION IN STOKE NEWINGTON

Stoke Newington and its surrounding area has, particularly since the end of the Second World War, provided a home for immigrants from across the world.

After the Jewish immigrants, the longest-established group was initiated by the '*Windrush* generation' of West Indians. After the War, Britain required workers to help rejuvenate its industries and to assist in the establishment of its newly expanding public services, so it looked to its former colonies to supply the necessary labour. The 1948 British Nationality Act offered all British Commonwealth citizens the right to British passports and lifelong residency in Britain, and an economically depressed Jamaica was one of the first to respond.

SS *Windrush*, carrying around 500 Caribbean passengers, docked at Tilbury in June that year and substantial immigration followed from the West Indies. Within ten years of the arrival of *Windrush*, 125,000 Afro-Caribbean people lived in the UK, mainly in London. Although some of these new arrivals received low wages and suffered sub-standard working conditions, those who moved to Stoke Newington had usually secured decent, well-paid jobs in London Transport and in the newly established NHS and a number bought their own homes, mainly in the southern part of the parish in or near the Poets' Roads area.

The growing presence of the Afro-Caribbean immigrants in Stoke Newington ensured that the Church Street Assembly Rooms 'ska' music nights were, after Brixton, the highest-attended such musical events in London. The Four Aces club (*see* later in this chapter) opened in 1966 on Dalston Lane in response to the demand for ska, reggae and soul, and music shops in the area began stocking these records to satisfy the growing interest in reggae – from acts like the Skatalites, Desmond Dekker, the Upsetters and, later, Bob Marley and the Wailers – from white teenagers in Stoke Newington.

However, at that time the National Front was active in East London and, although the influence of this racist 'party' was minimal in Stoke Newington, it did retain a few local followers. In his article on Allen Road (*see* p.160),

Ken Worpole observes: 'Well into the 1970s most pubs in Hackney operated a discreet "colour bar". Some pubs made black people unwelcome, and so were avoided. Others allowed black people to drink and mix in the public bar, but not in the saloon.' Ken cites the Allen Arms, a local pub on Allen Road and now demolished, as being very different and it was a bar that welcomed everyone, irrespective of colour or ethnicity. Its jukebox contained black jazz, soul and jive records, including Miles Davis, Nat King Cole, Ella Fitzgerald, James Brown and an extensive collection of Tamla Motown. It also played Irish records, in response to requests from another group of immigrants who had recently arrived in the area.

The remnants of racial discrimination in the parish evaporated, and the original immigrants and their descendants are today an integral part of Stoke Newington life, the Allen Arms having led the way in this respect. Ken concludes his article by saying that Allen Road 'managed to hold its own as a lively street by day and night … (and was) a pioneer of Hackney's growing multi-racial community'. In the 2011 Census, 8 per cent of the population of Hackney defined itself as 'black/British Caribbean'.

Around the same time, a wave of immigration arrived from India, Pakistan and Bangladesh. Mainly Muslim, although a smaller number were Hindi and Sikh, these people with an Asian background ('Asian/Asian British') constitute today almost 10 per cent of Hackney's population. Also, those who self-describe as 'black/British African', many originally from Somalia, settled in the Dalston area in the 1960s, and they and their descendants now make up almost 11 per cent of the borough's population.

A large number of Kurds came to Hackney, principally to Stoke Newington where many remain, after fleeing persecution in parts of Turkey and in Iran and Iraq during the late 1980s and early '90s. Often described as 'the world's largest stateless people', Kurds have their own language, and their origins pre-date that of the Celtic peoples who arrived in Europe around the eighth century BC. Most are Sunni Muslims, a minority are followers of the Alevis – a mystical variant of Shia Islam – and others are Christian or non-believers. The Turkish and Kurdish Community Centre is an organisation established in 1989 for the benefit of all Turks and Kurds living in London.

In July every year the Centre organises a day-long festival of music and arts. In recent years, the DayMer Festival, an annual festival celebrating Turkish–Kurdish unity, has been held in Clissold Park. Although it would be a mistake to believe that discord and disagreement are entirely absent from the relationship between some members of these two groups, in Stoke Newington there does appear to exist a high degree of unanimity and co-operation.

Stoke Newington has also welcomed people, often younger professionals, from Spain, Italy, France, Serbia, Switzerland and other European countries, as well as Australians, Latin Americans and a host of other places. However, the most numerous 'immigrant' group (like many other arrivals, the majority are now at least second-generation in the UK) in the immediate Stoke Newington area is the Charedim, or Hassidim: ultra-orthodox Jews.

Jewish people have been resident here in numbers since the early years of the twentieth century. Their population began to increase after the Second World War with the arrival of the Hassidim, and there are now estimated to be around 30,000 Hassidic people, mainly living within the confines of Stamford Hill, sometimes referred to as 'the square mile of piety'.

A MUSLIM–JEWISH PARTNERSHIP

In my capacity as editor of N16 Magazine, over the last twenty years I have discussed, on several occasions, the fascinating relationship between local Muslims and the Hassidim with two of the leading members of these faith groups: Rabbi Herschel Gluck and Ismail Amaan. In the following paragraphs I offer a brief synopsis of our conversations.

Cazenove Road is, in some respects, an unremarkable Stoke Newington street. Beginning opposite the main entrance to Abney Park Cemetery, and with the Weavers Arms that sat on the corner now long gone, it wends its way past a small, idiosyncratic and largely retail parade – health food outlet, Hindu playgroup, art gallery, internet cafe, charity shop – and passes council estates opposite a Victorian terrace. Then it meanders past a couple of schools (*see* Common Values box below) that face some grander Victorian buildings, and eventually carves its way between a variety of older houses and council estates towards its termination on the Upper Clapton Road.

In other respects, however, it is one of London's most remarkable thoroughfares. Cazenove Road is not only at the heart of a vibrant Muslim community, largely of Asian background, but it is also home to the world's third-largest population (after Israel and Brooklyn) of ultra-orthodox Jews, or Hassidim. In such a setting and in today's wider political context, one might expect to encounter at least a degree of inter-faith hostility, suspicion and distrust, but the atmosphere here is one of calm co-existence and co-operation.

The principal reason for this unusual spirit of mutual understanding is the existence in Cazenove Road of the Muslim–Jewish Forum, an organisation established around twenty years ago by Ismail Amaan, then director of the North London Muslim Community Centre, and Rabbi Herschel Gluck, one-time Rabbi at the Walford Road Independent Synagogue and a well-regarded and respected figure in Stoke Newington.

The Forum is one of the world's few examples of these two communities joining together to discuss issues of common concern to adherents of both strongly held faiths and agreeing on how best to handle these to the mutual benefit of each group, and also to the pluralistic, multi-ethnic society in which they and we all live. Ismail comments on the Forum that it 'promotes unity in strength, although we don't see eye-to-eye on every issue', and the Rabbi adds, 'We are distinct but unite to assist one another.'

Both men have travelled widely to study and to promote their respective beliefs, and they are far from being insular, but their faiths are reflected in their appearance and it is not difficult to confuse them. Ismail is a smiling man of Asian background, with a small black skullcap and a trimmed black beard, while Herschel also laughs easily and has a flowing white beard, black coat and wide-brimmed hat that mark him out as a member of the Hassidic community.

Their backgrounds are also very different, reflecting their religious cultures. Ismail moved with his family from the Midlands to Stoke Newington, attended state school, enjoyed sport (particularly cricket) and mixed easily with people of other beliefs and religions. Herschel attended Charedic faith schools, dedicated himself to study of the Torah and, in keeping with ultra-orthodox practice, mainly engaged socially with his Hassidic peers, believing that 'we should be able to share our traditions with future generations' and require 'a special "sacred space" to facilitate this'. He also studied for four years under an eminent Charedic scholar in Brooklyn.

However, he is an affable conversationalist on his frequent strolls around Stoke Newington, has been named Hackney's 'Man of the Year' and is, unlike many of his co-religionists, an outgoing and sociable ambassador for his faith.

Ismail retains many friends in the area but today lives slightly further away from Stoke Newington.

Both these men have experienced personal abuse. In the case of Ismail, anti-Muslim abuse occasionally occurs after much-publicised 'terrorist attacks', while Herschel has received 'Heil Hitler' salutes and anti-Semitic insults. The latter are far from uncommon, and are aimed at Hassidim from passing drivers in Stamford Hill. However, such insults are unusual in the Stoke Newington area.

How, then, do they feel about living in multi-cultural Stoke Newington? 'I am happy to live here,' says Rabbi Gluck. 'We have a very nice community and very good relations with our neighbours.' Ismail agrees that 'the general physical environment has improved markedly'.

Both of these men deserve praise for their single-minded concentration on ensuring, to the best of their abilities, that their different faith groups have come together in a mutually tolerant manner, and also for their emphases on understanding and co-operation rather than on religious and cultural division.

'COMMON VALUES'

A further demonstration of the close inter-faith nature of this area is Simon Marks Primary School, located on Cazenove Road close to its junction with Kyverdale Road.

Simon Marks is an orthodox (but not ultra-orthodox) Jewish school that has every reason to be 'proud of its diversity and tolerance'. A member of the United Synagogue – the union of orthodox UK synagogues – the school currently has 117 primary school pupils, of which around half are Jewish and the other children are non-Jewish, the latter comprising Muslim, Christian, Jehovah Witness and non-faith. The boys wear the 'kippah' – the traditional Jewish skullcap – and the pupils eat kosher food, observe Jewish holidays, learn Hebrew, leave school early on Fridays in time for the Jewish Sabbath and, unlike the many neighbouring ultra-orthodox schools, there is no gender separation at Simon Marks.

The headteacher – Gulcan Metin-Asdoyuran – is from a Turkish Muslim background and mentioned to the *Observer*, in a February 2020 interview, that she has 'struggled' to create links with the ultra-orthodox schools. However, there is a Muslim school across the road, with whom they marked Holocaust Memorial

Day, and Metin said, 'We interact more with them than with the independent (ultra-orthodox) schools.' Although the school is surrounded by a tall fence and is patrolled by security guards, she said that there have been no reported incidents of anti-Semitism at the school.

However, when I recently mentioned the headteacher's comments to Herschel, he indignantly disagreed with her remark about the school 'struggling' to communicate with the ultra-orthodox community. He told me that on several occasions he has attempted to engage Simon Marks in a communal discussion on the matter but to no avail.

Another Simon Marks teacher, a practising Muslim, defined the ethos of the school: 'We should celebrate diversity. There are lots of values in common between Judaism and Islam.' This inclusive and heartening communality of belief is shared by many others who constitute the multi-ethnic populations of Stoke Newington.

'THE STOKE NEWINGTON EIGHT'

The counterculture of the 1960s had flourished in Stoke Newington. With its message of love and peace, the sweet smell of dope drifting over the communal flats and squats, the diffuse sense of 'dropping out' and stoned nonconformity ('What are you rebelling against?' 'What've you got?') and all the rest of what was often criticised as the self-indulgent lifestyles of these mainly middle-class students and 'liberated' young locals, this new movement had found – as had many before it – that Stoke Newington was an ideal haven in which to differ from the social norm and, in this particular case, to celebrate the 'Age of Aquarius'.

While many of these 'baby boomers' had been content to 'make love, not war', listen to Hendrix and Van Morrison, and float gently out of their skulls on spliffs and various other stimulants ('far out, man'), there was a minority that had adopted, to a greater or lesser degree, the causes of the far left and its challenge to the oppressive rule of 'the Man', and had embraced self-styled 'revolutionary' activities. Many of the latter were arguably naive in their crusading zeal, but were sincere and committed to their beliefs in the possibility of revolutionary social change. There were, however, only a few who took action on these principles with the planning and dedication, or so it was alleged, which was adopted by the Angry Brigade in the early 1970s.

Between August 1970 and August 1971, the Angry Brigade had declared its own war on the British state and, while their bombing campaign had allegedly found their targets on twenty-five occasions, their bombs were relatively small explosives designed to damage property but not injure anyone. In this last aim, at least, they succeeded. The bombs had exploded in a variety of places, including targeting foreign embassies of what were considered repressive regimes, the sexism of the Miss World competition, the home of Tory Employment Minister Robert Carr and several banks. Indeed, on 26 October 1970, one of these bombs had gone off at Barclay's Bank in Stoke Newington High Street, in the building that is today home to the Stoke Newington Book Shop. With an embarrassed British government and police force increasingly on their trail, however, this group of inexperienced urban guerillas could not hold out for much longer.

In the late afternoon of 21 August 1971, eight of the Met's finest forced their way into the top floor of 395 Amhurst Road, just off Stoke Newington Road, and discovered, according to the police, thirty-three sticks of gelignite, a Sten gun, two revolvers, ammunition, names and addresses of leading Tory politicians and (a nice touch) a John Bull children's printing outfit for writing Angry Brigade comminiqués. They arrested the flat's four occupants – John Barker, Hilary Creek, Anna Mendelssohn and Jim Greenfield – as well as the next day's visitors, Chris Bott and Stuart Christie, the latter a more experienced anarchist who had been imprisoned in Madrid as a teenager for attempting to blow up Franco, later wrote his autobiography *Granny Made Me an Anarchist*, and died in 2020. They later picked up two more suspected Brigade members, Angela Mason and Kate McLean.

These alleged members of the Angry Brigade were soon dubbed in the tabloid press 'the Stoke Newington Eight', although the alleged 'leader', Jake Prescott, had been jailed the previous year. The arrest was front-page news in Britain, with a typical headline reading 'Dropouts with brains tried to launch bloody revolution.'

The trial began on 30 May 1972 and did not conclude until 6 December that year, making it the longest criminal trial in British legal history. The proceedings involved 200 prosecution witnesses, 688 exhibits and over 1,000 pages of evidence. Although some of the forensic and fingerprint evidence was dubious, and it was argued that the police had planted some of the evidence, four of the eight – those who had been present in the flat when the police entered – were found guilty, on majority jury verdicts, of conspiracy and possession of illegal material, and each was sentenced initially to fifteen years. They then became 'the Stoke Newington Four'.

Before the trial, the judge had told the jury that the prosecution did not have to prove that the defendants bombed anything, but only that they had conspired to do so. The sentences were reduced to ten years after the jury protested at the severity of the sentences, and Justice James told the convicted four that they had 'a warped understanding of sociology'. The other four so-called members of the Angry Brigade – Christie, Mason, Bott and McClean – were acquitted. Stuart Christie became a publisher and writer, and Angela Mason went on to become Director of Stonewall and was awarded an OBE for services to gay rights.

For better or worse, one of the lasting consequences of the trial of the Stoke Newington Eight was that, as the evidence produced by the police had come under question in some quarters and because the officers may also have lacked the necessary experience in cases of this nature, a specialist Bomb Squad should be established. This was instituted, and today it has evolved into the Anti-Terrorist Branch.

Jake Prescott, the 'fifth' (and possibly first) of the Stoke Newington Four who were convicted, was the only working-class member. Perhaps the last word on this subject should lie with Melford Stevenson, who later told *The Guardian*: 'He (Prescott) was the one who was angry, and the people he met were the Slightly Cross Brigade.'

◆ ◆ ◆

Coincidentally, the Angry Brigade were not the only internationally known 'revolutionaries' to have operated in Stoke Newington during the 1970s.

The Red Army Faction, or Baader-Meinhof Group, was a Marxist–Leninist German group that emerged in the late 1960s to challenge the manifest evils of 'state repression'. It is claimed that, during its twenty-year existence, it was responsible for thirty-four deaths, forty attempted murders, over 2,000 bomb and arson attacks, the abduction of leading German businessmen and politicians, and more besides. Formed by Andreas Baader and Ulrike Meinhof in the late 1960s, the group maintained a constantly changing membership that was markedly more enduring and notorious than was the Angry Brigade, and 'collateral damage' (the death of non-committed bystanders) was accepted as part of its 'armed struggle'.

An early member was Astrid Huberta Isolde Marie Luise Hildegard Proll, better known as **Astrid Proll**. Proll was involved in Red Army bank robberies in the early 1970s, and she was, among other group activities, a getaway driver for Baader. In 1971, she was arrested and charged in Hamburg with attempted murder and spent three years in prison awaiting trial. During her incarceration she suffered from poor health and a nervous breakdown. Her trial was deferred and she was sent, under police guard, to a Bavarian sanatorium.

She escaped from the sanatorium and, like many Germans before her, ended up in Hackney but with an assumed name. She worked at the recently demolished Lesney toy factory in Hackney Wick and in a local garage. She was then employed for a while by Hackney Council as a park warden in Clissold Park, and later she taught welding skills to young people from the area.

In September 1978, this urban warrior and fugitive from German justice was arrested by Special Branch and extradited back to Germany, where she received a five-year sentence but was released on compassionate grounds. She returned to Britain, worked as a picture editor in a national newspaper, and today this 74-year-old ex-revolutionary is a politics teacher in Germany.

Proll no doubt looks back with nostalgic affection on her time in Stoke Newington, when she was picking up discarded rubbish from the grass, brushing the pathway to Clissold House, talking to the deer in Clissold Park and collecting her wages from an unsuspecting Hackney Council Parks and Green Spaces Department.

THE IRA IN STOKE NEWINGTON

In the 1970s, parts of London sustained periodic bombing, violent attacks and killings that were carried out by Active Service Units of the Provisional IRA. Although there were few attacks on the city and its inhabitants between 1977 and 1989, the years from 1990 to early 1993 witnessed a resurgence of bombings and deaths in the capital. During these active years, and on at least two occasions, various members of these units were found to have based themselves and explosives in Stoke Newington.

Over fourteen months during 1974–75, an IRA unit staged a particularly bloody and destructive campaign in London, which resulted in forty explosions and thirty-five deaths in the capital, including pubs, military barracks, the attempted assassination of the Prime Minister Edward Heath and the fatal shooting of right-wing activist Ross McWhirter, who had offered a £50,000 reward for information that would lead to their arrest.

On 6 December 1975 four men driving a stolen car fired machine-gun shots through a restaurant window in Mayfair. They were chased by police cars through the streets of the West End before they took refuge by forcing themselves into a council flat in Balcombe Street in Marylebone. They took the two residents hostage, barricaded themselves in and demanded safe passage to Ireland. The siege of the flat lasted for six days until the IRA men surrendered and were arrested.

In his book *Late Extra!*, David Mander recounts a news story from the *Hackney Gazette* headlined 'Crossed line pinpointed IRA bomb factory' and dated one week after the men's surrender. This reported, 'A frightened mother told the Gazette this week how IRA terrorists in Stoke Newington threatened to kill her teenage son after he heard them discussing bombing plans.' The boy had apparently got a crossed line on his telephone on which he heard two Irishmen discussing a bombing, and he had been warned by the men, on pain of death, not to reveal the conversation.

Seemingly, the mother had contacted the newspaper after the end of the siege, and the men had not divulged to the police details of where they lived. The police pinned down the location of the crossed line and, on 17 December, they raided the address on the top floor of a flat at 99 Milton Grove in Stoke Newington. They discovered that the flat had been occupied by two of the IRA members at Balcombe Street – Martin O'Connell and Henry Duggan – and also found in the flat explosives, detonators and bomb-making equipment, plus a list of possible future targets.

The four members of 'the Balcombe Street gang' – who admitted they had carried out the Guildford and Woolwich pub bombings that had killed seven and injured scores more – were each sentenced to thirty years' imprisonment. They were released following the Good Friday Agreement in April 1999.

◆ ◆ ◆

The Balcombe Street Siege had received front-page national press coverage and, although it resulted in the imprisonment of leading Provisional activists, it had brought the IRA cause back into the public spotlight. In the early 1990s, two further incidents revealed that the Provos were again using Stoke Newington as one of the principal London-based centres for their bombing activities.

On 14 November 1992, during a routine check of vehicles at the Shacklewell end of Stoke Newington Road, the police discovered that a large Volvo lorry was carrying 3.2 tons of explosive. The driver and a passenger ran away, and one (or perhaps both) escaped. A pursuing local police officer was twice shot by one of the men and was hospitalised, but he made a full recovery. Close to the scene, police arrested an Irish lorry driver, Patrick Kelly, who immediately professed his innocence.

At the subsequent trial, Kelly pleaded not guilty to attempted murder and conspiracy to cause an explosion, but he was sentenced to twenty-five years' imprisonment. Kelly, who throughout had denied any knowledge of the explosives, then developed skin cancer and was refused treatment in British hospitals. Jeremy Corbyn and others supported his removal to an Irish hospital, and Kelly died in 1997.

Just two months after the explosive material had been discovered, in January 1993 the Met received a coded message from the Provisional IRA informing them that a bomb that they had planted was about to go off at Harrods department store in Knightsbridge. The police began to clear the area but the bomb exploded, injuring four people and causing an estimated £1 million worth of damage.

In March that year, and in connection with the Harrods bomb, police raided a house in Stoke Newington's Walford Road. This was the home of Patrick Hayes, an Englishman and alleged Provisional IRA activist. Another English alleged IRA sympathiser, Jan Taylor, was in the house at the time and, although Hayes fired three shots at the police, he missed his targets and both men were arrested. In the house the police discovered a quantity of Semtex, hand guns and detonators. Hayes subsequently led them to a lock-up garage, where they found home-made explosives.

At their trial, both men were sentenced to thirty years, and evidence indicated that Hayes had an involvement in a recent train bomb and also in helping to plan the devastating Baltic Exchange explosion in the City. At the trial, Hayes claimed that Patrick Kelly had been falsely imprisoned after the lorry incident in Stoke Newington 'on the basis of his nationality', but this allegation was dismissed. As with 'the Balcombe Street Gang', Hayes and Taylor were freed after the Good Friday Agreement.

The Provisional IRA announced a ceasefire from August 1994 to February 1996. In 1999 the ceasefire became permanent, and Stoke Newington was no longer a bomb depository and boarding house for radical Irish nationalists.

RONNIE AND REGGIE

Before I move on to discuss the ever-changing cultural, artistic and even life-affirming events of recent years in Stoke Newington, it is salutary to note that, particularly during the 1960s and '70s, violent crime was no stranger to this parish. Although crime is and always has been endemic in inner-city areas, its organised and callously murderous variant appears absent from today's Stoke Newington life. In those days, however, and although their activities did not directly affect too many residents, this seemingly sedate, bourgeois parish was part of the manor of two criminally dangerous gangsters: the Kray Twins.

These notorious brothers were born and originally operated in the East End, which starts a mile or two to the south-east of Stoke Newington. There have been so many books, films and documentaries produced about the Krays that their 'career' is widely known, so I will restrict myself here to their relationship with Stoke Newington. The twins' crime empire was built on their accumulation of bars and clubs, as well as protection, fraud and extortion rackets, in the East End, but by the early 1960s they had extended their scope to include the West End as well as northward to Hackney.

One of 'their' clubs was the Regency at 240a Amhurst Road in Stoke Newington, barely five minutes' walk from the local police station. The club was started in 1959 by brothers John and Anthony Barry as the Regency Suite and, mainly due to the influence of the Krays, in the 1960s violent East End criminals rubbed shoulders at the Regency with such celebrities as Lord Boothby, Princess Margaret and others.

In 1963 the twins had moved their headquarters from Vallance Road in Bethnal Green to Stoke Newington, and they acquired two adjoining flats on Cazenove Road. The Krays' henchmen then visited the Barry brothers, suggesting that they pay 'protection money' of £50 per week, to which offer, of course, the Barrys quickly agreed. The club then became the Krays' local hangout. Reggie's estranged wife, Frances Shea, daughter of a previous Regency manager, committed suicide in 1967, and this unbalanced Reggie's already fragile mental state to the extent that he became involved in a growing number of violent confrontations at the Regency. These alarming incidents persuaded Ronnie to move the twins' operations to a hotel in Seven Sisters Road until things calmed down, but they soon returned to the Regency.

Jack 'The Hat' McVitie was a minor criminal whose behaviour was increasingly out of order, as far as the Krays were concerned. His arrival at the Regency carrying a sawn-off shotgun was the final straw. On 29 October 1967 the twins invited him to a 'party' at a basement flat on Evering Road, and the events that followed led to the Krays' nemesis. They cleared out the partygoers and waited for Jack to turn up. He arrived at the flat and, after an argument, Reggie pulled out a gun, aimed it at Jack, and fired, but the gun jammed. Taunted by Ronnie, Reggie then pulled out a knife and stabbed Jack repeatedly until he died. It's hard to believe today that this flat – close by Rectory Road station and just one block south from where I live – was the scene of one of the most notorious murders of the last sixty years.

Jack's body was never found. It was apparently thrown off a boat at Newhaven, buried in an Essex farmhouse or is today part of the Bow flyover (where he is, as dark local humour has it, 'a man of standing') but, wherever it was abandoned, the murder was the evidential excuse the police needed. The twins never recovered from Reggie's actions that evening. It was effectively the end of the Krays and of Stoke Newington's involvement with organised crime, at least as far as the Krays were concerned.

As for the Regency, during the 1980s it became an Afro-Caribbean joint known as 'Willows', and some of its clientele were allegedly linked to Sandringham Road's 'Murder Mile'. However, today the old club is an upmarket block of private flats that, like a few other places in the Stoke Newington area, appears discreetly anonymous, as if trying to live down its criminally 'colourful' past.

SQUATTING IN STOKE NEWINGTON

From the 1960s until relatively recently, squats were a common feature of Stoke Newington life.

Squatting has been frequently maligned but it has a long and far from ignoble history. From the Peasants Revolt of 1381 via the mid-seventeenth

-century occupation of St George's Hill by the Diggers to the present day, squatting has been as much a form of political dissent as it has been a means of securing free accommodation.

It has also been socially necessary, as the years immediately following the end of the Second World War demonstrate. During that period, and particularly in London, the bomb damage that their homes had suffered left many city dwellers, ex-servicemen and their families without places to live. The government's slow reaction to this surge in homelessness led initially to families moving into vacant barracks and then to the occupation of disused army camps. This mass 'squatting' movement involved an estimated 45,000 people.

The housing crisis of the late 1960s witnessed another wave of squatting when, lacking affordable accommodation in the city, people moved into vacant houses, often in groups. The political dimension to squatting became apparent with the arrival of hippy commune squats, and this was reinforced by the London Street Commune's much-publicised takeover of a mansion at 144 Piccadilly. Over the following years, squatting was increasingly regarded (by squatters, mainly) as a revolutionary act. A number of London councils reacted to the invasions of their empty council flats by pouring concrete down sinks and toilets, and similar spoiling tactics. However, by the early 1980s there were 30,000 squatters in London and this number increased in the Thatcher years, as the right to buy council houses led to a decrease in the availability of affordable council accommodation.

In Stoke Newington, these years were the high point of squatting in the area. I recall attending the 1994 Homeless Festival in Clissold Park, directly across the road from an early Victorian terrace beside St Mary's Church and which was at the time almost entirely occupied by squatters. The crowd of around 10,000 contained numerous 'crusties', with their hair in ringlets and most with small dogs, as well as homeless young people and several comfortably housed but interested supporters such as I, and we were entertained by rock band The Levellers. Eventually, the police turned up and – for no apparent reason – brought the proceedings to a halt. There was little love between the crusties and the Old Bill. Soon after this, many crusties left the area in search of cheaper, more amenable areas that were not undergoing gentrification.

However, in 2002 another similarly minded group of young people occupied a vacant shop in Kynaston Road, began a 'social centre' and squatted the premises. Although initially unwelcome, the Radical Dairy (as they named the centre) gradually won over many residents, who visited and sent their children to the building, which offered free film shows, kids' art workshops, crèches, classes in Spanish and computing, and a good deal more.

However, the more the Dairy became accepted into the local scene – and it existed for over six months – the greater grew the police presence and harassment. Inevitably, and in an unnecessarily rough manner, the members of the Dairy squat were evicted as the owner had finally gained legal approval for this action. These squatters had tried to establish a community focus but had been thwarted, much to the displeasure of the majority of the local residents who much appreciated the existence of the Dairy.

In the early years of the new millennium, bodies such as the Social Centre Network were advising squatters on the development of vacant buildings into local community centres. Squatting *per se* was not then a criminal offence, although entering a building for purposes of permanent occupation was illegal. However, in 2012 'trespass' for permanent residence was declared illegal, and this has seen the jailing of squatters and, obviously, a decline in the number of squats.

Today there is little evidence in Stoke Newington of squatting on a noticeable scale, as any available accommodation is quickly grabbed by people who can afford to live here or by council tenants who have reached the top of Hackney Council's waiting list.

MUSIC VENUES

As I've previously mentioned in this book, Stoke Newington has never been short of public houses and similar places of entertainment. Even back in the sixteenth century, an ale-befuddled peasant in Church Street's Falcon tavern was probably crooning 'In my old Stoke Newington home', accompanied by the equally tuneless warbling of his fellow serfs.

However, it was not until the early 1960s that organised contemporary musical evenings took off in this parish. The earliest such venues began to appear mainly in the south of the borough and slightly beyond, including the Pegasus and the Four Aces. Two other venues that, at their peak of popularity, attracted local crowds and many from well outside the immediate area were the Rochester Castle and the Vortex.

Heading up Green Lanes from Newington Green, and well before reaching Clissold Park, on the western side of the road sat the **Pegasus**. Established in

1848, the bar was a well-regarded music venue from the early 1960s. In its early musical incarnation it featured acts such as Matt Monro – known as the 'Singing Bus Driver' – whose smooth baritone tones made him a national TV favourite in the 1960s. The audience then consisted of local 'jack the lads', East End criminals and villains, and the occasional music fan. In the 1970s the performers reflected the more sophisticated yet raucous bands and tastes of the time and, when punk rock arrived, local lad and soon-to-be Sex Pistols front man Johnny Rotten was stabbed during a fight outside the Pegasus.

In the early 1980s, on Friday nights Juice on the Loose, fronted by Ron Kavana, regularly provided pounding rhythm 'n' blues and rock 'n' roll, while on Saturdays the four-octave bluesy voice of Sarah-Jane Morris as well as Big Chief, a band then led by the illustrious saxophonist Dick Heckstall-Smith, played equally well-received jazz and blues. The diverse nature of the audience mellowed somewhat later in the 1980s when two more TV favourites took over the bar and named it after themselves: Chas 'n' Dave's. After they relinquished ownership, the Pegasus became for a while a gay bar, and it closed for good in 2004. Today, and again to mirror the changing times, it is a Turkish social club.

◆ ◆ ◆

Entertaining and rowdy as the Pegasus was, its cultural significance could never match that of the **Four Aces** club. Located on Dalston Lane, but with its influence stretching across the UK and beyond, the club was set up in 1966 by Jamaican-born Newton Dunbar to provide ska and reggae, featuring mainly live acts, for Afro-Caribbeans in north London.

The club originally used the foyer of the old Dalston Theatre, built in 1886 as home to a circus, then as the North London Colosseum and finally as a cinema, before lying unused. The Four Aces was opened up in the 1990 as the Club Labyrinth, which housed rave parties and DJs playing hardcore, jungle and drum and bass.

In its earlier years, the Four Aces hosted performances by the great and the good, including Desmond Dekker, Jimmy Cliff, Prince Buster, The Upsetters, Percy Sledge, Ben E. King, Jimmy Ruffin, The Ronettes and plenty of other international and local bands. It was also visited by such music legends as Bob Marley, Mick Jagger, Joe Strummer, Stevie Wonder and Bob Dylan. Afro-

Caribbeans and their descendants travelled across London and from all over the UK to attend gigs. The place was unique.

It was frequently 'visited' by the police, although Dunbar's fourteen prosecutions resulted in no convictions, but it finally closed in 1997. Hackney Council had obtained a Compulsory Purchase Order, and despite protests from the Georgian Society, other preservation groups and a petition against closure signed by 25,000 people, the old theatre and the Four Aces was demolished in 2007. In its place today stand 550 luxury flats beside the C.L.R. James Library.

As Newton Dunbar said: 'The demolition of the Four Aces laid down the roots for the subsequent gentrification of Dalston.'

♦ ♦ ♦

Although a glance today around the cavernous old place would make this difficult to believe, the **Rochester Castle** in the mid- to late 1970s was one of the leading pub rock and punk venues in north London.

Sitting on the site of the Green Dragon, a coaching tavern from 1702, and just south of the High Street's junction with Church Street, this unmistakeable pub was built in 1801. It was refurbished in late Victorian times and acquired by J.D. Wetherspoon in 1982, making it the oldest existing Wetherspoon's in the UK. Its clientele is as diverse as its wide range of ales, and it's a popular bar and a handy meeting and drinking place for locals. This is, if course, helped by its cheap prices and generally relaxed atmosphere but, ironically given its recent history, like all J.D. pubs it does not play music.

Before Tim Martin got his hands on it, the music policy at the Rochester was very different. The 'stage' was to the left near the entrance, and it hosted local and emerging performers and bands such as Ian Dury, Squeeze, Tom Robinson Band, The Jam, XTC (who had a regular spot), The Police, an early Adam and the Ants, and even Wayne (who later became Jayne) County and the Electric Chairs, as well as several more groups of varying talent or lack thereof. The Sex Pistols were also rumoured to have graced the stage but, although Sid Vicious lived in Stoke Newington's Carysford Road and attended Clissold School, there is little evidence for this. It would be nice, though, to think that Sid thrilled a crowd of punks with his endearing version of 'My Way', but this seems unlikely.

These days, the Rochester remains the bar of choice for many Stoke Newington musos, who enjoy their nostalgic reminiscences over a pint or several. So everything changes but remains, more or less, the same. Apart, of course, from the live music. However, with any luck, Wetherspoon's will abandon its non-music policy, and the Rochester Castle will once again assume its deserved musical stature as Stoke Newington's answer to the Fillmore East.

◆ ◆ ◆

In the autumn 2001 issue of *N16 Magazine*, *Guardian* jazz critic John Fordham described the **Vortex** Jazz Club, then on Church Street, as 'a cultural public service to a non-mainstream art form' and described its founder, David Mossman, as 'a hero, there's no other word for it'.

David, an ex-cab driver, opened the Vortex in 1987 as a jazz bar in the heart of Stoke Newington Church Street. A lover of jazz, he ran the club virtually single-handedly and promoted gigs almost every night, until pressure from the landowner signalled the imminent end of the venue. This was despite protests from many local residents and musicians, a 2,500-strong petition and fundraising events at Ocean and the Union Chapel, all of which were intended to keep the Vortex where it belonged: in Church Street. Unfortunately, the campaign failed and the Vortex closed in 2005.

After a short period when it was squatted and became an informal social centre, the squatters were evicted by police. Then the refurbishment began and a Nando's restaurant, which is still there, took over the space. Popular as the restaurant may be, it somewhat lacks the creative originality and international celebrity of its previous occupant.

David then channelled his prodigious energies into the reopened Vortex at its new venue in Dalston's Gillett Square. The Vortex in the 1990s had been internationally renowned, and many jazz greats, as well as aspiring local musicians, performed at the venue. Although David died in 2018, the new Vortex continues to maintain its high reputation in the world of jazz, blues and experimental music. However, during its time on Church Street it was the jewel in the musical crown of Stoke Newington.

◆ ◆ ◆

Today, there are several other bars and venues across Stoke Newington that provide live music and/or DJs, on a regular or occasional basis. These include the Royal Sovereign on Northwold Road, the White Hart on the High Street and the Mascara Bar on Stamford Hill Road. On Church Street, Ryan's Bar and the Auld Shillelagh are only two of the options.

During the various festivals in the late 1990s and 2000s, live music of all kinds was available in virtually every bar and many restaurants in Stoke Newington. I particularly recall sitting outside Yum Yum's earlier premises some years ago, when I (Scottish), my wife (North American) and two friends (Serbian and French) were being entertained outside a Thai restaurant by a live three-piece Mexican mariachi band. Music knows few frontiers in Stoke Newington.

CREATIVITY AND THE ARTS

As well as not lacking in musically entertaining public houses, neither does Stoke Newington suffer from the absence of creative and artistically inclined people. Those who were born or have made their homes here in recent years include numerous writers, novelists, journalists, television and stage actors, visual artists and photographers, musicians and performers, comedians, poets and others of a similar persuasion.

Many of these people have achieved fame far beyond this borough, while others have been content to express themselves to local audiences and opinions. To name these artists and performers would be invidious and almost certainly impossible, so I here provide a brief context to help appreciate the importance of the creative arts in Stoke Newington.

The written word – in its many varieties – has been long celebrated in Stoke Newington. Earlier in this book I have mentioned the work of, for instance, **Daniel Defoe, Mary Wollstonecraft, Anna Laetitia Barbauld, Anna Sewell** and **Edgar Allan Poe**, all of whom were connected, to a greater or lesser degree, to Stoke Newington. The Polish novelist Josef Teodor Konrad Korzeniowski, otherwise known as **Joseph Conrad** (*Nigger of the 'Narcissus', Heart of Darkness*) and regarded as having been one of the finest writers in the English language, also lived for a while in Dynevor Road, Stoke Newington.

In more recent years, the Clapton-born, Nobel Prize-winning playwright **Harold Pinter** (*The Birthday Party*), and the actor and playwright

Steven Berkoff, both attended Hackney Downs school, as did the increasingly acclaimed left-wing novelist **Alexander Baron** (*King Dido*) who lived in Foulden Road off Stoke Newington High Street. Booker Prize winner (*G*), novelist, art critic (*Ways of Seeing*) and poet **John Berger** was born and brought up in Filey Road in Stoke Newington. The pantheon of eminent writers from this parish is a formidable one, and each author can be considered in his or her field as a contrarian 'dissenter'. There are currently several more local writers and journalists who will no doubt soon receive due wider recognition.

Publishers have come and gone in the area, to some degree the most memorable being **Centerprise**, which opened in Dalston Lane in 1971 and then moved to Kingsland High Street, just south of Crossway. First opened as a radical bookshop and cafe, it quickly became the radical intellectual hub of the area. As a publisher, Centerprise covered many areas, including feminism, Irish nationalism, local autobiographies, Latin American revolutionary thought and much more. As a left-wing collective, it promoted education and the dissemination of radical ideas across Hackney, but it was closed by Hackney Council after a rent dispute in 2012.

There are also a good many active and 'resting' actors currently resident in the parish, as well as a couple of independent theatres. The **Arcola** theatre was started by Mehmet Ergun in Arcola Street (opposite the original Mangal restaurant), just east of Stoke Newington Road, on the site of an old shirt factory and on a shoestring. Only eleven years later, the success of the Arcola propelled its move to the old Reeves and Sons Artists Paints factory in Dalston, where it is now a thriving, much-expanded theatre. The **Tower** theatre has recently moved from Canonbury to Northwold Road, opposite the old almshouses, and has occupied part of a building that was variously an old Methodist church, a synagogue and, in its last incarnation, Sunstone Health Club.

These are so many visual artists in Stoke Newington that, rather than cite names, it is easier and just as revealing to mention some of the galleries. The visual arts scene has been particularly prominent in the cobbled streets of **Belfast Road**, a small passageway just north of the railway station, which links the High Street with Windus Road. Many local artists have held their exhibitions here, in particular at the **Campbell Works** gallery and at **Madame Lillie's** round the corner on Cazenove Road. Other venues have included the **Edwards Lane** gallery behind Stoke Newington library, the old **Sea Cadets** building on the corner of Church Street and Yoakley Road, **Stoke Newington Studios** on Victorian Grove, **Tram Depot** on Lower Clapton Road (*see* p.113) and other permanent and more transient studios. Exhibitions have also been staged at a local recording studio, **Reels Rebel** on Bouverie Mews, and at other local spaces and studios.

And, of course, there are the local politicians, led by **Diane Abbott** who, as MP for Hackney North and Stoke Newington, was in 1987 the first black woman to have been elected to the House of Commons. Diane has been the parish MP for a continuous thirty-three years. Other politicians have come and gone, but Diane survives. **Ken Livingstone** was a councillor for Stoke Newington in the late 1970s, before he moved on. Local resident **Paul Foot**, a politically left activist, journalist and nephew of Labour ex-leader Michael Foot, was the Socialist Alliance candidate for the position of Mayor of Hackney in 2002, the first time a Mayor was directly elected by popular vote to the position. Paul, however, lost out to **Jules Pipe**, another ex-Stoke Newington councillor, who won a further two mayoral elections before resigning to help lead London.

STOKE NEWINGTON FESTIVALS

There are a good many other similarly creative 'dissidents' in Stoke Newington, and I imagine that many of them, as did many local residents, gleefully embraced the boisterous and contagiously entertaining spirit of the annual Stoke Newington Festival.

The first Festival was held in June 1994 as the **Stoke Newington Midsummer Festival.** It was organised by a group of local businesses, financed by grants and sponsorship, and with the assistance of local police and Hackney Council. For the next year's Festival and from then on, it was run by a small committee of local residents. The Festival culminated on a Sunday in June, when the police closed off Church Street from Albion Road to the High Street, and local bars and cafes joined in the celebrations that included food and drink stalls, music and bands playing on specially erected street stages and in pubs, and all manner of performances taking place on Church Street.

By the late-1990s, the Church Street Festival had become one of London's leading and most anticipated one-day events, with around 50,000 people, mainly locals but also thousands from across London, thronging Church Street, the side roads and Clissold Park to enjoy the day.

In 2002, however, due to a combination of circumstances the Festival was cancelled and, aside from **Stokefest,** which ran from 2003 to 2009 in Clissold Park, it was not to reappear. Meanwhile in 2002, I and others had formed a separate committee to launch a Fringe Festival, in conjunction with *N16 Magazine*, on the High Street to complement the main event. Suddenly, due to the cancellation of the Festival, we found ourselves as the only fringe festival in the country without a main festival to support it.

The **N16 Fringe** continued as an annual weekend of largely free music of all types across Stoke Newington, in numerous venues across the parish, but came to an end in 2009. The Fringe culminated in a sell-out, stunning performance in St Mary's New Church by folk music legend Martin Carthy and his daughter Eliza Carthy. After this, we called it a day.

The following year, 2010, saw the first **N16 Literary Festival**. Again held at bars and venues across the area, its first year was so successful that it was repeated in 2011. Now a nationally celebrated event, the Stoke Newington Literary Festival has hosted some of the finest international and local writers, critics, poets, novelists and others, and it is becoming regarded as one of the country's leading annual events in the world of literature. The eleventh festival was due to take place in July 2020 but, given the constraints of the Covid-19 pandemic, it had to be cancelled.

These festivals contained so many intriguing, outstanding and scarcely credible performances and events that it would be impossible here to do them any justice. Such a task would require another book. However, suffice to say that they were and are yet another example of the creativity, talent and spirit of enterprise that exists in this small corner of north-east London.

COMMON GROUND

As I began this book with a brief discussion of Stoke Newington Common, the Common seems an appropriate place on which to conclude my reflections on the history of Stoke Newington.

There are two facts concerning the Common that, if they have heard anything about the place, most people should know. The first fact, as I mention in Chapter One, is that it is one of the most important Palaeolithic archaeological sites in Europe. The second fact is that it was the home of a young man who became one of the first internationally idolised pop stars of the 1970s, this being Stoke Newington's 'Electric Warrior', Marc Bolan.

'20TH CENTURY BOY'

On the southern side of Stoke Newington Common sits a terrace of mid-Victorian houses. At its eastern end, facing Fountayne Road, house no. 25 was home to young Mark Feld, who lived there with his working-class Jewish parents until he was 15 years old, and before he changed his name to the rocktastic **Marc Bolan**.

Today, a brown plaque on the house's front wall celebrates Marc's origins and, as I live round the corner, I frequently stroll past fans taking each other's pictures under the plaque. Although Marc was killed in a car crash in 1977, his global fame lives on, and his is the most illustrious and enduringly popular name in popular culture to have emerged from Stoke Newington.

He attended nearby Northwold School, where he and his fellow pupil Helen Shapiro – another early pop star who later toured with the Beatles and whose single 'Walking Back to Happiness' topped the UK's music charts in the early 1960s – formed the band Susie and the Hula Hoops, with young Marc on tea chest bass. A chubby, assertive kid with attitude and a quiff, Marc attended Shacklewell's William Wordsworth Secondary Modern and spent his spare time hanging out at Stamford Hill Jewish Youth Club.

Marc listened avidly to contemporary music with his friend Keith Reed – also a budding pop star who co-founded Procol Harum and wrote the band's mid-1960s smash hit 'A Whiter Shade of Pale' – and they often visited the Hackney Empire to watch the filming of TV series *Oh Boy!*. A Mod, dressed in Italian suits and Levis, Marc and his buddies had frequent punch-ups with their local rivals. Malcolm McLaren, also from this parish, observed, 'Stoke Newington … was a very potent place to be. It sported some of the first Teddy Boys.'

At the age of 15, Marc was already making his name on the wider London scene, and he was featured in *Town* magazine as 'a face to watch' in London's embryonic Mod scene. A couple of years after this exposure, he changed his name and became an early hippie, with long curly hair, silver buckles and a beatific persona. He formed Tyrannosaurus Rex in 1967. The band was a success, but his later formation of T.Rex led to meteoric international acclaim ('Get It On', anyone?), and his early formative days perhaps disappeared from the radar of this supremely confident kid from the wilds of Stoke Newington Common.

Although in Chapter One I describe the Common as a 'treasured family heirloom', I'd probably have been less charitable about the place if I'd lived here in 1979.

That was the final year of Jim Callaghan's Labour government, when worker unrest was commonplace. Like many other British workers, the binmen in this parish went on strike, and their favoured spot for piling up rubbish was on Stoke Newington Common. By the time the strike ended, the Common was piled high with all types of rubbish, and rats were everywhere. The general condition of the Common had been degenerating for years, but this was easily its nadir.

The unappealing condition of the Common had not exactly been improved when, only a few years previously and despite objections from local residents and retailers, London Transport had created a 'gyratory system'. This system not only turned Stoke Newington High Street into a northbound, one-way street but also carved a one-way southbound route – a northern extension of Rectory Road – through the Common, as had been done with the railway 100 years previously. Due to the apparent requirement for speedy transport links, the Common is now divided (or trifurcated?) into three separate areas.

One of the contributing causes to the less than exuberant morale and declining profit margins of Stoke Newington retailers in the 1970s and '80s – to which I allude in the Foreword to this book – was this one-way system, as well as its parking restrictions. Traffic travelling north along the High Street, and which may previously have stopped there for a bit of shopping, tended increasingly to leave their chores until they had reached Stamford Hill or Tottenham. Likewise, southbound traffic was forced by the gyratory system to bypass the High Street altogether until they re-emerged from Evering Road onto Stoke Newington Road, so they began to shop closer to the Dalston area. This was not good news for small local traders.

Since the arrival of the new millennium, however, criticism of the gyratory system has grown to such a clamorous extent that Transport for London and

Hackney Council have proposed new plans for the existing 'gyratory', which include making it more shopper/cyclist/retailer-friendly and also re-examining the benefit to the area of the entire one-way system. At the time of writing, nothing has yet been decided, but the omens appear promising.

◆ ◆ ◆

Stoke Newington Common has over the last few years re-emerged as a pleasantly green and well-tended public space. Largely due to the tireless efforts of the Stoke Newington Users Group (SNUG), the tree/bush/flower planting and landscaping skills of the Tree Musketeers and a renewed interest in the Common from Hackney Council, the Common is once more an attractive and popular public space.

SNUG presents regular music concerts and performances, and promotes an annual event on the Common that includes a variety of activities for children and adults as well as stalls selling various local foods and artefacts. SNUG also created a children's playground on the Common, and this is in constant use by the kids who attend the many nurseries and schools in the immediate area.

The Common has survived the setbacks and vicissitudes of recent years, and today it is used and enjoyed by the diverse, multicultural residents of this area. In some respects, the renaissance of this public space mirrors that of the wider parish of Stoke Newington, which has also undergone an economic and cultural rebirth, and one which in the 1980s would have been difficult to imagine.

Its new affluence has not been welcomed by all, particularly by some longer-term residents, but generally Stoke Newington is a friendlier, more culturally amenable and livelier area in which to reside and enjoy one's life than it was when I arrived here thirty years ago. Its current wealthier status has attracted many newcomers, but has also made it unaffordable for some people who were born and brought up in the area. This is, to say the very least, unfair, but is often a predictable side-effect of gentrification and today's inner-city life.

However, those of us who live here find Stoke Newington one of London's most interesting and invigorating areas. This 'village' has experienced profound changes over the 1,000 years since it was first named and identified in the Domesday Book. These have been caused by numerous factors but 'dissent', as expressed in the many and various ways I have defined the term in this book, has always lain at the heart of Stoke Newington life.

Long may this continue to be the case.

FURTHER READING

What follows is a selection of some of the sources I used in compiling this book, which is essentially a personal introduction to Stoke Newington and described mainly from the perspective of 'dissent'. There were a good many other books, websites and newspaper articles which I consulted, but this brief list includes some of those I found most useful.

Several of these books are mainly about Hackney but they do contain, to a greater or lesser degree, information on Stoke Newington. Other titles are concerned with London's cultural history, and these provide a wider context in which to assess the changing nature of Stoke Newington. These latter titles include *London: A social history* by Roy Porter, *The London Encyclopedia* by Ben Weinreb and Christopher Hibbert, *A Short History of London* by Simon Jenkins, *Beyond the Tower: A history of East London* by John Marriott, *Battle for the East End: Jewish responses to fascism in the 1930s* by David Rosenberg, Cynthia Cockburn's *Looking at London: Stories of War, Escape and Asylum* and Peter Fryer's *Staying Power: The History of Black People in Britain*. There are plenty more.

Readers searching for explanatory works on the tumultuous seventeenth century – the ascendancy of the Stuarts, the execution of Charles I, the Wars of the Three Kingdoms, the Protectorate, the Restoration, the brief reign of James VII and the 'Glorious Revolution' – and its critical relationship with a variety of Protestant dissenters, have access to an almost bewildering array of sources. However, in my view the two most revealing and accessible books on this period were both written by Christopher Hill: *The Century of Revolution, 1603–1714* and *The World Turned Upside Down: Radical ideas during the English revolution.*

Closer to home, here are a few books, several compiled and published by the estimable Hackney Society, which you will find of interest: *Glimpses of Ancient Hackney and Stoke Newington* by Benjamin Clarke, *Hackney and Stoke Newington Past* by Isobel Watson, *Lost Hackney* by Elizabeth Robinson, *Loddiges of Hackney: the largest hothouse in the world* by David Solman, *Late Extra! Hackney in the News* by David Mander, *Hackney: Modern, Restored, Forgotten, Ignored* edited by Lisa Rigg, *The Victorian Villas of Hackney* by Michael Hunter, *From Tower to Tower Block: The buildings of Hackney, Twentieth century buildings in Hackney* by Elizabeth Robinson, *Hackney At War* by Jennifer Golden, *Cinemas and Theatres of Hackney* by Gavin McGrath, *The Lime Green Mystery: an oral history of Centerprise* by Rosa Schling, *Hackney Memories* by Alan Wilson, *Hackney: portrait of a community 1967–2017* edited by Laurie Elks, *Hackney: An Uncommon History in Five Parts* edited by Margaret Wiles … and so the list continues.

Also, two of this country's leading writers have published in recent years books which, to much acclaim and to laudatory national reviews, evocatively and perceptively capture Hackney life. These are Iain Sinclair's *Hackney, That Rose-Red Empire: A Confidential Report* ('an explosion of literary fireworks', *Times*) and Patrick Wright's *A Journey Through Ruins: The Last Days Of London* ('sheer good writing, sense and humanity', *TLS*).

There is also a range of books specifically featuring Stoke Newington, including *Dramas and Dissent: twelve hectic years in Stoke Newington* edited by Rab MacWilliam (and which is a thematic collection of articles first published in *N16 Magazine*), *The Growth of Stoke Newington* by Jack Whitehead, *Clissold Park* edited by Ken Worpole and Clissold Park Users Group, *A Guide to Abney Park Cemetery* by Paul Joyce, *Discover Stoke Newington* edited by Friends of Hackney Archives, *Street Names of Stoke Newington* by F. W. Baxter in 1927 and transcribed online by Amir Dotan, *Stoke Newington* compiled by Gavin Smith, *Stoke Newington, Stamford Hill and Upper Clapton* by David Mander and Bill Manley … and again the titles continue.

For an instructive cartographic overview of the transformation of Stoke Newington from the mid–nineteenth century until the onset of the First World War, compare and contrast the Ordnance Survey Maps of the area for the years 1868, 1894 and 1914, republished by Alan Godfrey Maps. These also contain illuminating and interpretative texts by David Mander and Jenny Golden, and they well reveal the profound structural changes in the parish over that brief period.

If the existence of these published works and others is insufficient evidence of the widespread interest and fascination in this north-east London area, then I suggest you type 'Stoke Newington' into Google. I would quickly run out of space here if I tried to list the number of websites devoted to this parish and its history. From national archives.co.uk, british-archives.ac.uk and nationalarchives.gov.uk to stokenewingtonhistory.com, clissoldpark.com, abney-park.org.uk, stmaryslodge.co.uk, woodberrywetlands.org.uk, hackneygazette.co.uk and stokenewingtonquakers.org.uk, all of Stoke Newington life, past and present, is on the Web.

Finally, Hackney Archives, based in the CLR James Library on Dalston Lane, is considered by many to be the best equipped and most comprehensive public archive collection in London. If you are searching for more detailed or more specialist information than is available in this introductory book, then you should be able to find this at the Archives.

POSTSCRIPT

As I have attempted to demonstrate in this book, Stoke Newington has been one of England's leading centres of dissent for over 400 years. However, even with such a proud historical heritage, this little parish could do nothing to disagree with or prevent its invasion by the Covid-19 pandemic, which in 2020 established its iron will on most countries in the world. In the UK, the rigid lockdowns and other socioeconomic constraints imposed on the population by an inept government were of an extent rarely before encountered.

Everyone was affected by the devastating spread of the Covid-19 virus, including book publishers. I delivered the final draft of this book in March 2020, as the viral impact was becoming ominously apparent, and the book was then scheduled for October publication. Due to external factors, and despite the publisher's very best efforts in dealing with this most hostile of economic climates, the book was moved to March 2021 publication. I agreed entirely with this decision.

This being a work of history, the book is significantly less affected by Covid-19 than would be a book on, say, current affairs. However, I have updated the text where necessary, and ensured that its publication delay will in no way diminish its relevance for readers wishing to understand how and why this village, now a busy, Inner-London suburb, has retained its historical identity in the face of the hazards and changing circumstances of contemporary urban life.

In future editions, this Covid-19 crisis may well be reduced to simply another minor obstacle which Stoke Newington confronted and overcame. I very much hope and expect this to be the case. We shall see.

INDEX

i) Page numbers in bold type refer to Text Boxes

ii) 'Passim' refers to a) passing references or b) to numerous occasions (eg Church Street)

ii) This Index refers only to Chapters One to Seven. I have not included references to Foreword ('Slouching towards to Stokey'), Introduction, 'Where is Stoke Newington', Postscript or Further Reading

iv) Generally, the entries indicate only names, places and similar (eg Acts of Parliament etc)